RIVER VALLEY RECIPES

D1710509

WHEAT AND CONE FLOWERS

for those who cook...
and for those who don't...

Rock River Valley Council of Girl Scouts

Acknowledgements

The beautifully detailed line drawings throughout the book were generously contributed by Mike Abbott, who is well known for his sensitive wildlife drawings.

Special thanks goes to Vance Barrie of the Rockford Park District who helped us locate talented area photographers who donated their work for this book.

Our area streams and rivers have diverse personalities and a special beauty in all seasons. Our thanks to the local photographers who captured these moods and seasons so well. We're grateful for their help.

COLOR PHOTOGRAPHS

Cover – Anonymous
Page 17 – Pamela Hess
Page 35 – Lynn Northrup
Page 53 – Patricia Rednour
Page 71 – Steve Edwards
Page 89 – Helen Morgan
Page 107 – Anonymous
Page 141 – Gedeon Trias
Page 175 – Tom Siefken

BLACK AND WHITE PHOTOGRAPHS

Page 18 – Camp Medill McCormick Development Plans
Page 36 – Kent Creek Fairgrounds Park, 1914. Photo from the library of the Rockford Park District
Page 54 – The Troophouse at Camp Medill McCormick
Page 72 – Tinker Swiss Cottage, circa 1920. Photo from the library of the Rockford Park District
Page 90 – Whippoorwill Dining Hall at Camp Medill McCormick
Page 108 – Photo by Charles Rhodes
Page 142 – The Tepees at Camp Medill McCormick
Page 176 – A platform tent at Camp Medill McCormick

First Printing: 15,000
Copyright ©Rock River Valley Council of Girl Scouts, Inc.
P. O. Box 1616, Rockford, Illinois 61110-0116
Library of Congress Number: 88-24663
ISBN: 0-87197-242-5

Dedication

For nearly fifty years, more than 100,000 Girl Scouts have passed through the gates of Camp McCormick and stored up a treasure of fond memories. This book is dedicated to the young women of the past, present, and future, and to the extended family that supports Girl Scouting.

Camp McCormick is located along the Rock River, seventeen miles southwest of Rockford in Ogle County. The property is composed of 415 acres of woods and meadow, with a five-acre primitive island in the river for the girls to explore. It is, and has always been, our only camp property.

The property was given to the Girl Scouts by Ruth Hanna McCormick Sims in 1939. It has been used by many thousands of girls over the years for day programs, weekend overnight camping, and week-long summer experiences. Many local and area educational and community groups have enjoyed the facilities.

Because camping is important in nurturing personal development, Rock River Valley Council is committed to renovating, upgrading, and expanding the outdoor program facilities at Camp McCormick. The proceeds of this cookbook will be used to assist in these new plans.

FIELD SPARROW

Contents

Appetizers 7
Beverages 23
Salads 29
Main Dishes 47
Vegetables 83
Breads 99
Desserts 113
Potluck 155
Outdoor Cooking 159
Potpourri 181

Microwave Tips 189
Cheese Chart 190
Quantities To Serve 50 192
Substitution Chart 195
Equivalent Chart 196
Contributors' Index 198
Index 200
Order Form 207

Microwave recipes are identified with this symbol.

The editors have attempted to present these tried-and-true family recipes in a form that allows approximate nutritional values to be computed. Persons with dietary or health problems or whose diets require close monitoring should not rely solely on the nutritional information provided. They should consult their physicians or a registered dietitian for specific information.

Abbreviations for Nutritional Analysis

Cal – Calories	Chol – Cholesterol	Potas – Potassium
Prot – Protein	Carbo – Carbohydrates	gr – gram
T Fat – Total Fat	Sod – Sodium	mg – milligram

Nutritional information for recipes is computed from values furnished by the United States Department of Agriculture Handbook. Many specialty items and new products now available on the market are not included in this handbook. However, producers of new products frequently publish nutritional information on each product's packaging and that information may be added, as applicable, for a more complete analysis. If the nutritional analysis notes the exclusion of a particular ingredient, check the package information.

Unless otherwise specified, the nutritional analysis of these recipes is based on the following guidelines.

- All measurements are level.
- Artificial sweeteners vary in use and strength so should be used "to taste," using the recipe ingredients as a guideline.
- Artificial sweeteners using aspertame (NutraSweet and Equal) should not be used as a sweetener in recipes involving prolonged heating which reduces the sweet taste. For further information on the use of these sweeteners, refer to package information.
- Alcoholic ingredients have been analyzed for the basic ingredients, although cooking causes the evaporation of alcohol thus decreasing caloric content.
- Buttermilk, sour cream, and yogurt are commercial-type.
- Chicken, cooked for boning and chopping, has been roasted; this method yields the lowest caloric values.
- Cottage cheese is cream-style with 4.2 percent creaming mixture. Dry-curd cottage cheese has no creaming mixture.
- Eggs are all large.
- Flour is unsifted all-purpose flour.
- Garnishes, serving suggestions and other optional additions and variations are not included in the analysis.
- Margarine and butter are regular, not whipped or presoftened.
- Milk is whole milk, 3.5 percent butterfat. Lowfat milk is 1 percent butterfat. Evaporated milk is produced by removing 60 percent of the water from whole milk.
- Oil is any cooking oil. Shortening is hydrogenated vegetable shortening.
- Salt to taste as noted in the method has not been included in the nutritional analysis.

Appetizers

DOWNY
WOODPECKER

CHEESE BALL

Yields: 24 tablespoons *Pan Size: bowl*

- 8 ounces cream cheese, softened
- 2 teaspoons salad dressing
- 1/8 teaspoon horseradish
- 1 (2 1/2-ounce) package dried beef, chopped
- 3 green onion tops, chopped
- 1/2 cup chopped walnuts

Combine cream cheese, salad dressing, horseradish, dried beef and green onion tops in bowl; mix well. Shape into ball. Wrap in clear plastic wrap. Chill for several hours or until firm. Roll cheese ball in chopped walnuts. Chill until serving time.

APPROX PER TABLESPOON: Cal 60; Prot 2.2 gr; T Fat 5.5 gr; Chol 12.6 mg; Carbo 0.9 gr; Sod 153.5 mg; Potas 28.6.

BRAUNSCHWEIGER PATÉ

Yields: 24 ounces *Pan Size: bowl*

- 1 small onion, chopped
- 1 pound braunschweiger
- 8 ounces reduced-calorie cream cheese, softened
- Steak sauce to taste
- Worcestershire sauce to taste

Combine onion, braunschweiger, cream cheese, steak sauce and Worcestershire sauce in bowl; mix well. Chill, covered, for 24 hours. Serve with assorted crackers.

Nutritional information not available.

GREEN GODDESS DIP

Yields: 32 tablespoons *Pan Size: blender*

- 1 clove of garlic
- 1/2 bunch fresh parsley, chopped
- 1/2 bunch green onions with tops, chopped
- 1 tablespoon anchovy paste
- 1 pint mayonnaise
- 1 tablespoon lemon juice

Combine all ingredients in blender container. Blend until smooth. Add salt to taste. Chill, covered, for several hours. Delicious served with fresh vegetable chunks or chips.

APPROX PER TABLESPOON: Cal 104; Prot 0.3 gr; T Fat 11.2 gr; Chol 10.0 mg; Carbo 0.9 gr; Sod 87.5 mg; Potas 30.3 mg.

HOT BROCCOLI DIP

Yields: 10 servings *Pan Size: glass dish* 

- 1 (10-ounce) package frozen chopped broccoli
- 1 onion, chopped
- 1 (4-ounce) can sliced mushrooms
- 2 tablespoons margarine
- 1 (6-ounce) roll garlic cheese
- 1/2 can mushroom soup
- 1 teaspoon Tabasco sauce
- 1/4 teaspoon salt

Cook broccoli using package directions; drain. Saute onion and mushrooms in margarine in skillet. Place broccoli, mushrooms and onion in microwave dish. Add remaining ingredients and pepper to taste. Microwave on High for 30 seconds or until cheese is melted, stirring frequently. Serve hot with corn chips.

APPROX PER SERVING: Cal 121; Prot 5.8 gr; T Fat 9.1 gr; Chol 18.0 mg; Carbo 4.8 gr; Sod 327.2 mg; Potas 122.2 mg.

MICROMEALS' CHILI SALSA DIP

Yields: 88 tablespoons *Pan Size: 8-cup measure* 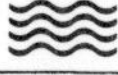

- 1 pound lean, hot breakfast sausage
- 1 large onion, finely chopped
- 1 (8-ounce) can tomato sauce
- 1 (12-ounce) jar chili salsa dip
- 1 (7-ounce) round Gouda cheese

Combine sausage and onion in glass measure. Microwave on High for 6 to 7 minutes or until sausage is cooked; drain. Add tomato sauce and salsa; mix well. Place round Gouda cheese in 10-inch pie plate or shallow 1 1/2-quart serving dish. Pour salsa mixture over cheese. Microwave on High for 5 to 6 minutes or until hot and cheese melts. Serve with corn chips.

APPROX PER TABLESPOON: Cal 22; Prot 1.1 gr; T Fat 1.8 gr; Chol 4.4 mg; Carbo 0.4 gr; Sod 54.0 mg; Potas 21.9 mg. Nutritional information does not include chili salsa dip.

LIVER DIP

Yields: 32 tablespoons *Pan Size: bowl*

A success at many gatherings. Even those who dislike liver love this dip!

1 (8-ounce) package liver sausage
8 ounces cream cheese, softened
2 teaspoons lemon juice
1 teaspoon Worcestershire sauce
Chopped onions to taste

Combine liver sausage, cream cheese, lemon juice and Worcestershire sauce in bowl; mix well. Add salt, pepper and chopped onions to taste. Chill, covered, until serving time. Serve with pumpernickel crackers.

APPROX PER TABLESPOON: Cal 49.3; Prot 1.5 gr; T Fat 4.6 gr; Chol 19.1 mg; Carbo 0.4 gr; Sod 111.4 mg; Potas 23.0 mg.

LYNDA'S TACO DIP

Yields: 8 to 10 servings *Pan Size: baking sheet*

1 or 2 cans refried beans
8 ounces cream cheese, softened
1 bottle mild taco sauce
1 onion, chopped
1 cup black olives, sliced
1 to 2 cups shredded Cheddar cheese
2 large tomatoes, chopped

Spread refried beans over bottom of baking sheet. Combine cream cheese with taco sauce; spread evenly over beans. Sprinkle with chopped onion, black olives, cheese and tomatoes. Serve immediately.

Nutritional information not available.

TERRY HODGES' TOMATO DIP

Yields: 64 tablespoons *Pan Size: bowl*

Friends gave us this recipe when we lived in New Mexico.

4 medium tomatoes, diced
1 (4-ounce) can green chilies, chopped
2 tablespoons oil
2 tablespoons wine vinegar
Garlic powder to taste

Combine tomatoes, chilies, oil and vinegar in bowl; mix well. Add garlic powder and salt and pepper to taste. Let stand, covered, in refrigerator for at least 12 hours. Serve with Doritos or corn chips.

APPROX PER TABLESPOON: Cal 5.9; Prot 0.1 gr; T Fat 0.4 gr; Chol 0.0 mg; Carbo 0.5 gr; Sod 0.4 mg; Potas 22.3 mg.

SHRIMP DIP

Yields: 40 tablespoons *Pan Size: bowl*

8 ounces cream cheese, softened
2/3 cup mayonnaise
1/4 to 1/2 cup chopped celery
2 green onions, chopped
1 (6-ounce) can tiny shrimp, drained and chopped

Combine cream cheese and mayonnaise in bowl until smooth. Add remaining ingredients; mix well. Chill for 1 hour before serving. Serve with Town House crackers.

APPROX PER TABLESPOON: Cal 54; Prot 1.5 gr; T Fat 5.2 gr; Chol 15.3 mg; Carbo 0.4 gr; Sod 44.4 mg; Potas 17.5 mg.

STANLEY FOLZ'S NACHO STUFF

Yields: 150 tablespoons *Pan Size: skillet*

1 pound ground beef
2 large onions, chopped
1 pound Velveeta cheese, melted
1 pound sharp Cheddar cheese, melted
1 (2 1/2-pound) can tomatoes, drained, chopped
2 (4-ounce) cans green chili peppers, diced

Brown ground beef in skillet; drain. Saute onions until soft. Add melted cheeses, stirring constantly. Add remaining ingredients. Cook over medium heat until flavors blend, stirring constantly. Serve hot with tortilla chips.

APPROX PER TABLESPOON: Cal 61; Prot 4.0 gr; T Fat 4.3 gr; Chol 14.4 mg; Carbo 1.7 gr; Sod 161.6 mg; Potas 73.2 mg.

APPLE DIP

Yields: 24 tablespoons *Pan Size: mixer bowl*

8 ounces cream cheese, softened
1 1/2 to 2 teaspoons vanilla extract
3/4 cup firmly packed brown sugar
1/4 cup sugar
1/2 cup chopped dry roasted peanuts

Combine cream cheese, vanilla, brown sugar and sugar in mixing bowl; beat until well blended. Add roasted peanuts; mix well. Chill until serving time. Serve with sliced apples and/or other fruit.

APPROX PER TABLESPOON: Cal 122; Prot 2.3 gr; T Fat 8.6 gr; Chol 21.0 mg; Carbo 9.7 gr; Sod 61.9 mg; Potas 57.9 mg.

ORANGE-SOUR CREAM DIP

Yields: 40 tablespoons *Pan Size: mixer bowl*

1 (6-ounce) can frozen orange juice concentrate, thawed
1 1/4 cups milk
1 (3-ounce) package vanilla instant pudding mix
1/8 teaspoon cinnamon
1/8 teaspoon nutmeg
1/4 cup sour cream

Combine orange juice concentrate, milk and pudding mix in mixer bowl. Beat for about 2 minutes or until smooth. Stir in cinnamon, nutmeg and sour cream. Chill, covered, for 2 hours. Serve with assorted fresh fruit chunks for dipping.

APPROX PER TABLESPOON: Cal 30; Prot 0.6 gr; T Fat 0.7 gr; Chol 1.9 mg; Carbo 5.6 gr; Sod 18.4 mg; Potas 55.5 mg.

CARAMEL DIP

Yields: 24 servings *Pan Size: mixer bowl*

8 ounces cream cheese, softened
3/4 cup packed brown sugar
1/4 cup sugar
2 tablespoons vanilla extract
1/2 cup chopped pecans
1 (3-pound) bag apples, cored, sliced
1/4 cup lemon juice

Combine cream cheese, sugars and vanilla in mixer bowl. Beat until well blended. Add pecans; mix well. Chill, covered, for several hours. Dip apple slices in lemon juice to prevent browning. Dip apples in caramel dip for a tasty treat.

APPROX PER SERVING: Cal 117; Prot 1.1 gr; T Fat 5.6 gr; Chol 10.5 mg; Carbo 17.1 gr; Sod 26.3 mg; Potas 107.3 mg.

FRUIT DIP

Yields: 24 tablespoons *Pan Size: small bowl*

12 ounces cream cheese, softened
1/4 cup firmly packed brown sugar
Few drops of vanilla extract

Combine all ingredients in bowl; mix well. Serve with chunks of fresh fruit.

APPROX PER TABLESPOON: Cal 62; Prot 1.1 gr; T Fat 5.3 gr; Chol 15.7 mg; Carbo 2.5 gr; Sod 36.1 mg; Potas 18.4 mg.

CLAMS CASINO

Yields: 12 servings | *Pan Size: clam shells* | *Preheat: 275 degrees*

2 (6-ounce) cans minced clams
1/2 cup chopped onion
5 tablespoons butter
6 tablespoons bread crumbs
6 tablespoons dried parsley
7 tablespoons mayonnaise
1 (2-ounce) jar minced pimento
1/4 cup minced green bell pepper

Drain clams, reserving juice. Saute onion in butter in skillet. Add clams, bread crumbs, parsley, mayonnaise, pimento and green pepper; mix well. Add 1/2 of the reserved clam juice. Serve warm with rye or melba toast rounds or fill clam shells with mixture. Place on baking sheet. Bake until bubbly. An elegant hors d'oeuvre for a small dinner party.

APPROX PER SERVING: Cal 126; Prot 2.9 gr; T Fat 11.6 gr; Chol 30.2 mg; Carbo 3.0 gr; Sod 291.4 mg; Potas 76.9 mg.

HOT CRAB SPREAD

Yields: 32 tablespoons | *Pan Size: 2-cup casserole* | *Preheat: 375 degrees*

8 ounces cream cheese, softened
1 tablespoon milk
1 (7-ounce) can flaked crab meat
2 tablespoons finely chopped onion
2 tablespoons finely chopped parsley
2 teaspoons cream-style horseradish
1/4 teaspoon salt
Dash of pepper
1/3 cup sliced almonds

Combine cream cheese and milk in bowl. Add crab meat; mix well. Add onion, parsley, horseradish, salt and pepper; mix well. Spoon into 2-cup ovenproof dish. Sprinkle with sliced almonds. Bake for 15 minutes. Serve hot with cocktail rye. This may be made a day ahead, refrigerated, then heated before serving.

APPROX PER TABLESPOON: Cal 44; Prot 2.0 gr; T Fat 3.7 gr; Chol 14.6 mg; Carbo 0.9 gr; Sod 94.2 mg; Potas 32.7 mg.

CRAB MEAT DELUXE

Yields: 40 tablespoons *Pan Size: serving plate*

- 16 ounces cream cheese, softened
- 1 (7-ounce) can crab meat, drained
- 1 (8-ounce) bottle of chili sauce

Shape cream cheese into flat circle on serving plate. Place crab meat over top. Pour chili sauce over all. Serve immediately with assorted crackers.

APPROX PER TABLESPOON: Cal 53; Prot 1.8 gr; T Fat 4.4 gr; Chol 17.1 mg; Carbo 1.8 gr; Sod 135.9 mg; Potas 35.1 mg.

SHRIMP MOUSSE

Yields: 15 servings *Pan Size: double boiler*

- 9 ounces calorie-reduced cream cheese, softened
- 1 can tomato soup
- 1 package unflavored gelatin
- 1/4 cup water
- 1 cup lite Miracle Whip salad dressing
- 1/2 cup chopped green onions, tops included
- 1 cup diced celery
- 2 cups diced cooked shrimp

Combine cream cheese and soup in top of double boiler. Cook over hot water for 20 minutes or until well blended, stirring constantly. Remove from heat. Dissolve gelatin in water in small bowl. Add salad dressing and gelatin to cream cheese mixture, mixing well. Add onions, celery and shrimp; mix well. Pour into greased 6-cup mold. Chill, covered, for several hours to 24 hours. Unmold onto serving dish. Serve with assorted crackers.

Nutritional information not available.

CLASSIC COCKTAIL SAUCE

Yields: 16 tablespoons *Pan Size: bowl*

- 3/4 cup tomato catsup
- 1 to 2 tablespoons horseradish
- 2 tablespoons lemon juice
- 1/8 teaspoon Tabasco sauce

Combine all ingredients in bowl; mix well. Serve immediately, or chill to use as needed. Serve over shrimp or cream cheese and crab meat.

APPROX PER TABLESPOON: Cal 13; Prot 0.3 gr; T Fat 0.1 gr; Chol 0.0 mg; Carbo 3.2 gr; Sod 119.2 mg; Potas 49.0 mg.

CRANBERRY COCKTAIL MEATBALLS

Yields: 65 meatballs *Pan Size: shallow baking pan* *Preheat: 350 degrees*

1 cup cornflake crumbs
1/4 cup minced parsley
2 tablespoons instant minced onion
1/2 teaspoon garlic powder
1 teaspoon salt
2 eggs
2 tablespoons soy sauce
1/4 teaspoon pepper
1/3 cup catsup
2 pounds lean ground beef
1 (16-ounce) can cranberry sauce
1 (12-ounce) can chili sauce
2 tablespoons brown sugar
1 tablespoon lemon juice

Combine crumbs, parsley, onion, garlic powder, salt, eggs, soy sauce, pepper, catsup and ground beef in bowl; mix well. Shape into small meatballs. Place in shallow baking pan. Bake until meatballs are well done. Drain off grease. Place in serving dish. Combine cranberry sauce, chili sauce, brown sugar and lemon juice in saucepan. Cook over medium heat until heated through, stirring occasionally. Pour over meatballs. Serve hot.

APPROX PER MEATBALL: Cal 56; Prot 2.9 gr; T Fat 2.3 gr; Chol 17.2 mg; Carbo 6.1 gr; Sod 165.2 mg; Potas 65.0 mg.

MINIATURE CREAM PUFFS

Yields: 24 servings *Pan Size: baking sheet* *Preheat: 400 degrees*

Nice size for all, especially children, and good served as appetizer or easy dessert.

1 cup water
1/2 cup butter
1 cup flour
4 eggs

Bring water and butter to a rolling boil. Stir in flour. Stir over low heat for 1 minute or until mixture forms ball. Remove from heat. Add eggs, 1 at a time, beating until smooth after each addition. Drop by rounded teaspoonfuls onto ungreased baking sheet. Bake for 20 to 25 minutes or until puffed and brown. Cool on wire rack. Fill with ham salad, egg salad, chicken salad, whipped cream or cooked pudding.

APPROX PER SERVING: Cal 66; Prot 1.7 gr; T Fat 4.8 gr; Chol 54.0 mg; Carbo 4.1 gr; Sod 57.0 mg; Potas 16.8 mg. Nutritional information does not include fillings.

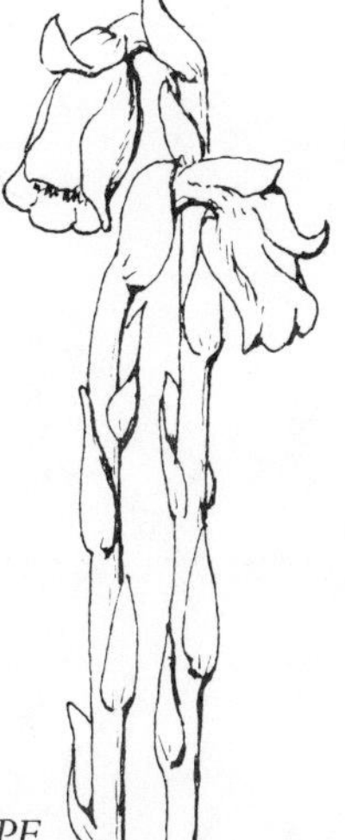
INDIAN PIPE

MINI TOSTADOS

Yields: 50 servings *Pan Size: skillet*

1 (16-ounce) can kidney beans
2 pounds ground beef
1/2 cup chopped onion
1/2 cup catsup
1 to 2 tablespoons chili powder
1 teaspoon salt
1 pound large corn chips
1 cup sour cream
1 cup shredded Cheddar cheese

Drain kidney beans; mash well. Brown ground beef in skillet; drain. Stir in onion, catsup, chili powder, salt and beans. Serve warm on corn chips; top with dollop of sour cream. Sprinkle with shredded Cheddar cheese.

APPROX PER SERVING: Cal 118; Prot 5.1 gr; T Fat 7.7 gr; Chol 19.4 mg; Carbo 7.3 gr; Sod 158.7 mg; Potas 89.5 mg.

NACHO APPETIZERS

Yields: 16 servings *Pan Size: pizza pan* *Preheat: 350 degrees*

1 pound ground beef
1 package taco seasoning
1 small can jalapeno bean dip
1/2 cup shredded Cheddar cheese
1/2 cup shredded Monterey Jack cheese
Nacho chips

Brown ground beef in skillet; drain. Add taco seasoning according to package directions. Spread bean dip in center of pizza pan. Sprinkle 1/4 cup each cheese over dip. Add taco meat sauce over cheeses. Top with remaining cheeses. Bake for 10 minutes. Remove from oven. Surround with nacho chips sprinkled with additional cheeses, if desired. Serve with Guacamole Dip.

Nutritional information not available.

BIRD TRACKS

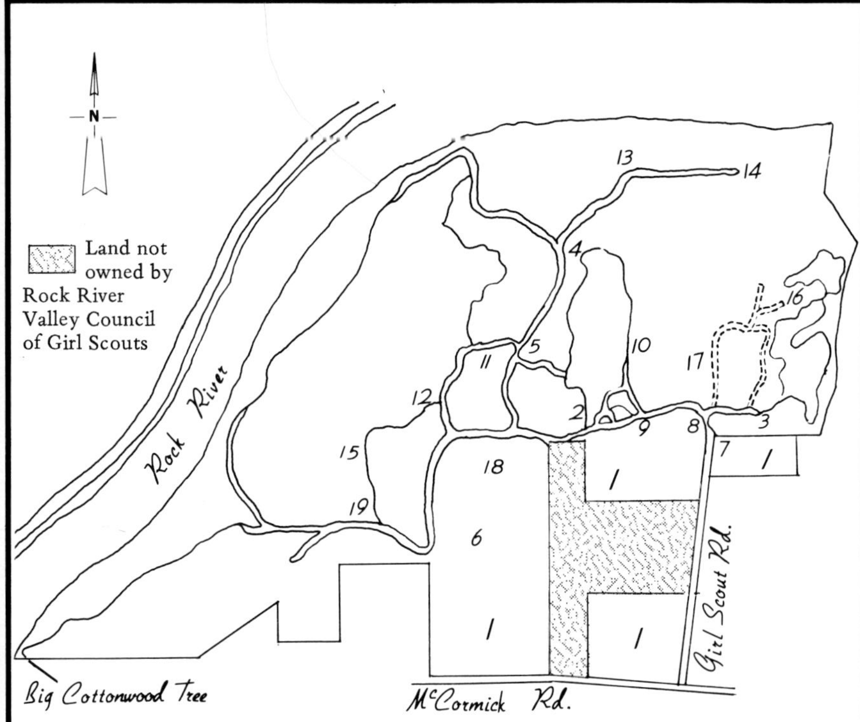

CAMP MEDILL McCORMICK DEVELOPMENT PLANS

1. Farmland — new
2. Troophouse
   - improve kitchen
   - restore balcony
   - new latrine
   - storm windows
3. Greenwood
   - improve floor
   - convert to environmental center
4. Whippoorwill Dining Hall
   - improve dining hall & kitchen
   - install new dishwasher
5. Administration Building — new
   - house infirmary, showers, trading post, and resident camp administration
6. Multi-troop Building — new
   - for 2–3 troops
   - covered swim pool with showers
   - wildlife observation deck
7. Maintenance Building — new
   - workshop
   - ski storage
   - camp check-in
   - wood storage
   - camp parking lot
8. Ranger Residence — new
9. Rabbit
   - convert to arts & craft center
10. O Pee Chee Unit
    - new unit shelter
    - warming building
    - all weather sports surface
11. Deertrail Unit
    - new unit shelter
12. Arrowhead Unit
    - new unit shelter
13. Riverside Unit
    - improve unit shelter
14. Trail's End Unit
    - new latrine
15. Teepees — new
16. Trails — new
17. Team's Course — new
18. Restored Prairie — new
19. Amphitheater

RITA'S CHEESE SQUARES

Yields: 24 servings | *Pan Size: baking sheet* | *Preheat: 250 degrees*

1 loaf unsliced sandwich bread
1 (5-ounce) jar Old English cheese spread
1/2 cup butter, softened

Remove crusts from bread; cut into 1-inch cubes. Beat cheese and butter together with a fork. Frost bread cubes on all sides except bottom with cheese-butter. Place on baking sheet. Bake for 15 to 20 minutes. May be prepared and refrigerated or frozen. Thaw and bring to room temperature before baking.

APPROX PER SERVING: Cal 130; Prot 3.7 gr; T Fat 6.2 gr; Chol 16.9 mg; Carbo 14.8 gr; Sod 284.7 mg; Potas 44.4 mg.

STUFFED MUSHROOMS

Yields: 20 servings | *Pan Size: 9 x 13 inch* | *Preheat: 350 degrees*

1 pound fresh mushrooms
1/4 cup chopped onion
1/4 cup chopped green bell pepper
3 tablespoons margarine
1 1/2 cups soft bread crumbs
1/2 teaspoon salt
1/2 teaspoon thyme
1/4 teaspoon tumeric
1/4 teaspoon pepper
1 tablespoon margarine

Remove and reserve mushroom stems. Saute 1/3 cup chopped stems with onion and green pepper in 3 tablespoons margarine. Add crumbs, salt, thyme, tumeric and pepper, stirring until flavors blend. Stuff mushroom caps with hot mixture. Melt 1 tablespoon margarine in baking pan. Place stuffed caps in pan. Bake for 15 minutes. Serve immediately.

APPROX PER SERVING: Cal 39.5; Prot 1.1 gr; T Fat 2.5 gr; Chol 0.1 mg; Carbo 3.4 gr; Sod 106.7 mg; Potas 106.3 mg.

COLLEEN HAWKINSON'S COLD VEGETABLE PIZZA

Yields: 48 servings *Pan Size: 11 x 17 inch* *Preheat: 400 degrees*

I was fortunate enough to win first place in Appetizers in the 1986 Rockford Register Star Cook-Off Contest with this recipe.

2 (8-count) cans refrigerator crescent rolls
16 ounces cream cheese, softened
1 cup mayonnaise
1 1/2 teaspoons dillweed
1 teaspoon onion powder
3 cups chopped fresh vegetables
1/4 cup chopped black olives
1 1/2 cups shredded Cheddar cheese
Bacon bits or cherry tomatoes (optional)

Arrange rolls in greased baking pan. Bake for 10 minutes; cool. Combine cream cheese and mayonnaise in bowl. Spread over crescent rolls. Sprinkle with dillweed and onion powder. Arrange vegetables, olives and cheese over rolls. Top with bacon bits, or garnish with cherry tomatoes. This is best if made 3 to 4 hours before serving.

Nutritional information not available.

VEGETARIAN PIZZA

Yields: 24 servings *Pan Size: 10 x 15 inch* *Preheat: 350 degrees*

2 cans Pillsbury crescent rolls
16 ounces cream cheese, softened
1 cup mayonnaise
1 1/2 teaspoons dillweed
1 1/2 teaspoons onion powder
Green onions, chopped
Carrots, chopped
Green bell pepper, chopped
Olives, chopped
Celery, chopped
Tomatoes, chopped

Grease baking pan. Spread Pillsbury crescent rolls out flat on pan. Bake for 10 minutes. Let cool. Combine cream cheese, mayonnaise, dillweed and onion powder in bowl; mix well. Spread on baked layer. Top with vegetables.

Nutritional information not available.

VEGETARIAN SANDWICHES

Yields: 8 sandwiches *Pan Size: baking sheet* *Preheat: 350 degrees*

1 (4-ounce) can pitted ripe olives, chopped
1 1/2 cups shredded Cheddar cheese
1/2 cup chopped onion
1/2 to 3/4 cup mayonnaise
1/4 teaspoon curry powder
4 English muffins, split

Combine olives, cheese, onion, mayonnaise and curry powder in bowl; mix well. Spread on English muffins. Place on foil-lined baking sheet. Bake for 10 minutes or until cheese is melted and bubbly. May be served as open-faced hot sandwiches or may be quartered for bite-sized snacks.

APPROX PER SANDWICH: Cal 320; Prot 7.8 gr; T Fat 25.8 gr; Chol 35.7 mg; Carbo 15.2 gr; Sod 463.5 mg; Potas 43.5 mg.

FINGER JELL-O

Yields: 96 servings *Pan Size: 9 x 13 inch*

2 envelopes unflavored gelatin
2/3 cup warm water
1 (6-ounce) package Jell-O
2 cups boiling water

Dissolve gelatin in 2/3 cup warm water. Dissolve Jell-O in 2 cups boiling water. Combine mixtures in bowl. Pour into glass dish. Chill until set. Cut with cookie cutters.

APPROX PER SERVING: Cal 7; Prot 0.3 gr; T Fat 0.0 gr; Chol 0.0 mg; Carbo 1.6 gr; Sod 5.8 mg; Potas 3.8 mg.

CINNAMON PECANS

Yields: 40 servings *Pan Size: baking sheet* *Preheat: 300 degrees*

1/2 cup sugar
1/4 teaspoon salt
2 tablespoons cinnamon
2 cups pecan halves
1 egg white, unbeaten

Combine sugar, salt and cinnamon in small bowl. Dip pecans into unbeaten egg white, then into sugar mixture. Place on ungreased cookie sheet. Bake for 30 minutes. Store in covered container.

APPROX PER SERVING: Cal 51; Prot 0.6 gr; T Fat 4.2 gr; Chol 0.0 mg; Carbo 3.4 gr; Sod 14.6 mg; Potas 36.8 mg.

MICROWAVE CARAMEL CORN

Yields: 12 cups *Pan Size: 2-quart glass dish* 

1 cup packed brown sugar
1/4 cup light corn syrup
1/2 cup margarine
1/4 teaspoon salt
1 teaspoon vanilla extract
1/2 teaspoon soda
3 or 4 quarts popped popcorn
1 cup peanuts

Combine brown sugar, syrup, margarine and salt in glass dish. Microwave on High for 2 minutes or until mixture comes to a boil, stirring down 3 times. Microwave on High for 2 minutes longer. Add vanilla and soda; stir well. Combine popcorn and peanuts in microwave-safe cooking bag; shake vigorously. Pour cooked mixture over popcorn; shake vigorously. Microwave on High for 1 1/2 minutes; shake vigorously. Microwave for 1 1/2 minutes longer; shake again. May need 1 1/2 minutes longer, depending on strength of microwave. Shake, then pour onto waxed paper, spreading out to cool. Store in covered container.

APPROX PER CUP: Cal 254; Prot 4.2 gr; T Fat 14.0 gr; Chol 0.0 mg; Carbo 30.4 gr; Sod 228.1 mg; Potas 168.3 mg.

ZILLAH'S ORANGE POPCORN BALLS

Yields: 30 popcorn balls *Pan Size: saucepan*

3 cups sugar
1 (6-ounce) can frozen orange juice concentrate
1/3 cup water
1/3 cup light corn syrup
1 tablespoon butter
1 1/2 cups popped popcorn

Combine sugar, orange juice concentrate, water, corn syrup and butter in saucepan. Bring to a boil. Cook to 255 degrees on candy thermometer, hard-ball stage; do not stir. Pour over popcorn in bowl; stir well. Butter hands; form into small balls, working steadily. Wrap popcorn balls in plastic wrap to store.

APPROX PER POPCORN BALL: Cal 190; Prot 0.8 gr; T Fat 0.6 gr; Chol 1.2 mg; Carbo 46.9 gr; Sod 5.8 mg; Potas 71.2 mg.

Beverages

BARRED
OWL

JOHNNY APPLESEED SHAKES

Yields: 3 servings

Kids love this and it's nutritious too!

1 pint vanilla ice cream, slightly softened
1 cup apple juice
1/4 teaspoon cinnamon
1/4 teaspoon nutmeg

Place ice cream, apple juice, cinnamon and nutmeg in blender container. Cover container. Blend on High for 30 seconds or until smooth and well blended. Pour into glasses. Serve immediately.

APPROX PER SERVING: Cal 258;
Prot 2.6 gr; T Fat 15.9 gr; Chol 56.2 mg;
Carbo 56.2 gr; Sod 33.4 mg; Potas 177.2 mg.

COLD EGGNOG

Yields: 4 cups *Pan Size: blender*

Tested and approved by the kids! Easy enough for them to make.

3 cups cold milk
3 eggs
3 tablespoons sugar
1 teaspoon vanilla extract
1 cup crushed ice

Place milk, eggs, sugar, vanilla and ice in blender container; cover. Blend until thick and creamy. Enjoy!

APPROX PER CUP: Cal 219;
Prot 11.3 gr; T Fat 10.7 gr; Chol 215.2 mg;
Carbo 19.3 gr; Sod 137.5 mg;
Potas 312.3 mg.

ORANGE JULIETTE

Yields: 4 servings *Pan Size: blender*

1/4 cup sugar
1 (6-ounce) can frozen orange juice concentrate
1 cup milk
1 cup water
1 teaspoon vanilla extract
10 ice cubes

Combine sugar, orange juice concentrate, milk, water, vanilla and ice cubes in blender container; cover. Blend on High for 30 seconds or until ice is crushed.

APPROX PER SERVING: Cal 178;
Prot 3.5 gr; T Fat 2.2 gr; Chol 8.5 mg;
Carbo 37.1 gr; Sod 31.7 mg;
Potas 463.1 mg.

CHAMPAGNE PUNCH

Yields: 30 servings *Pan Size: punch bowl*

1 quart orange juice
2 cups ginger ale, chilled
1 quart Champagne, chilled
1 cup vodka
1 (16-ounce) can pineapple tidbits, undrained
1 pint orange sherbet

Pour orange juice, ginger ale, Champagne and vodka in punch bowl. Add pineapple tidbits and sherbet; mix lightly. Serve cold immediately. Ladle into punch cups.

APPROX PER SERVING: Cal 82; Prot 0.4 gr; T Fat 0.2 gr; Chol 0.0 mg; Carbo 12.8 gr; Sod 2.6 mg; Potas 99.7 mg.

FRUITY PUNCH

Yields: 25 servings *Pan Size: punch bowl*

2 cups sugar
3 cups water
3 bananas, mashed
1 (23-ounce) can pineapple juice
1 (12-ounce) can frozen orange juice concentrate
1 (16-ounce) can frozen lemonade concentrate
1 liter 7-Up

Combine sugar and water in bowl. Add bananas; mix well. Add pineapple juice, orange juice and lemonade; mix well. Freeze for several hours. Remove from freezer 1 hour before serving time. Add 7-Up. Serve immediately.

APPROX PER SERVING: Cal 157; Prot 0.7 gr; T Fat 0.1 gr; Chol 0.0 mg; Carbo 39.9 gr; Sod 1.1 mg; Potas 224.1 mg.

ISLANDER PUNCH

Yields: 18 servings *Pan Size: punch bowl*

4 cups sugar
6 cups water
1 (6-ounce) can frozen orange juice concentrate
Juice of 3 lemons
6 bananas, mashed
1 (46-ounce) can pineapple juice
2 (1-quart) bottles of club soda

Combine sugar and water in saucepan. Bring to a boil; boil for 3 minutes. Cool. Combine orange juice, lemon juice, bananas and pineapple juice in large bowl. Add sugar water; mix well. Pour into 2 half-gallon containers; cover. Freeze. Remove from freezer 1 hour before serving time. Add club soda. Serve immediately.

APPROX PER SERVING: Cal 269; Prot 1.1 gr; T Fat 0.2 gr; Chol 0.0 mg; Carbo 68.7 gr; Sod 1.9 mg; Potas 351.9 mg.

REAL GOOD PUNCH

Yields: 50 servings *Pan Size: punch bowl*

- 4 tea bags
- 3 cups boiling water
- 2 cups sugar
- 1 1/2 quarts cold water
- 1 (46-ounce) can apricot nectar
- 2 (12-ounce) cans unsweetened pineapple juice
- 1 pint lemon juice
- 2 quarts 7-Up or ginger ale

Steep tea bags in boiling water for 5 minutes in saucepan. Add sugar, stirring to dissolve. Remove tea bags. Pour into freezer container. Add cold water, apricot nectar, pineapple juice and lemon juice; mix well. Freeze for 12 to 24 hours. Remove from freezer 5 hours before serving time. Add 7-Up. Serve immediately.

APPROX PER SERVING: Cal 76; Prot 0.2 gr; T Fat 0.1 gr; Chol 0.0 mg; Carbo 19.7 gr; Sod 0.3 mg; Potas 79.9 mg.

RECOGNITION PUNCH

Yields: 16 cups *Pan Size: punch bowl*

- 1 cup boiling water
- 1 (3-ounce) package cherry gelatin
- 1 quart orange-pineapple juice
- 1 quart apple juice
- 1 (28-ounce) bottle of ginger ale
- 1 quart orange sherbet

Combine boiling water with gelatin in punch bowl. Add orange-pineapple juice and apple juice. Pour in ginger ale. Float scoops of sherbet on top. Serve immediately.

APPROX PER CUP: Cal 162; Prot 1.3 gr; T Fat 0.7 gr; Chol 0.0 mg; Carbo 38.9 gr; Sod 23.0 mg; Potas 193.0 mg.

REFRESHING TEA PUNCH

Yields: six 8-ounce servings *Pan Size: blender*

- 1 (10-ounce) package frozen strawberries, thawed
- 1 (6-ounce) can frozen lemonade concentrate, thawed
- 1/2 cup sugar
- 1/2 cup instant tea
- 6 cups water

Combine strawberries, lemonade concentrate, sugar and tea in blender container. Blend on High until smooth. Pour into pitcher. Add cold water. Serve over ice immediately. Garnish with whole strawberries and lemon slices.

APPROX PER SERVING: Cal 187; Prot 0.3 gr; T Fat 0.1 gr; Chol 0.0 mg; Carbo 48.4 gr; Sod 1.4 mg; Potas 79.1 mg.

SLUSH-SLUSH PUNCH

Yields: forty 5-ounce cups *Pan Size: freezer container*

1 (46-ounce) can pineapple juice
1 (16-ounce) can crushed pineapple
6 ripe bananas, mashed
1 (6-ounce) can frozen orange juice concentrate
1 (16-ounce) can Hawaiian Punch
7 ounces coconut
1 (1-liter) bottle of 7-Up

Combine pineapple juice, crushed pineapple, bananas, orange juice, Hawaiian Punch and coconut in freezer container. Freeze for 3 to 4 hours. Remove from freezer; mix with spoon. Freeze until serving time. Let stand until slushy. Fill glasses half full with mixture; add 7-Up. Serve immediately.

APPROX PER CUP: Cal 206; Prot 0.6 gr; T Fat 0.9 gr; Chol 0.0 mg; Carbo 5.0 gr; Sod 6.3 mg; Potas 177.7 mg.
Nutritional information does not include Hawaiian Punch.

APRICOT SLUSH

Yields: 30 cups *Pan Size: freezer container*

7 cups water
2 cups sugar
4 tea bags
2 cups boiling water
1 (12-ounce) can frozen orange juice concentrate
1 (12-ounce) can frozen lemonade concentrate
2 cups apricot brandy
15 cups ginger ale

Bring 7 cups water and sugar to a boil in saucepan; boil for 5 minutes. Cool. Steep tea bags in boiling water for 10 minutes; remove tea bags. Cool. Combine sugar water, tea, orange juice, lemonade and brandy in large freezer container; mix well. Freeze overnight. Fill serving glass half full with slush. Add ginger ale. Serve immediately.

APPROX PER CUP: Cal 142; Prot 0.4 gr; T Fat 0.0 gr; Chol 0.0 mg; Carbo 36.3 gr; Sod 0.7 mg; Potas 110.6 mg.
Nutritional information does not include Brandy.

SUMMER SLUSH

Yields: 10 cups *Pan Size: freezer container*

This is a drink you can always have on hand. It's in the freezer and ready to serve. Very refreshing in the summer.

- 7 cups water
- 2 cups sugar
- 2 cups water
- 4 green tea bags
- 1 (12-ounce) can frozen lemonade concentrate
- 1 (12-ounce) can frozen orange juice concentrate
- 7-Up, ginger ale or Squirt

Bring 7 cups water and sugar to a boil in saucepan. Cool. Bring 2 cups water and tea bags to a boil in separate saucepan. Cool; remove tea bags. Combine 2 mixtures, lemonade and orange juice in large freezer container; mix well. Freeze for 24 hours, stirring mixture 3 times. Fill glasses half full with slush. Add 7-Up, ginger ale or Squirt. Serve immediately.

APPROX PER CUP: Cal 312;
Prot 1.2 gr; T Fat 0.1 gr; Chol 0.0 mg;
Carbo 79.5 gr; Sod 2.1 mg;
Potas 331.8 mg.
Nutritional information does not include soda.

TERRIFIC COCOA

Yields: 80 servings

This is a staple in the camping box and also in the kitchen cupboard all year long!

- 1 (8-quart) box powdered milk
- 1 pound instant chocolate drink mix
- 1 (6-ounce) jar coffee creamer
- 3/4 cup confectioners' sugar

Combine powdered milk, chocolate, coffee creamer and confectioners' sugar in bowl; mix well. Fill cup 1/3 full with dry mixture. Add hot water; stir to mix. Serve hot immediately.

Nutritional information not available.

Salads

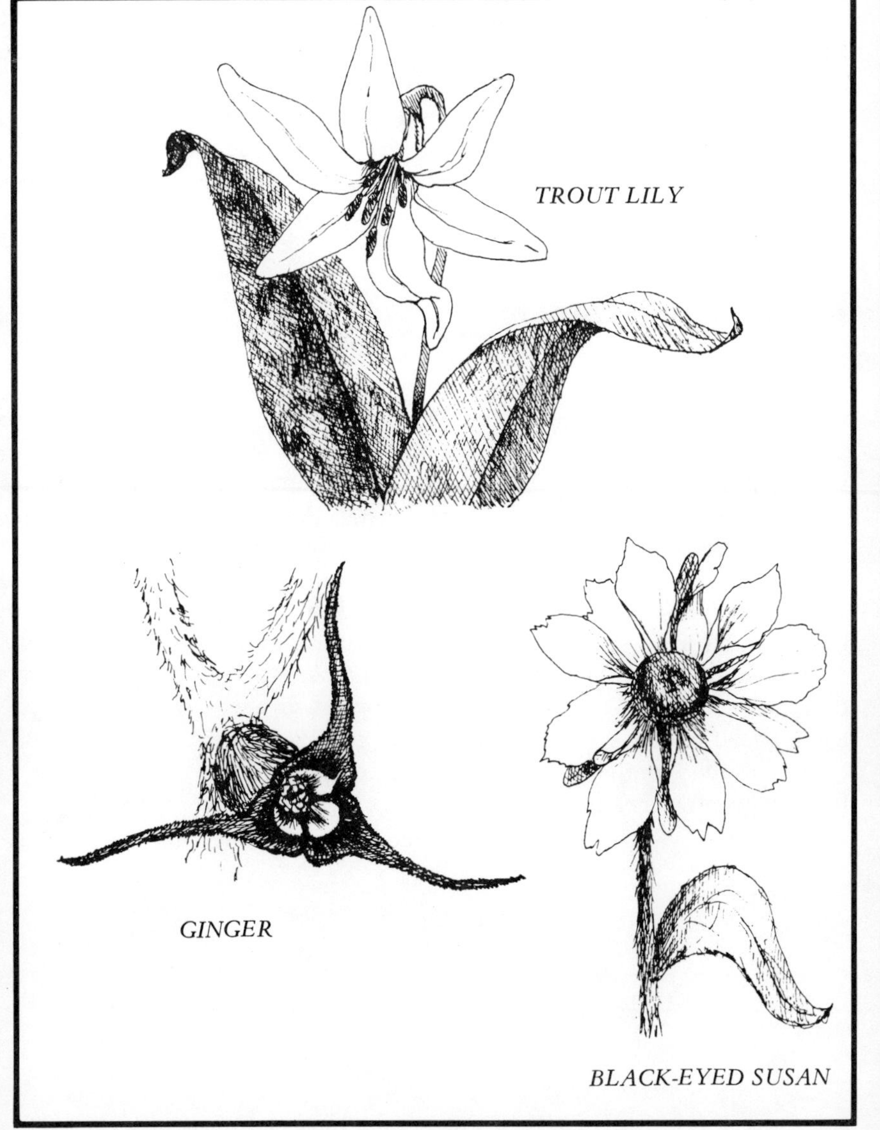

TAFFY APPLE SALAD

Yields: 10 servings *Pan Size: 2 quart*

1 (20-ounce) can crushed pineapple
2 cups miniature marshmallows
1/2 cup sugar
1 egg, well beaten
1 tablespoon flour
8 ounces Cool Whip
1 1/2 cups Spanish peanuts (with skins on)
2 cups diced unpeeled apples

Drain pineapple, reserving juice. Combine pineapple and marshmallows in glass dish. Refrigerate overnight. Combine reserved juice, sugar, egg and flour in saucepan. Cook until bubbly. Refrigerate overnight. Combine sauce with Cool Whip, peanuts, pineapple mixture and apples. Chill for 1 hour before serving.

APPROX PER SERVING: Cal 338; Prot 7.1 gr; T Fat 17.2 gr; Chol 25.4 mg; Carbo 43.2 gr; Sod 106.6 mg; Potas 246.4 mg.

PARTY FRUIT SALAD

Yields: 10 servings

1 (20-ounce) can pineapple
1/2 cup sugar
1/2 cup water
1 egg, beaten
1 1/2 tablespoons cornstarch
1 1/2 tablespoons flour
1 cup miniature marshmallows
1 cup sliced grapes
1 cup sliced bananas
1 cup chopped apples
1 cup whipping cream, whipped

Drain pineapple, reserving juice. Combine reserved juice, sugar, water and egg in saucepan. Combine cornstarch and flour. Add to pineapple juice mixture, stirring constantly. Bring to a boil. Cook until thick, stirring constantly. Add pineapple. Chill in refrigerator for several hours or overnight. Add marshmallows, grapes, bananas and apples; mix well. Fold in whipped cream gently. Chill.

APPROX PER SERVING: Cal 231; Prot 1.9 gr; T Fat 9.8 gr; Chol 57.0 mg; Carbo 36.5 gr; Sod 17.1 mg; Potas 178.9 mg.

BUBBLING FRUIT

Yields: 4 servings

1 (8 3/4-ounce) can peach slices, drained
1 (8-ounce) can pineapple chunks
1/2 cup halved seedless green grapes
1 medium banana, sliced
1/4 cup coconut
1/2 cup ginger ale, chilled

Combine peaches, pineapple, grapes, banana and coconut in large bowl; stir well. Chill, covered, for several hours. Spoon fruit into individual serving dishes. Pour a small amount of ginger ale into each dish. Serve immediately.

APPROX PER SERVING: Cal 137; Prot 1.1 gr; T Fat 1.9 gr; Chol 0.0 mg; Carbo 31.9 gr; Sod 13.8 mg; Potas 309.5 mg.

CHAMPAGNE SALAD

Yields: 12 servings

8 ounces cream cheese, softened
3/4 cup sugar
1 (16-ounce) container sliced frozen strawberries
1 (20-ounce) can crushed pineapple, drained
2 large bananas, diced
3/4 cup chopped pecans
8 ounces Cool Whip

Combine cream cheese and sugar in bowl; mix well. Add strawberries, pineapple, bananas and pecans. Add Cool Whip gently. Freeze for several hours. May be kept frozen until just before serving.

APPROX PER SERVING: Cal 326 Prot 3.0 gr; T Fat 17.3 gr; Chol 21.0 mg; Carbo 43.5 gr; Sod 53.1 mg; Potas 229.0 mg.

CHERRY SALAD

Yields: 8 servings *Pan Size: 9 x 12 inch*

1 (6-ounce) package cherry Jell-O
1 cup boiling water
1/4 cup pecans, chopped
1 (21-ounce) can cherry pie filling
1 (20-ounce) can crushed pineapple, with juice
1/4 to 1/2 cup chopped celery

Dissolve Jell-O in boiling water. Pour into glass dish. Add remaining ingredients; stir until well mixed. Chill until firm.

APPROX PER SERVING: Cal 248; Prot 2.7 gr; T Fat 2.7 gr; Chol 0.0 mg; Carbo 55.4 gr; Sod 77.8 mg; Potas 168.9 mg.

CRANBERRY WALDORF SALAD

Yields: 12 servings *Pan Size: 2-quart mold*

3 (3-ounce) packages peach Jell-O
3 cups boiling water
2 cups cranberry juice
2 tablespoons lemon juice
1 1/4 teaspoons salt
1 1/2 cups diced apple
1 1/2 cups diced celery
1/2 cup chopped English walnuts

Combine Jell-O, boiling water, cranberry juice, lemon juice and salt in bowl. Stir until Jell-O is dissolved. Chill until partially set. Add apple, celery and walnuts; mix well. Chill until firm or overnight. Unmold onto serving plate. Serve with dollops of mayonnaise or sour cream. Garnish with cranberries or walnuts.

APPROX PER SERVING: Cal 148; Prot 2.8 gr; T Fat 3.3 gr; Chol 0.0 mg; Carbo 28.9 gr; Sod 290.3 mg; Potas 92.1 mg.

MARLOW SALAD

Yields: 15 servings

1/2 cup pineapple juice
3 eggs, slightly beaten
1/4 cup vinegar
32 large marshmallows
1 (16-ounce) can fruit cocktail, drained
1 (6-ounce) can crushed pineapple
1 cup whipping cream, whipped

Combine pineapple juice, eggs and vinegar in top of double boiler. Cook until thick, stirring constantly. Add marshmallows; stir until almost dissolved. Pour over fruit cocktail and crushed pineapple in large dish. Let stand in refrigerator until cool. Fold whipped cream gently into mixture. Chill for several hours.

APPROX PER SERVING: Cal 157; Prot 2.1 gr; T Fat 7.2 gr; Chol 71.8 mg; Carbo 22.4 gr; Sod 23.5 mg; Potas 116.1 mg.

MILLIONAIRE SALAD

Yields: 12 servings

1 (21-ounce) can cherry pie filling
1 (9-ounce) carton Cool Whip
1 can sweetened condensed milk
1 (16-ounce) can pineapple chunks, drained
1 cup chopped walnuts
1 cup miniature marshmallows

Combine cherry pie filling, Cool Whip, condensed milk, pineapple, walnuts and marshmallows in glass serving dish. Chill for several hours.

APPROX PER SERVING: Cal 367; Prot 5.6 gr; T Fat 15.0 gr; Chol 15.2 mg; Carbo 55.0 gr; Sod 56.7 mg; Potas 229.3 mg.

PRETZEL SALAD

Yields: 15 servings *Pan Size: 9 x 13 inch* *Preheat: 400 degrees*

12 ounces cream cheese, softened
1 1/4 cups sugar
2 2/3 cups pretzels, coarsely chopped
1 1/2 sticks butter, melted
3/4 (12-ounce) carton Cool Whip
1 (6-ounce) package strawberry Jell-O
2 cups hot pineapple juice
1 (16-ounce) package frozen strawberries

Combine cream cheese and sugar in bowl; mix well. Set aside. Combine pretzels and melted butter in glass dish, pressing into sides of dish. Bake for 10 minutes. Spread cream cheese mixture over pretzels, a small amount at a time. Spread Cool Whip over cream cheese. Chill for several hours. Dissolve Jell-O in hot pineapple juice in bowl. Add strawberries. Let stand until partially set. Pour over chilled mixture. Chill for several hours or overnight.

APPROX PER SERVING: Cal 395; Prot 3.5 gr; T Fat 23.5 gr; Chol 53.6 mg; Carbo 45.2 gr; Sod 211.3 mg; Potas 131.3 mg.

STRAWBERRY PRETZEL DELIGHT

Yields: 15 servings *Pan Size: 9 x 13 inch* *Preheat: 350 degrees*

3/4 cup margarine, melted
2 cups crushed pretzels
2 tablespoons sugar
8 ounces cream cheese, softened
2 cups Cool Whip
1 cup sugar
2 (3-ounce) packages strawberry Jell-O
2 cups hot water
2 (10-ounce) packages frozen strawberries

Combine margarine with crushed pretzels and 2 tablespoons sugar in bowl. Press into baking pan. Bake for 10 minutes. Cool. Combine cream cheese with Cool Whip and 1 cup sugar. Pour over crumb crust. Chill. Dissolve Jell-O in hot water with frozen strawberries; mix well. Chill until partially set. Pour over cream cheese layer. Chill until firm. Serve cut into squares.

APPROX PER SERVING: Cal 307; Prot 2.7 gr; T Fat 23.3 gr; Chol 16.8 mg; Carbo 37.9 gr; Sod 300.7 mg; Potas 84.6 mg.

STRAWBERRY-RHUBARB MOLD

Yields: 12 servings *Pan Size: 6-cup mold*

4 cups diced fresh rhubarb
1/2 cup water
1/2 cup sugar
2 (3-ounce) packages strawberry gelatin
1 (16-ounce) can crushed pineapple, undrained
1 (10-ounce) package frozen sliced strawberries

Cook rhubarb with water and sugar in saucepan over low heat until soft and smooth. Add gelatin; stir until dissolved. Stir in pineapple and strawberries. Pour into mold. Chill until firm.

APPROX PER SERVING: Cal 156; Prot 1.9 gr; T Fat 0.1 gr; Chol 0.0 mg; Carbo 39.1 gr; Sod 46.7 mg; Potas 209.6 mg.

SKATING ON KENT CREEK, FAIR GROUNDS,
JANUARY, 1914.

SOUR CREAM JELL-O SALAD

Yields: 8 servings *Pan Size: 6-cup mold*

This Jell-O does not "melt" when you take it to potlucks or outdoor meals. It will also "set up" quickly in a ring mold.

1 (6-ounce) package orange Jell-O
1 cup boiling water
1 cup sour cream
1 (20-ounce) can crushed pineapple
1 (11-ounce) can mandarin oranges, drained

Combine Jell-O with water in bowl; stir until dissolved. Add sour cream; mix well. Add pineapple with juice and oranges; mix well. Pour into oiled mold. Chill until firm.

APPROX PER SERVING: Cal 214; Prot 3.4 gr; T Fat 6.2 gr; Chol 12.6 mg; Carbo 39.1 gr; Sod 84.3 mg; Potas 203.1 mg.

SEVEN-LAYER JELL-O

Yields: 15 servings *Pan Size: 9 x 13 inch*

1 (3-ounce) package black cherry gelatin
1 (3-ounce) package lime gelain
1 (3-ounce) package orange gelatin
1 (3-ounce) package strawberry gelatin
1 (3-ounce) package red cherry gelatin
1 (3-ounce) package lemon gelatin
1 (3-ounce) package orange-pineapple gelatin
1 (13-ounce) can evaporated milk

Prepare gelatins, 1 at a time, in order listed, preparing each layer as the previous layers chill. Prepare black cherry, lime, orange and strawberry gelatins according to package directions, using 3/4 cup boiling water and 3/4 cup cold water. Prepare red cherry, lemon and orange-pineapple gelatins using 1/2 cup boiling water and 1/2 cup cold water. Stir 1/2 cup evaporated milk into each just before pouring over congealed layer. Use a glass dish. Chill for 30 to 45 minutes before adding next layer.

APPROX PER SERVING: Cal 182; Prot 5.5 gr; T Fat 2.0 gr; Chol 7.8 mg; Carbo 37.4 gr; Sod 155.9 mg; Potas 159.7 mg.

SEVEN-UP SALAD

Yields: 15 servings *Pan Size: 9 x 13 inch*

1 (8-ounce) can crushed pineapple
2 (3-ounce) packages lemon Jell-O
2 cups boiling water
2 cups 7-Up
3 bananas, sliced
1 cup miniature marshmallows
1 egg, beaten
2 tablespoons flour
2 tablespoons butter, melted
1/2 cup sugar
1 cup whipping cream, whipped
1 cup grated Cheddar cheese

Drain pineapple, reserving juice. Add enough water to juice to measure 1 cup. Combine Jell-O and boiling water in bowl; stir until dissolved. Add 7-Up; mix well. Chill for 1 hour. Combine pineapple, bananas and marshmallows in glass dish. Add chilled Jell-O. Combine egg, flour, butter, sugar and pineapple juice in saucepan. Cook over low heat until thick. Set aside to cool. Fold whipped cream gently into sauce. Spread evenly over Jell-O. Sprinkle cheese on top.

APPROX PER SERVING: Cal 204; Prot 2.3 gr; T Fat 8.0 gr; Chol 42.7 mg; Carbo 32.9 gr; Sod 65.6 mg; Potas 148.5 mg.

MANHATTAN DELI SALAD

Yields: 20 servings

1 (16-ounce) package spiral pasta, cooked
1 1/4 cups pitted ripe olives, sliced
1 cup chopped green bell pepper
1/4 pound hard salami, cut into thin strips
1 small red onion, cut into rings
1/4 to 1/2 cup grated Parmesan cheese
1/4 cup finely chopped parsley
1 (8-ounce) bottle of Wishbone Italian salad dressing

Combine all ingredients in order listed in bowl; mix well. Chill, covered, for several hours. Serve cold.

APPROX PER SERVING: Cal 197; Prot 5.6 gr; T Fat 11.0 gr; Chol 6.7 mg; Carbo 18.9 gr; Sod 367.6 mg; Potas 93.0 mg.

EASY SEAFOOD SALAD

Yields: 4 servings

Dieter's delight if diet or light mayonnaise is used.

- 1 (6-ounce) can shrimp, drained
- 1 (6-ounce) can water-pack tuna, drained
- 1 (6-ounce) can crab meat, drained
- 1 cup chopped celery
- 1 cup peas
- 2 tablespoons chopped onion
- 1/2 cup mayonnaise

Combine shrimp, tuna, crab meat, celery, peas and onion in bowl. Add mayonnaise; mix well. Chill, covered, until serving time.

APPROX PER SERVING: Cal 390; Prot 33.8 gr; T Fat 24.5 gr; Chol 157.8 mg; Carbo 7.9 gr; Sod 828.7 mg; Potas 428.6 mg.

TUNA-CASHEW SALAD

Yields: 6 servings

- 1 cup diced onion
- 1 cup diced ripe olives
- 1 cup diced celery
- 2 small carrots, shredded
- 1 (6-ounce) can water-pack tuna
- 1 cup salad dressing
- 1 cup cashews
- 1 (3-ounce) can chow mein noodles

Combine onion, olives, celery, carrots and tuna in bowl. Add salad dressing; mix well. Add cashews and chow mein noodles; mix well. Chill until serving time.

APPROX PER SERVING: Cal 587; Prot 16.1 gr; T Fat 48.2 gr; Chol 47.1 mg; Carbo 22.1 gr; Sod 588.2 mg; Potas 417.6 mg.

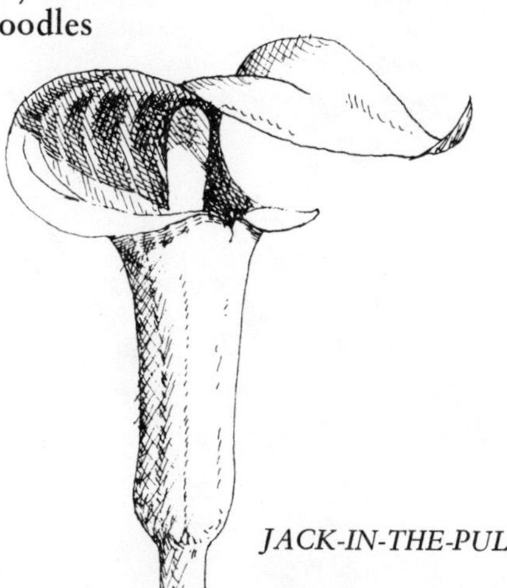

JACK-IN-THE-PULPIT

AMERIENTAL SALAD

Yields: 15 servings *Pan Size: large bowl*

2/3 cup sugar
1/3 cup salad oil
2/3 cup vinegar
1/2 teaspoon salt
1/2 teaspoon pepper
1 (16-ounce) can French-style green beans
1 (16-ounce) can Shoe Peg corn
1 (7-ounce) can water chestnuts
1 (7-ounce) can water chestnuts
1 (16-ounce) can bamboo shoots
1 medium onion, chopped
1 1/2 cups chopped celery
1 small jar chopped pimento

Combine sugar, salad oil, vinegar, salt and pepper in saucepan. Bring to a boil; simmer until sugar is dissolved. Drain vegetables. Combine in large bowl. Add onion, celery and pimento; mix well. Pour marinade over vegetables; mix well. Marinate, covered, in refrigerator overnight, stirring occasionally. Serve cold.

APPROX PER SERVING: Cal 160; Prot 3.8 gr; T Fat 5.4 gr; Chol 0.0 mg; Carbo 27.1 gr; Sod 287.2 mg; Potas 344.3 mg.

SARAH'S BROCCOLI SALAD

Yields: 7 servings

1 large bunch broccoli, cut in chunks
4 to 6 hard-boiled eggs, chopped
1 (12-ounce) jar green olives, chopped
1 teaspoon salt
1 teaspoon garlic powder
3/4 cup low-calorie mayonnaise

Combine broccoli, eggs and olives in bowl. Sprinkle with salt and garlic. Add enough mayonnaise to moisten well. Chill for several hours. Serve as side salad on picnics or summer meals. Very tasty!

APPROX PER SERVING: Cal 267; Prot 8.9 gr; T Fat 23.0 gr; Chol 229.5 mg; Carbo 8.6 gr; Sod 1842.2 mg; Potas 335.7 mg.

CRUNCHY BROCCOLI SALAD

Yields: 10 servings

1 (16-ounce) package frozen chopped broccoli, thawed
3 hard-cooked eggs, cut up
1/3 cup chopped onion
1 small jar stuffed olives, sliced
1 cup chopped celery
1 (7-ounce) can sliced water chestnuts
1 cup mayonnaise

Combine broccoli, eggs, onion, olives, celery and water chestnuts in bowl; mix well. Add mayonnaise. Season with dillweed and salt to taste. Chill for several hours. Serve cold.

APPROX PER SERVING: Cal 232; Prot 4.4 gr; T Fat 20.8 gr; Chol 91.5 mg; Carbo 8.6 gr; Sod 363.1 mg; Potas 221.4 mg.

BROCCOLI AND CAULIFLOWER SALAD

Yields: 10 servings

1 pound broccoli, chopped
1 pound cauliflower, chopped
1 small onion, chopped
1/3 cup vinegar
1/3 cup sugar
2/3 cup mayonnaise
1 teaspoon salt

Combine broccoli, cauliflower and onion in bowl; toss well. Combine vinegar, sugar, mayonnaise and salt in small bowl; mix well. Pour over vegetables. Chill, covered, overnight.

Nutritional information not available.

MARINATED CARROTS

Yields: 8 servings

1 cup vinegar
1 cup sugar
1/3 cup oil
3 (16-ounce) cans sliced carrots
1 cup chopped green bell pepper
1 (2-ounce) jar pimento, cut up
3 green onions with tops, chopped

Combine vinegar, sugar and oil in saucepan. Bring to a boil. Cool. Combine carrots, green pepper, pimento and onion in covered dish. Pour cooled marinade over vegetables; mix well. Chill, covered, for 24 hours.

APPROX PER SERVING: Cal 234; Prot 1.3 gr; T Fat 9.4 gr; Chol 0.0 mg; Carbo 36.3 gr; Sod 279.4 mg; Potas 239.2 mg.

COLESLAW

Yields: 6 servings

2 tablespoons sugar
1/8 teaspoon salt
2 tablespoons vinegar
1/4 cup mayonnaise
4 cups shredded cabbage

Combine sugar, salt, a dash of pepper and vinegar in bowl. Add mayonnaise; mix well. Pour over cabbage in bowl; toss well. Serve on lettuce leaves. Garnish with paprika.

APPROX PER SERVING: Cal 99; Prot 0.9 gr; T Fat 7.6 gr; Chol 6.5 mg; Carbo 8.1 gr; Sod 114.0 mg; Potas 148.1 mg.

RAVE COLESLAW

Yields: 20 servings

1 1/2 cups salad dressing
1 tablespoon lemon juice
1 teaspoon cinnamon
1/2 cup evaporated milk
3 tablespoons sugar
1 teaspoon vanilla extract
1/2 cup sour cream
1 head cabbage, finely shredded

Combine salad dressing, lemon juice, cinnamon, evaporated milk, sugar, vanilla and sour cream in large bowl; mix well. Toss with cabbage; mix well. Raisins, drained pineapple, apple bits or pecans are nice additions, if desired.

APPROX PER SERVING: Cal 124; Prot 1.7 gr; T Fat 9.5 gr; Chol 13.5 mg; Carbo 9.2 gr; Sod 129.6 mg; Potas 188.7 mg.

K. F. C. COLESLAW

Yields: 20 servings

1/4 cup milk
1/4 cup cider vinegar
1/2 cup sugar
1 cup salad dressing
2 teaspoons salt
1 medium head cabbage, chopped
3 carrots, chopped
1 green bell pepper, chopped

Combine milk, vinegar, sugar, salad dressing and salt in blender container. Process for 5 minutes. Combine cabbage, carrots and green bell pepper in serving bowl; mix well. Toss with dressing, mixing well. Chill before serving.

APPROX PER SERVING: Cal 95; Prot 1.3 gr; T Fat 5.3 gr; Chol 6.4 mg; Carbo 11.8 gr; Sod 304.2 mg; Potas 30.7 mg.

FIESTA COLESLAW

Yields: 15 servings

1 (16-ounce) can crushed pineapple, drained
1 head cabbage, shredded
2 cups raisins
1 cup mayonnaise

Combine pineapple, cabbage and raisins. Add mayonnaise just before serving. Season to taste.

APPROX PER SERVING: Cal 203; Prot 1.5 gr; T Fat 12.1 gr; Chol 10.5 mg; Carbo 25.1 gr; Sod 106.7 mg; Potas 325.0 mg.

FROZEN COLESLAW

Yields: 20 servings

1 teaspoon salt
1 medium cabbage, shredded
3 stalks celery, chopped
1/2 green bell pepper, chopped
1 cup white vinegar
1/2 cup water
2 cups sugar
1 teaspoon celery seed
1 teaspoon mustard seed

Sprinkle salt over cabbage. Let stand for 1 hour. Squeeze out liquid. Combine cabbage, celery and green pepper in freezer container. Combine vinegar, water, sugar, celery seed and mustard seed in saucepan. Bring to a boil. Cool. Pour over cabbage mixture; mix well. Freeze, covered, until serving time.
Will keep in refrigerator for about 2 weeks without freezing.

APPROX PER SERVING: Cal 96; Prot 1.0 gr; T Fat 0.1 gr; Chol 0.0 mg; Carbo 24.6 gr; Sod 128.3 mg; Potas 195.5 mg.

OVERNIGHT SALAD

Yields: 10 servings

1 large head cauliflower, chopped
1 large bunch broccoli, chopped
1 medium red onion, sliced
1 cup cherry tomatoes
1 cup pitted black olives
1 (8-ounce) bottle Zesty Italian dressing

Layer cauliflower and broccoli in bowl. Top with onion, tomatoes and olives. Add enough dressing to moisten well. Marinate in refrigerator overnight.

APPROX PER SERVING: Cal 206; Prot 4.6 gr; T Fat 17.5 gr; Chol 0.0 mg; Carbo 11.6 gr; Sod 623.6 mg; Potas 505.9 mg.

LAYERED SALAD

Yields: 16 servings *Pan Size: 9 x 13 inch*

1 head lettuce, finely chopped
1 cup diced celery
1 green bell pepper, diced
1 onion, diced
1 (10-ounce) package frozen peas
3 cups mayonnaise
1 tablespoon sugar
4 cups shredded Cheddar cheese
10 slices crisp-fried lean bacon, crumbled

Line glass dish with lettuce. Layer celery, green pepper, onion, peas, mayonnaise, sugar, cheese and bacon in order listed. Chill until ready to serve.
VARIATIONS: Add layer of 3 or 4 stalks chopped celery on top of lettuce base;
Use 3/4 lettuce for base and 1/4 just before mayonnaise;
Add 2 or 3 teaspoons sugar on top of mayonnaise;
Substitute Parmesan cheese for Cheddar cheese.

APPROX PER SERVING: Cal 468; Prot 10.3 gr; T Fat 45.2 gr; Chol 61.5 mg; Carbo 7.1 gr; Sod 533.4 mg; Potas 186.2 mg.

ROMAN SALAD

Yields: 6 servings

1/2 head lettuce, chopped
3/4 cup chopped celery
1/2 cup sliced radishes
5 ounces frozen peas, thawed
1/4 cup chopped onion
1/3 pound crisp-cooked bacon, crumbled
3/4 cup salad dressing
1/3 cup grated Cheddar cheese

Layer lettuce, celery, radishes, peas, onion and bacon in order listed in bowl. Spread top with salad dressing. Sprinkle Cheddar cheese over all. Let stand, covered, overnight in refrigerator. Toss lightly before serving.

APPROX PER SERVING: Cal 220; Prot 5.4 gr; T Fat 17.9 gr; Chol 26.2 mg; Carbo 10.5 gr; Sod 335.1 mg; Potas 229.3 mg.

SPRING PARFAIT SALAD

Yields: 8 servings

2 (3-ounce) packages lemon Jell-O
1 cup boiling water
3 cups diced celery
2/3 cup diced green bell pepper
1/3 cup diced carrot
2 cups diced cucumber
1/2 cup sliced radishes
1 cup salad dressing
1/2 cup drained crushed pineapple
Juice of 1 lemon

Dissolve Jell-O in boiling water in bowl. Chill until partially set. Combine celery, green pepper, carrot, cucumber and radishes in bowl. Add salad dressing; mix well. Add pineapple and lemon juice; mix well. Add to Jell-O. Pour into mold. Chill until set.

APPROX PER SERVING: Cal 251; Prot 3.5 gr; T Fat 12.9 gr; Chol 15.0 mg; Carbo 33.0 gr; Sod 318.1 mg; Potas 424.2 mg.

EVIE GRUBEN'S PANTRY SHELF PEA SALAD

Yields: 8 servings

1/2 cup oil
1/4 cup tarragon vinegar
2 teaspoons salt
2 teaspoons sugar
1/4 teaspoon pepper
1/2 cup grated carrot
2 (16-ounce) cans peas, drained
2 cups diced celery
2 cups diced cucumber
1/2 cup minced green onion
1/3 cup chopped pimento

Combine oil, vinegar, salt, sugar and pepper in bowl; mix well. Add carrot, peas, celery, cucumber, onion and pimento; mix well. Chill at least for 1 hour.

APPROX PER SERVING: Cal 222; Prot 5.0 gr; T Fat 14.1 gr; Chol 0.0 mg; Carbo 20.5 gr; Sod 863.2 mg; Potas 341.7 mg.

HEALTHY SALAD DRESSING

Yields: 6 ounces

Better tasting than commercial dressings, quick, easy!

1 (6-ounce) can frozen lemonade, limeade, or orange juice concentrate

Pour undiluted frozen concentrate over salad for delicious easy salad dressing. No need for salad oils. Orange juice concentrate makes excellent sweet-sour dressing for cooked red cabbage; will maintain color. May be thickened if necessary.

Nutritional information not available.

CROUTONS

Yields: 4 servings *Pan Size: baking sheet* *Preheat: 325 degrees*

Wonderful recipe; gives you a use for leftover breads instead of just throwing them out.

1/2 cup butter
1/4 cup lemon juice
2 tablespoons Worcestershire sauce
1 tablespoon parsley flakes
2 tablespoons minced garlic
1/2 cup Parmesan cheese
4 cups cubed bread

Melt butter on baking sheet in oven for 2 to 3 minutes. Remove from oven. Add lemon juice, Worcestershire sauce and parsley; mix well. Add garlic, Parmesan cheese and bread cubes; stir until cubes are well coated. Toast cubes in oven for 30 to 35 minutes, turning every 10 minutes to toast evenly. Great snack! Super for salads!

APPROX PER SERVING: Cal 431; Prot 10.9 gr; T Fat 28.7 gr; Chol 86.8 mg; Carbo 33.1 gr; Sod 751.0 mg; Potas 193.4 mg.

Main Dishes

TUFTED TITMOUSE

YUMMY BEEF BRISKET

Yields: 15 servings *Pan Size: roaster* *Preheat: 450 degrees*

1 (4 to 5-pound) beef brisket
1 envelope dry onion soup mix
1 cup catsup
1 clove of garlic, minced
1 (12-ounce) can Classic Coke

Rub brisket with soup mix; place in roaster. Bake, uncovered, for 30 minutes. Add mixture of catsup, garlic and Coke. Reduce oven temperature to 300 degrees. Bake, tightly covered, for 4 hours longer.

APPROX PER SERVING: Cal 310; Prot 30.7 gr; T Fat 16.5 gr; Chol 102.6 mg; Carbo 8.1 gr; Sod 431.5 mg; Potas 410.2 mg.

CROCK•POT ITALIAN BEEF

Yields: 10 servings *Pan Size: Crock·Pot*

1 (3-pound) beef rump roast
2 teaspoons oregano
1 to 2 teaspoons basil
1/4 to 1/2 teaspoon red pepper
1 envelope dry onion soup mix
3 cups water

Place roast in Crock·Pot. Sprinkle with seasonings and soup mix. Add water. Cook on Low for 10 to 12 hours. Serve roast slices on hot garlic bread. Save pan juices for dipping.

APPROX PER SERVING: Cal 261; Prot 27.5 gr; T Fat 15.0 gr; Chol 94.9 mg; Carbo 2.3 gr; Sod 353.1 mg; Potas 325.5 mg.

ITALIAN BEEF

Yields: 10 servings *Pan Size: roaster* *Preheat: 350 degrees*

1 (3 to 4-pound) lean beef roast
5 bay leaves
1 tablespoon oregano
5 tablespoons lemon juice
Garlic to taste
2 tablespoons pepper

Place roast in roaster. Add bay leaves, oregano, lemon juice, garlic, pepper and salt to taste. Pour 1 inch water into roaster. Bake, covered, for 3 1/2 hours or until very tender. Discard bay leaves. Shred roast. Serve on French bread.

APPROX PER SERVING: Cal 330; Prot 36.0 gr; T Fat 19.4 gr; Chol 118.1 mg; Carbo 0.6 gr; Sod 88.1 mg; Potas 0.0 mg.

PEPPER STEAK

Yields: 6 servings *Pan Size: large skillet*

1 1/2 pounds round steak
1 cup chopped onion
5 cups water
4 beef or onion bouillon cubes
1 or 2 green bell peppers, sliced
1 (16-ounce) can whole tomatoes
1/4 cup cornstarch
1 to 1 1/2 cups water

Cut round steak into bite-sized pieces. Brown steak with onion in deep skillet. Add 5 cups water and bouillon cubes. Cook for 15 minutes. Add green bell peppers and tomatoes. Simmer for 15 minutes. Dissolve cornstarch in water. Add to simmering stew. Cook until thickened, stirring constantly. Cook for 10 minutes longer. Serve over hot cooked noodles or rice.

APPROX PER SERVING: Cal 260; Prot 24.5 gr; T Fat 12.4 gr; Chol 75.8 mg; Carbo 11.9 gr; Sod 805.5 mg; Potas 525.3 mg.

SUNDAY DINNER STEAK

Yields: 8 servings *Pan Size: 9 x 13 inch* *Preheat: 250 degrees*

8 (4-ounce) cube steaks
1/2 cup flour
1/2 cup shortening
1 (4-ounce) can mushrooms
1 medium onion, sliced
1 envelope dry onion soup mix
1 (10-ounce) can beef gravy
1 gravy can water

Season steaks with pepper to taste; coat with flour. Brown in shortening in skillet. Place in greased baking dish. Top with undrained mushrooms, onion, soup mix and mixture of gravy and water. Bake, covered with foil, for 3 to 4 hours or until tender.

APPROX PER SERVING: Cal 388; Prot 24.6 gr; T Fat 26.8 gr; Chol 81.7 mg; Carbo 11.3 gr; Sod 416.1 mg; Potas 321.9 mg.
Nutritional information does not include gravy.

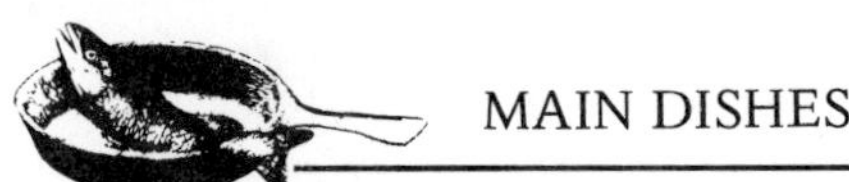

ITALIAN BEEF PIE

Yields: 8 servings *Pan Size: 3 quart* *Preheat: 300 degrees*

8 ounces Italian sausage
2 pounds lean chuck, cubed
6 tablespoons flour
2 teaspoons salt
1/4 teaspoon pepper
1 medium onion, chopped
1 beef bouillon cube
1/4 cup chili sauce
1/2 teaspoon Italian seasoning
3 cups water
8 medium carrots, cut into 1-inch pieces
6 medium potatoes, chopped
2 cups green beans
1 1/2 cups buttermilk baking mix
1/2 cup shredded Cheddar cheese
1/2 cup milk

Slice sausage 1/2 inch thick. Brown in skillet; drain. Set aside. Shake beef cubes with flour, salt and pepper. Brown in drippings in skillet. Remove and add to sausage. Saute onion in drippings. Stir in sausage, beef, bouillon, chili sauce, Italian seasoning and water. Bring to a boil. Spoon into baking dish. Stir in carrots, potatoes and green beans. Bake, covered, for 2 hours and 20 minutes. Combine baking mix and cheese in bowl. Add milk; mix well. Knead for 1/2 minute. Cut eight 3/4-inch wide strips. Weave strips over beef mixture, lattice fashion. Bake at 425 degrees for 20 minutes.

APPROX PER SERVING: Cal 566; Prot 35.1 gr; T Fat 21.6 gr; Chol 101.3 mg; Carbo 57.4 gr; Sod 1358.2 mg; Potas 1259.4 mg.

SIX-HOUR STEW

Yields: 8 servings *Pan Size: roaster* *Preheat: 250 degrees*

6 carrots, peeled
6 potatoes, peeled
2 pounds stew beef
4 stalks celery, sliced
3 onions, sliced
2 tablespoons sugar
3 tablespoons tapioca
1 (30-ounce) can tomatoes
1 (12-ounce) can tomato juice

Cut carrots and potatoes into 1-inch cubes. Layer beef, celery, potatoes, carrots and onions in roaster. Sprinkle sugar and tapioca over layers. Add tomatoes and tomato juice. Bake, covered with foil, for 6 hours.

APPROX PER SERVING: Cal 432; Prot 29.1 gr; T Fat 12.8 gr; Chol 73.8 mg; Carbo 51.5 gr; Sod 377.5 mg; Potas 1639.0 mg.

HUNGARIAN GOULASH

Yields: 6 servings *Pan Size: large skillet*

2 pounds beef round, cut into 1-inch cubes
1 cup sliced onion
1 small clove of garlic, minced
1/4 cup shortening
3/4 cup catsup
2 tablespoons Worcestershire sauce
1 tablespoon brown sugar
2 teaspoons salt
2 teaspoons paprika
1/2 teaspoon dry mustard
Dash of cayenne pepper
1 1/2 cups water
2 tablespoons flour
1/4 cup water
3 cups hot cooked noodles

Cook beef with onion and garlic in shortening in skillet until beef is brown and onion is tender. Stir in catsup, Worcestershire sauce, sugar, salt, paprika, mustard, cayenne pepper and 1 1/2 cups water. Simmer, covered, for 2 to 2 1/2 hours. Blend flour with 1/4 cup water. Stir into beef mixture gradually. Bring to a boil, stirring constantly. Cook for 1 minute. Serve over noodles.

APPROX PER SERVING: Cal 488; Prot 33.6 gr; T Fat 26.4 gr; Chol 114.8 mg; Carbo 27.7 gr; Sod 1150.2 mg; Potas 565.0 mg.

CYNDIE'S SWEDISH MEATBALLS

Yields: 24 meatballs *Pan Size: skillet*

1 egg, beaten
1/2 teaspoon allspice
1/2 teaspoon salt
1 slice whole wheat bread, crumbled
1/4 cup milk
1 pound ground beef
1 can cream of mushroom soup
1/4 cup Madeira

Combine egg, seasonings, freshly ground pepper to taste and bread soaked in milk in bowl; mix well. Add ground beef; mix well. Shape into small balls. Brown in skillet. Remove meatballs. Add soup and Madeira to skillet; stir to deglaze. Return meatballs to skillet. Simmer, covered, for 20 to 30 minutes. Serve over noodles.

APPROX PER MEATBALL: Cal 64; Prot 4.0 gr; T Fat 4.1 gr; Chol 24.7 mg; Carbo 1.9 gr; Sod 160.6 mg; Potas 58.0 mg.

SWEDISH MEATBALLS

Yields: 6 servings *Pan Size: skillet*

- 1/4 cup finely chopped onion
- 1 tablespoon butter
- 1 large potato, boiled, mashed
- 3 tablespoons fine dry bread crumbs
- 1 pound lean ground beef
- 1/3 cup heavy cream
- 1 teaspoon salt
- 1 egg
- 1 tablespoon finely chopped parsley
- 2 tablespoons butter
- 2 tablespoons oil
- 1 tablespoon flour
- 3/4 cup light cream

Saute onion in 1 tablespoon butter in skillet until translucent. Combine sauteed onion, mashed potato, bread crumbs, ground beef, heavy cream, salt, egg and parsley in large bowl; beat until fluffy. Shape into small meatballs; arrange on baking sheet. Chill for 1 hour. Fry in mixture of 2 tablespoons butter and oil in skillet over medium-high heat until golden; drain. Keep meatballs warm in 200-degree oven. Stir mixture of flour and light cream into skillet. Cook until thickened, stirring constantly. Return meatballs to skillet. Heat to serving temperature.

APPROX PER SERVING: Cal 436; Prot 16.6 gr; T Fat 36.3 gr; Chol 160.1 mg; Carbo 10.9 gr; Sod 508.5 mg; Potas 345.3 mg.

JO MARSHALL'S SWEET-SOUR MEATBALLS

Yields: 30 meatballs *Pan Size: baking sheet* *Preheat: 400 degrees*

- 3 eggs, beaten
- 1 1/2 cups dry oatmeal
- 1 small green bell pepper, chopped
- 1 small onion, chopped
- 2 pounds ground beef
- 1 teaspoon salt
- 1 (32-ounce) jar grape jelly
- 1 (32-ounce) bottle of catsup

Combine eggs, oatmeal, green bell pepper, onion, ground beef and salt in large bowl; mix well. Shape into 1 1/2-inch balls. Place on foil-lined baking sheet. Bake until light brown. Heat jelly and catsup in large saucepan to the boiling point. Add baked meatballs. Simmer for 15 to 20 minutes. Serve over hot cooked macaroni, noodles or rice.

APPROX PER MEATBALL: Cal 204; Prot 7.4 gr; T Fat 5.5 gr; Chol 45.7 mg; Carbo 32.5 gr; Sod 427.8 mg; Potas 232.0 mg.

THIS HOUSE IS BUILT

This house is built
With rafters strong as the bonds of long friendships,
With walls that are warm as a mother bird's wing,
With windows that lure the sunbeams to dancing,
With hearth-stone inviting young voices to sing.

This house was built
For girls questing knowledge from hillsides and valleys,
Who look at the future with eyes that are clear,
Whose hands reach out to the hands of all nations...
Let no girl be stranger who enters here.

Written by Theresia Zack Hanitz
to celebrate the 1943 Dedication
of the Troophouse at Camp McCormick

MICROWAVE MEAT LOAF

Yields: 6 servings *Pan Size: glass baking dish* 

1 1/2 pounds lean ground beef
1 small onion, chopped
1/3 cup seasoned dry bread crumbs
1 egg
1/4 cup milk

Combine ground beef, onion, bread crumbs, egg, milk and salt and pepper to taste in large bowl; mix lightly with wooden spoon. Shape into 2-inch thick oval in shallow glass baking dish. Cover with waxed paper. Microwave on High for 6 minutes. Turn dish 1/4 turn. Microwave for 6 minutes longer. Let stand for 5 minutes.

APPROX PER SERVING: Cal 408; Prot 31.2 gr; T Fat 13.2 gr; Chol 126.0 mg; Carbo 38.5 gr; Sod 441.7 mg; Potas 384.5 mg.

HAM AND CHEESE STUFFED MEAT LOAF

Yields: 6 servings *Pan Size: loaf pan* *Preheat: 325 degrees*

1 egg
1/2 cup catsup
1/4 teaspoon salt
Dash of pepper
1 tablespoon minced onion
1/2 teaspoon Worcestershire sauce
3 slices bread, cubed
1 pound lean ground beef
3 (1-ounce) slices deli ham
3 ounces Swiss cheese, sliced
1/4 cup catsup

Combine egg, 1/2 cup catsup, salt, pepper, onion and Worcestershire sauce in bowl. Add bread cubes; mix well. Crumble ground beef into mixture; mix well. Turn onto sheet of plastic wrap; flatten into 1-inch thick rectangle. Place ham slices on mixture leaving 1 inch from edge. Top with cheese. Roll as for jelly roll; seal edge and ends. Place in greased pan; top with 1/4 cup catsup. Bake for 1 1/4 hours.

APPROX PER SERVING: Cal 287; Prot 25.9 gr; T Fat 13.2 gr; Chol 122.5 mg; Carbo 15.2 gr; Sod 754.5 mg; Potas 366.7 mg.

EVA SWENSON'S MEAT LOAF

Yields: 8 servings *Pan Size: loaf pan* *Preheat: 350 degrees*

1 pound ground beef
1/2 pound ground pork
1/2 pound ground veal
2 cups soft bread crumbs
1/2 cup milk
1 onion, grated
2 eggs
1 cup chili sauce
2 teaspoons salt
1/4 teaspoon mixed herbs

Combine meats, crumbs, milk, onion, eggs, chili sauce and seasonings in bowl; mix well. Shape into loaf; place in pan. Bake for 1 1/2 hours.

APPROX PER SERVING: Cal 338; Prot 24.3 gr; T Fat 18.6 gr; Chol 141.5 mg; Carbo 17.5 gr; Sod 991.5 mg; Potas 419.5 mg.

GROUND BEEF AND POTATO CASSEROLE

Yields: 4 servings *Pan Size: 8 x 12 inch* *Preheat: 350 degrees*

1 pound ground beef
5 medium potatoes, peeled, sliced
1 can vegetable beef soup
1 cup water
1 teaspoon salt
1 (3-ounce) can French-fried onion rings

Crumble ground beef into 12-inch skillet. Brown over medium-high heat; drain. Combine with potatoes, soup, water and salt in baking pan. Bake, covered, for 30 minutes. Stir. Bake, uncovered, for 55 to 60 minutes or until potatoes are tender and liquid is absorbed. Sprinkle onion rings over top. Bake for 5 minutes or until heated. May microwave ground beef on High for 4 to 6 minutes; drain and mix as above. Microwave, loosely covered, for 14 to 18 minutes; stir. Top with onion rings. Microwave for 1 to 3 minutes.

APPROX PER SERVING: Cal 560; Prot 27.9 gr; T Fat 22.6 gr; Chol 91.1 mg; Carbo 60.6 gr; Sod 1565.7 mg; Potas 1274 mg.

OLIVE MEXICAN FIESTA

Yields: 8 servings *Pan Size: 2 quart* *Preheat: 400 degrees*

- 1 pound ground beef
- 1/2 cup chopped onion
- 1 (16-ounce) can tomatoes
- 1 (8-ounce) can tomato sauce
- 1 envelope chili sauce mix
- 1 (15-ounce) can kidney beans, drained
- 1 (12-ounce) can corn, drained
- 3 tablespoons chopped green chilies
- 1 cup sliced black olives
- 1 (8-ounce) package tortilla chips
- 1 cup shredded Cheddar cheese

Brown ground beef with onion in large skillet; drain. Stir in tomatoes, tomato sauce and chili sauce mix. Simmer, uncovered, for 5 minutes. Stir in beans, corn, chilies and olives. Layer tortilla chips and ground beef mixture alternately in casserole. Top with cheese; arrange tortilla chips around edges. Bake for 15 minutes.

APPROX PER SERVING: Cal 468; Prot 21.2 gr; T Fat 27.3 gr; Chol 61.2 mg; Carbo 37.9 gr; Sod 765.6 mg; Potas 608.1 mg.
Nutritional information does not include chili sauce mix.

VELVEETA MOSTACCIOLI

Yields: 6 servings *Pan Size: 9 x 13 inch* *Preheat: 350 degrees*

- 1 pound ground beef
- 1 envelope Italian spaghetti sauce mix
- 1 (29-ounce) can tomatoes
- 1 (6-ounce) can tomato paste
- 8 ounces mostaccioli noodles
- 6 ounces Velveeta cheese, sliced

Cook ground beef in skillet until brown and crumbly; drain. Stir in sauce mix, tomatoes, tomato paste and salt and pepper to taste. Cook noodles using package directions. Layer noodles, ground beef mixture and cheese in greased baking pan. Bake for 40 minutes.

APPROX PER SERVING: Cal 438; Prot 25.8 gr; T Fat 18.7 gr; Chol 71.5 mg; Carbo 41.4 gr; Sod 668.2 mg; Potas 825.5 mg.
Nutritional information does not include spaghetti sauce mix.

JOANN JOHNSON'S CHILI PRONTO

Yields: 4 servings *Pan Size: large bowl* 

I adapted this recipe from my favorite conventional chili recipe.

1 1/2 pounds lean ground beef
2 tablespoons chili powder
1 medium green bell pepper, chopped
1 large onion, chopped
1 (16-ounce) can tomatoes, drained, cut up
1 can tomato soup
2 (16-ounce) cans red kidney beans

Crumble ground beef into glass bowl. Microwave, covered with plastic wrap, on High for 5 minutes; drain. Sprinkle with half the chili powder; add green bell pepper and onion. Microwave for 5 minutes or until ground beef is no longer pink and vegetables are tender; drain well. Add tomatoes, soup, undrained beans, remaining chili powder and salt to taste. Microwave, covered, on High for 16 to 18 minutes, stirring once. Garnish with shredded Cheddar cheese and sour cream. Serve with crackers.

Nutritional information not available.

HOMECOMING CHILI

Yields: 25 servings *Pan Size: roaster* *Preheat: 300 degrees*

A post game tradition with the faculty after homecoming game in Pecatonica.

5 pounds ground beef
1 large onion, chopped
2 cloves of garlic
1 quart whole tomatoes
3 (6-ounce) cans tomato paste
2 quarts tomato juice
1 cup diced green bell pepper
3 (16-ounce) cans chili beans
1 tablespoon pepper
1 teaspoon cumin
2 tablespoons chili powder
3 envelopes chili seasoning mix

Cook ground beef with onion and garlic in roaster over medium heat until brown and crumbly, stirring frequently; drain. Add tomatoes, tomato paste, tomato juice, green pepper, beans, seasonings and salt to taste; mix well. Bake for 6 hours or to desired consistency, stirring occasionally. Serve with salsa, sour cream, chopped black olives, hot cooked rice, additional chili powder, and shredded Cheddar cheese for garnishing individual servings.

APPROX PER SERVING: Cal 232; Prot 17.8 gr; T Fat 13.6 gr; Chol 61.3 mg; Carbo 10.0 gr; Sod 261.1 mg; Potas 647.6 mg.
Nutritional information does not include chili beans and chili seasoning.

EGG ROLLS

Yields: 6 servings *Pan Size: skillet*

1 1/2 pounds ground beef
1 tablespoon ginger
2 (15-ounce) cans Chinese vegetables, drained, chopped
1 (8-ounce) package frozen cocktail shrimp
1 tablespoon soy sauce
1 package egg roll wraps
Oil for frying

Cook ground beef in skillet until brown and crumbly; drain. Add ginger and Chinese vegetables. Add shrimp and soy sauce. Simmer, uncovered, for 15 minutes; drain well. Place 1 egg roll wrapper on floured surface; place 1/4 cup ground beef mixture in center. Fold 1 corner over filling; fold sides over corner and roll up. Repeat until all ingredients are used. Fry in hot oil until brown and crisp. Drain on paper towels.

Nutritional information not available.

BIRTHDAY SUPPER PIZZA FONDUE

Yields: 6 servings *Pan Size: skillet*

1 clove of garlic, mashed
3/4 pound ground beef
1/2 cup finely chopped onion
2 (10 1/2-ounce) cans Chef Boy-ar-dee pizza sauce with cheese
1/2 teaspoon garlic powder
4 ounces mozzarella cheese, shredded
1 tablespoon cornstarch
1/2 teaspoon oregano
10 ounces mild Cheddar cheese, shredded

Spray heavy skillet with nonstick cooking spray; rub with garlic. Cook ground beef and onion in skillet until beef is brown and crumbly; drain. Add pizza sauce and garlic powder; mix well. Heat until bubbly. Toss mozzarella cheese with cornstarch and oregano. Add cheeses 1/2 cup at a time; stir until melted after each addition. Serve with Italian or garlic bread cubes for dipping.

APPROX PER SERVING: Cal 374; Prot 25.9 gr; T Fat 28.0 gr; Chol 101.5 mg; Carbo 4.0 gr; Sod 432.7 mg; Potas 187.9 mg.

Nutritional information does not include pizza sauce.

EASY LASAGNA

Yields: 8 servings *Pan Size: 9 x 13 inch* *Preheat: 350 degrees*

1 pound ground beef
1/2 cup chopped onion
1 (28-ounce) can tomatoes, cut up
1 teaspoon salt
1/4 teaspoon pepper
1/2 teaspoon oregano
2 eggs, beaten
16 ounces low-fat cottage cheese
1 (10-ounce) package frozen spinach, cooked
8 ounces lasagna noodles
1/2 cup Parmesan cheese
8 to 10 (1-ounce) slices mozzarella cheese

Brown ground beef with onion in skillet, stirring until crumbly; drain. Add undrained tomatoes, seasonings and garlic powder to taste. Heat for several minutes. Beat eggs with cottage cheese and well-drained spinach. Layer uncooked noodles, ground beef mixture, spinach mixture, Parmesan cheese and mozzarella cheese, 1/2 at a time, in baking pan. Bake for 45 to 60 minutes or until cheese is golden brown and noodles are tender. May reheat, covered, in microwave on High for 4 to 6 minutes.

APPROX PER SERVING: Cal 416; Prot 27.5 gr; T Fat 20.9 gr; Chol 139.7 mg; Carbo 29.1 gr; Sod 656.4 mg; Potas 577.6 mg.
Nutritional information does not include cottage cheese.

HAMBURGER PIE

Yields: 6 servings *Pan Size: 1½ quart* *Preheat: 350 degrees*

A good recipe for beginner cooks from a home economist.

1 medium onion, chopped
1 tablespoon shortening
1 pound ground beef
1 (20-ounce) can green beans, drained
1 can tomato soup
5 medium potatoes, cooked, mashed
1/2 cup warm milk
1 egg, beaten

Saute onion in shortening in skillet until brown. Add ground beef and salt and pepper to taste. Cook until brown and crumbly; drain. Add green beans and soup. Pour into greased casserole. Mash potatoes with milk, egg and salt and pepper to taste. Spoon in mounds over ground beef mixture. Bake for 30 minutes.

APPROX PER SERVING: Cal 362; Prot 20.2 gr; T Fat 14.1 gr; Chol 96.1 mg; Carbo 39.6 gr; Sod 595.5 mg; Potas 1016.7 mg.

BETH'S FORGOT-THE-YEAST PIZZA

Yields: 16 servings *Pan Size: two 12-inch* *Preheat: 425 degrees*

Popover-type crust saved the day when I forgot the yeast during a weekend at Camp McCormick.

2 pounds ground beef
1 or 2 onions, chopped
3 cups flour
2 teaspoons salt
2 teaspoons oregano
1/4 teaspoon pepper
4 eggs, beaten
1 1/3 cups milk
8 ounces mushrooms
2 cups pizza sauce
2 cups shredded Cheddar cheese

Brown ground beef in skillet, stirring until crumbly. Add onions. Saute lightly; drain. Combine flour, salt, oregano, pepper, eggs and milk in bowl; mix well. Pour into greased and floured pizza pans; tilt pans to coat bottoms. Arrange mushrooms and ground beef mixture over batter. Bake on low oven rack for 25 to 30 minutes or until deep golden brown. Top with sauce and cheese. Bake for 10 to 15 minutes longer.
Note: This is a popover-type crust.

APPROX PER SERVING: Cal 275; Prot 18.0 gr; T Fat 15.2 gr; Chol 118.3 mg; Carbo 15.7 gr; Sod 419.3 mg; Potas 273.7 mg.
Nutritional information does not include pizza sauce.

CONEY DOG SAUCE

Yields: 8 servings *Pan Size: saucepan*

1/2 pound ground beef
1 tablespoon chopped onion
1 tablespoon brown sugar
2 teaspoons vinegar
1 tablespoon prepared mustard
1/3 cup tomato paste
1/2 cup water

Brown ground beef with onion in saucepan; drain. Add remaining ingredients and salt to taste. Simmer until thickened, stirring frequently. Serve on hot dogs in buns.

APPROX PER SERVING: Cal 74.8; Prot 5.4 gr; T Fat 4.3 gr; Chol 19.2 mg; Carbo 3.8 gr; Sod 39.7 mg; Potas 155.3 mg.

CHUCK'S SPAGHETTI SAUCE

Yields: 6 servings *Pan Size: 3 quart*

2 pounds ground beef
2 tablespoons olive oil
1 large onion, chopped
2 or 3 cloves of garlic, chopped
1 (15 1/2-ounce) jar spaghetti sauce with mushrooms
2 (8-ounce) cans tomato sauce
1/2 teaspoon salt
2 tablespoons Worcestershire sauce
1 tablespoon Italian herbs
7 tablespoons Parmesan cheese
1/2 (7-ounce) jar stuffed green olives
2 (4-ounce) cans sliced mushrooms

Brown ground beef in olive oil in heavy pan. Add onion and garlic. Cook until tender; drain. Add spaghetti and tomato sauces and about 2 cups water. Add salt, Worcestershire sauce and Italian herbs. Simmer, covered, for 2 hours, stirring frequently. Add cheese. Cook for 30 minutes longer, adding water if necessary to make of desired consistency. Add olives and mushrooms. Cook for 30 minutes longer. Serve over hot cooked spaghetti with additional Parmesan cheese. Serve with French bread and green salad.

APPROX PER SERVING: Cal 479;
Prot 35.1 gr; T Fat 30.5 gr; Chol 125.5 mg;
Carbo 12.6 gr; Sod 1365.1 mg;
Potas 750.2 mg.
Nutritional information does not include spaghetti sauce.

PERFECT BARBECUES

Yields: 15 servings *Pan Size: skillet*

Perfect and consistent every time.

2 pounds ground beef
1 large onion, finely chopped
1 can tomato soup
1/2 cup water
1/2 green bell pepper, chopped
1/2 cup chopped celery
2 teaspoons white vinegar
1 (14-ounce) bottle of catsup
2 tablespoons brown sugar
1 teaspoon pepper
15 hamburger buns

Brown ground beef with onion in skillet. Add soup, water, vegetables, vinegar, catsup, brown sugar and pepper; mix well. Simmer, uncovered, for 20 minutes, stirring frequently. Serve on buns.

APPROX PER SERVING: Cal 336;
Prot 16.6 gr; T Fat 11.2 gr; Chol 42.6 mg;
Carbo 41.7 gr; Sod 770.1 mg;
Potas 364.7 mg.

PEGGY DEAN'S AMERICAN CHOP SUEY

Yields: 10 servings *Pan Size: skillet*

My mother lived with a family in Chicago during the war while working at a factory. She got this recipe from that family.

1 pound pork
1 pound beef
1 pound veal
2 tablespoons shortening
1 large stalk celery, chopped
4 large onions, chopped
1 (12-ounce) package fresh mushrooms
1 (16-ounce) can bean sprouts
1 quart tomato juice
1 quart water
1 teaspoon sugar
1 teaspoon salt
1 teaspoon pepper
1 teaspoon soy sauce
1 1/2 tablespoons bead molasses
2 to 3 tablespoons cornstarch

Cut meats into small pieces. Brown in shortening in skillet. Add vegetables, tomato juice, water and seasonings. Cook until vegetables are tender. Stir in cornstarch dissolved in a small amount of water. Cook until thickened, stirring constantly. Serve over hot cooked rice. Garnish with chow mein noodles.

APPROX PER SERVING: Cal 333; Prot 28.9 gr; T Fat 17.5 gr; Chol 89.3 mg; Carbo 15.3 gr; Sod 551.7 mg; Potas 837.5 mg.

GRAM'S BAKED PORK CHOPS

Yields: 4 servings *Pan Size: 9 x 13 inch* *Preheat: 350 degrees*

4 (4-ounce) pork chops
1/4 cup catsup
1 cup cornflakes, crushed

Trim chops; place in greased baking pan. Season with salt and pepper to taste. Spread chops with catsup. Top with cornflakes. Add a small amount of water to pan. Bake, uncovered, for 1 hour.

APPROX PER SERVING: Cal 378; Prot 20.2 gr; T Fat 28.3 gr; Chol 70.3 mg; Carbo 9.1 gr; Sod 286.9 mg; Potas 372.2 mg.

KRISSY SWANSON'S KROPP KAKOR

Yields: 8 servings *Pan Size: 12 quart*

Krissy's great grandfather came from Oland, Sweden. Kropp Kakor started from Oland.

5 pounds potatoes, peeled
1/2 to 3/4 cup flour
1/2 pound pork steak, finely chopped
1/2 pound salt pork, finely chopped
1/2 teaspoon allspice
1 onion, chopped

Grate potatoes finely; drain, reserving potato liquid. Squeeze potatoes dry in towel. Let potato liquid stand until starch sinks to bottom; pour off clear liquid. Combine grated potatoes, starch and flour in bowl; mix well. Test a small ball of mixture in pan of boiling water. If ball falls apart, add flour. Mix pork steak, salt pork, allspice and onion in bowl. Pat a small amount of potato mixture in palm of hand to resemble pancake. Spoon a small amount of pork mixture into center. Add potato mixture and shape into ball, enclosing filling completely. Place in pan of simmering water. Simmer for 1 hour; drain.

Nutritional information not available.

BARBECUE SAUCE FOR PORK

Yields: 4 cups *Pan Size: saucepan*

1 1/2 teaspoons salt
5 tablespoons brown sugar
2/3 cup catsup
1/2 cup vinegar
1 teaspoon pepper
1 1/3 cups water
1/2 teaspoon garlic salt
2 teaspoons ginger
2/3 cup tomato sauce
1/2 cup butter
1 teaspoon Worcestershire sauce
2 small onions, minced

Combine all ingredients in saucepan. Bring to a simmer. Simmer until of desired consistency, stirring occasionally. Store in refrigerator, if desired. May use on ribs or pork chops.

APPROX PER CUP: Cal 385; Prot 3.0 gr; T Fat 23.4 gr; Chol 71.0 mg; Carbo 45.2 gr; Sod 2413.4 mg; Potas 610.5 mg.

CORINE'S BARBECUE SAUCE FOR RIBS

Yields: 4 servings *Pan Size: skillet*

This is a very old barbecue sauce recipe from the south.

1/2 cup chopped onion
2 tablespoons margarine
1/2 cup chopped celery
1/4 cup chopped green bell pepper
1 cup tomato catsup
1 cup water
2 tablespoons brown sugar
2 tablespoons Worcestershire sauce
1/8 teaspoon pepper

Saute onion in margarine in skillet until transparent. Add celery, green pepper, catsup, water, brown sugar, Worcestershire sauce and pepper. Bring to a boil. Pour sauce over ribs or chicken. Bake, covered with foil, for 1 to 1 1/2 hours. Bake, uncovered, for 30 minutes longer.

Note: Prepare ribs or chicken by coating with seasoned flour and browning in shortening in skillet. Place in 9 x 13-inch baking dish. Sauce is enough for 3 pounds ribs or chicken.

APPROX PER SERVING: Cal 226; Prot 3.3 gr; T Fat 6.3 gr; Chol 0.0 mg; Carbo 42.1 gr; Sod 1419.6 mg; Potas 646.3 mg.
Nutritional information is for sauce only.

HAM BALLS

Yields: 30 meatballs *Pan Size: 9 x 13 inch* *Preheat: 350 degrees*

This is a favorite at Christmas time. Meatballs are good cold or in a sandwich.

1 pound ham
1 1/2 pounds pork
2 eggs, beaten
1 cup cracker crumbs
1/8 teaspoon pepper
1/2 cup packed brown sugar
1/2 teaspoon dry mustard
1/2 cup vinegar
1/4 cup water

Grind ham and pork together. Mix with eggs, crumbs and pepper. Shape into golf ball-sized balls. Brown meatballs in skillet; drain. Place in baking dish. Combine remaining ingredients in saucepan. Boil for 5 minutes. Pour over meatballs. Bake for 1 hour, basting and turning meatballs frequently. May serve hot, cold, or in sandwiches.

APPROX PER MEATBALL: Cal 113; Prot 6.4 gr; T Fat 7.1 gr; Chol 38.9 mg; Carbo 5.5 gr; Sod 110.1 mg; Potas 87.9 mg.

KITTY AUKER'S FETTUCINI ALFREDO

Yields: 4 servings *Pan Size: 1 quart*

I first had this dish with James Clavell's daughter, Micheala, in Hollywood, 1979.

2 tablespoons butter
1 cup whipping cream
1 cup freshly grated
Parmesan cheese
1 teaspoon oregano
1 teaspoon basil
1 pound spinach noodles
2 cups finely chopped ham
1 tablespoon butter
1 cup cooked peas

Melt 2 tablespoons butter in saucepan. Add 1/2 cup cream. Heat over low heat; do not boil. Add cheese and remaining 1/2 cup cream gradually, stirring until melted after each addition. Stir in oregano and basil. Keep warm over very low heat. Cook noodles using package directions. Saute ham in 1 tablespoon butter in skillet. Pour sauce over noodles. Top with ham and peas. Serve with French bread.

APPROX PER SERVING: Cal 1057; Prot 43.2 gr; T Fat 56.7 gr; Chol 294.1 mg; Carbo 91.6 gr; Sod 936.3 mg; Potas 457.9 mg.

HELEN'S HAM AND CHEESE STRATA

Yields: 12 servings *Pan Size: 9 x 13 inch* *Preheat: 350 degrees*

12 slices bread
1 pound sliced American
cheese
1 (10-ounce) package frozen
broccoli, cut into
bite-sized pieces
3 cups cubed cooked ham
3 tablespoons chopped onion
6 eggs, slightly beaten
3 1/2 cups milk
1/2 teaspoon dry mustard

Cut 12 circles from bread slices. Tear scraps into pieces; place in buttered baking pan. Layer cheese, broccoli and ham in pan. Sprinkle with onion. Arrange bread circles on top. Beat eggs with milk and dry mustard. Pour over layers. Chill, covered, overnight. May drizzle melted butter over bread circles before baking if desired. Bake for 1 1/2 hours.

APPROX PER SERVING: Cal 395; Prot 23.8 gr; T Fat 23.2 gr; Chol 195.6 mg; Carbo 22.2 gr; Sod 1079.4 mg; Potas 394.4 mg.

HAM PUFFS

Yields: 6 servings *Pan Size: baking sheet* *Preheat: 350 degrees*

- 6 puff pastry shells
- 1 medium onion, finely chopped
- 1 bunch green onions, finely chopped
- 8 ounces mushrooms, sliced
- 1/4 cup butter
- 2 cups chopped cooked ham
- 1/2 cup Italian black olives, sliced
- 1 (4-ounce) jar chopped pimento, drained
- 1/2 teaspoon salt
- 1/2 teaspoon Tabasco sauce
- 1/4 cup minced fresh parsley
- 2 egg yolks, beaten
- 1/2 cup whipping cream
- 1 tablespoon Madeira
- 2 tablespoons melted butter

Prepare pastry shells according to package directions; reserve tops. Saute onion, green onions and mushrooms in 1/4 cup butter in skillet until golden. Mix in ham, olives, pimento and seasonings. Cool slightly. Beat egg yolks with cream. Stir into ham mixture. Cook over very low heat until thickened, stirring constantly; do not boil. Stir in Madeira. Spoon into pastry shells; replace tops. Place on baking sheet; brush with 2 tablespoons melted butter. Bake for 15 minutes.

APPROX PER SERVING: Cal 386; Prot 13.2 gr; T Fat 33.6 gr; Chol 187.3 mg; Carbo 8.7 gr; Sod 777.5 mg; Potas 449.4 mg.

Nutritional information does not include puff pastry shells.

BREAKFAST CASSEROLE

Yields: 8 servings *Pan Size: 9 x 13 inch* *Preheat: 350 degrees*

- 1 pound pork sausage
- 10 slices white bread, cubed
- 1/2 cup shredded Cheddar cheese
- 1/2 cup shredded Swiss cheese
- 1 (4-ounce) can mushroom halves
- 6 eggs, beaten
- 1 cup milk
- 1 cup light cream
- 1 teaspoon salt
- 1/2 teaspoon Worcestershire sauce
- 1/2 teaspoon pepper

Cook sausage in skillet until brown and crumbly; drain. Layer bread, sausage, cheeses and mushrooms in greased baking pan. Combine eggs and remaining ingredients; pour over layers. Refrigerate, covered, overnight. Bake, covered, for 45 minutes.

APPROX PER SERVING: Cal 450; Prot 18.4 gr; T Fat 31.9 gr; Chol 14.0 mg; Carbo 265.9 gr; Sod 875.9 mg; Potas 247.4 mg.

BREAKFAST PIZZA

Yields: 6 servings *Pan Size: 12 inch* *Preheat: 400 degrees*

12 ounces pork sausage
1 (8-count) package refrigerator crescent rolls
2 hashed brown potato patties, thawed
4 eggs, beaten
2 cups shredded Cheddar cheese

Cook sausage in skillet until brown and crumbly; drain. Pat roll dough into lightly greased pizza pan, sealing rolls together. Sprinkle crumbled potato patties and sausage over dough. Pour eggs over top. Sprinkle with cheese. Bake for 20 minutes. Cut into wedges. May chill overnight before baking.

Nutritional information not available.

SAUSAGE BAKE

Yields: 4 servings *Pan Size: 1½ quart* *Preheat: 350 degrees*

2 (16-ounce) cans butter beans
1 can tomato soup
1 (6-ounce) package Polish sausage

Pour undrained beans into casserole; stir in soup. Cut sausage lengthwise; place over beans. Bake, uncovered, until brown. Serve with corn sticks or corn bread.

APPROX PER SERVING: Cal 539; Prot 20.9 gr; T Fat 17.9 gr; Chol 23.6 mg; Carbo 77.5 gr; Sod 3758.3 mg; Potas 1144.4 mg.

SICILIAN SAUSAGE SOUP

Yields: 8 servings *Pan Size: 8 quart*

1/2 pound sweet Italian bulk sausage
1 large onion, chopped
1 quart stewed tomatoes
3 1/2 cups chicken broth
1 teaspoon sweet basil
1/2 cup orzo (rice - shaped macaroni)
1/4 teaspoon salt
1/8 teaspoon pepper
1/2 cup Parmesan cheese

Cook sausage in skillet; drain. Saute onion in a small amount of drippings. Add to tomatoes in large saucepan. Add sausage, broth and basil. Bring to a boil. Stir in orzo, salt and pepper; reduce heat. Simmer for 30 minutes or until orzo is tender. Sprinkle individual servings with Parmesan cheese. Serve with garlic bread.

APPROX PER SERVING: Cal 160; Prot 8.9 gr; T Fat 8.1 gr; Chol 25.2 mg; Carbo 131.1 gr; Sod 714.3 mg; Potas 397.0 mg.

FAVORITE SPAGHETTI SAUCE

Yields: 12 servings *Pan Size: 4 quart*

Old family recipe of Michael Genaro, Austin, Texas.

1 large sweet onion, minced
3 large cloves of garlic, minced
3 tablespoons olive oil
6 (5-ounce) cans tomato sauce
1 tablespoon basil
1/2 to 1 tablespoon pepper

Saute onion and garlic in oil in saucepan over medium heat for 10 minutes. Add tomato sauce, basil and pepper; mix well. Bring to a boil; reduce heat. Simmer for 3 hours. May add Italian sausage, meatballs or mushrooms for last hour of cooking.

APPROX PER SERVING: Cal 196; Prot 7.3 gr; T Fat 4.4 gr; Chol 0.0 mg; Carbo 38.0 gr; Sod 2461.6 mg; Potas 1762.5 mg.

QUICK SPAGHETTI SAUCE

Yields: 4 servings *Pan Size: saucepan*

2 (6-ounce) cans tomato paste
3 cups water
2 tablespoons instant minced onion
1 tablespoon Parmesan cheese
1 beef bouillon cube
1 tablespoon sugar
1 teaspoon Italian seasoning
1/2 teaspoon salt
1/2 teaspoon garlic powder
1/8 teaspoon pepper

Combine all ingredients in heavy saucepan. Simmer, covered, for 20 minutes, stirring occasionally. Serve over hot cooked spaghetti or noodles. May add 1 pound ground beef cooked until brown and crumbly, and drained.

APPROX PER SERVING: Cal 90; Prot 3.7 gr; T Fat 0.8 gr; Chol 2.5 mg; Carbo 18.9 gr; Sod 551.8 mg; Potas 758.6 mg.

FLYING SQUIRREL

VENISON STEW

Yields: 4 servings *Pan Size: Crock·Pot*

4 carrots, sliced
3 potatoes, chopped
2 pounds 1-inch venison cubes
1 cup beef consomme
1 teaspoon salt
1 teaspoon instant minced onion
1 stalk celery, cut up
1 (4-ounce) can sliced mushrooms, drained

Combine all ingredients in Crock·Pot; stir until mixed. Cook, covered, on Low for 10 to 12 hours.

APPROX PER SERVING: Cal 437; Prot 53.0 gr; T Fat 9.4 gr; Chol 153.4 mg; Carbo 32.7 gr; Sod 983.3 mg; Potas 1610.3 mg.

PARTY CHICKEN CASSEROLE

Yields: 10 servings *Pan Size: 9 x 13 inch* *Preheat: 375 degrees*

1 (8-ounce) package stuffing mix
1 (1-pound) bag frozen broccoli
5 chicken breasts, cooked, chopped
1/2 cup slivered almonds
2 cans cream of mushroom soup
1/2 cup milk
1 cup mayonnaise
1 1/2 teaspoons curry powder
1 teaspoon lemon juice
1/2 cup shredded Cheddar cheese
3 tablespoons white cooking wine

Prepare stuffing mix using package directions. Place 1/2 of the stuffing mixture on bottom of buttered baking pan. Cook broccoli using package directions for several minutes; place broccoli on top of stuffing. Place chicken over broccoli. Sprinkle with almonds, if desired. Mix soup, milk, mayonnaise, curry powder, lemon juice, cheese and wine in bowl. Spread over chicken. Top with remaining stuffing mixture. Bake for 45 minutes.

APPROX PER SERVING: Cal 480; Prot 25.3 gr; T Fat 30.8 gr; Chol 70.1 mg; Carbo 26.4 gr; Sod 997.1 mg; Potas 492.1 mg.

TINKER SWISS COTTAGE, CIRCA 1920.

CHICKEN AND BISCUIT CASSEROLE

Yields: 6 servings *Pan Size: 2 quart* *Preheat: 425 degrees*

1 (3 1/2-pound) chicken, cut up
3 cups chicken broth
1 1/2 cups chopped celery
1 cup chopped onion
1 cup sliced carrots
1/3 cup butter
1/2 cup flour
1/2 teaspoon poultry seasoning
1 1/2 cups milk
1 cup flour
1/2 cup shredded Cheddar cheese
1 1/2 teaspoons baking powder
1/4 teaspoon salt
3 tablespoons butter
1/2 cup milk

Wash chicken; pat dry. Sprinkle with salt and pepper to taste. Place chicken pieces, broth, celery, onion and carrots in 4-quart saucepan; cover. Bring to a boil; reduce heat. Simmer for 45 minutes or until chicken is tender. Remove chicken; bone and cut into bite-sized pieces. Set aside. Reserve vegetables and 1 1/2 cups broth. Melt 1/3 cup butter in large saucepan. Stir in 1/2 cup flour and poultry seasoning until smooth. Remove from heat. Stir in 1 1/2 cups milk and reserved broth. Bring to a boil, stirring constantly. Cook for 1 minute, stirring constantly. Stir in reserved vegetables and chicken. Pour into casserole. Combine 1 cup flour, cheese, baking powder and 1/4 teaspoon salt in bowl. Cut in 3 tablespoons butter until crumbly. Stir in 1/2 cup milk until all ingredients are moistened. Drop biscuits by rounded tablespoonfuls onto chicken mixture. Bake for 20 to 25 minutes or until biscuits are brown.

APPROX PER SERVING: Cal 460; Prot 25.2 gr; T Fat 24.4 gr; Chol 128.2 mg; Carbo 34.7 gr; Sod 1010.1 mg; Potas 595.4 mg.

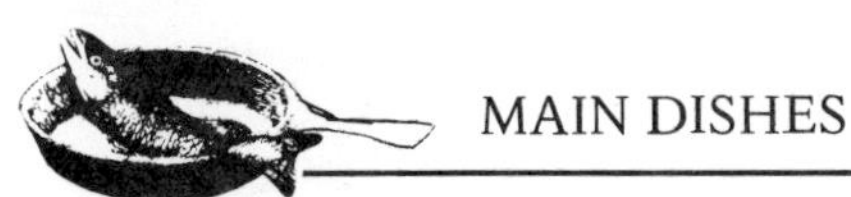

CHICKEN BREASTS IN SOUR CREAM

Yields: 8 servings *Pan Size: 7 x 11 inch* *Preheat: 275 degrees*

1 (2 1/2-ounce) package dried beef
8 chicken breast filets
8 slices bacon
1 cup sour cream
1 can cream of chicken soup
Paprika to taste

Tear dried beef into pieces. Place in baking dish. Roll up chicken breast filets. Wrap 1 slice bacon around each; place over dried beef. Mix sour cream with soup in bowl. Spoon over chicken. Sprinkle lightly with paprika to taste. Bake for 4 hours.

APPROX PER SERVING: Cal 434; Prot 39.9 gr; T Fat 27.7 gr; Chol 120.2 mg; Carbo 4.0 gr; Sod 919.6 mg; Potas 544.8 mg.

LEISA'S EASY AND INEXPENSIVE CHICKEN AND DUMPLINGS

Yields: 6 servings *Pan Size: large saucepan*

1 (3 1/2-pound) chicken
6 to 8 cups water
2 cans refrigerator biscuits

Place chicken in saucepan. Add enough water to cover. Cook for 1 1/2 hours or until tender. Remove chicken; reserve stock. Skin and bone chicken. Return chicken to stock. Bring to a boil. Season with salt and pepper and poultry seasoning to taste. Cut biscuits into quarters. Add to broth; push down. Cook for 15 minutes longer.

APPROX PER SERVING: Cal 403; Prot 22.6 gr; T Fat 9.6 gr; Chol 102.5 mg; Carbo 54.0 gr; Sod 1052.1 mg; Potas 237.8 mg.

RED FOX

CHICKEN-ESCAROLE SOUP

Yields: 6 servings *Pan Size: 6-quart saucepan*

I found this recipe in a farm magazine a few years ago.

1 (3 1/2-pound) chicken
2 stalks celery with leaves
4 sprigs of parsley
7 cups water
4 chicken bouillon cubes
3/4 cup sliced carrots
1/2 cup chopped onion
1 clove of garlic, chopped
1/3 cup rice
1/4 teaspoon pepper
8 ounces escarole
7 cups broth

Combine chicken, celery, parsley, water and bouillon cubes in saucepan. Cook until chicken is tender. Bone and chop chicken. Combine carrots, onion, garlic, rice, pepper, escarole and broth in saucepan. Cook until vegetables are tender. Add chicken. Cook until heated through.

APPROX PER SERVING: Cal 215; Prot 29.4 gr; T Fat 3.9 gr; Chol 107.5 mg; Carbo 15.5 gr; Sod 906.8 mg; Potas 490.1 mg.

FIVE-CAN CASSEROLE

Yields: 6 servings *Pan Size: casserole* *Preheat: 350 degrees*

1 (6-ounce) can boned chicken, drained, chopped
1 (6-ounce) can evaporated milk
1 (3-ounce) can chow mein noodles
1 can cream of celery soup
1 can cream of chicken soup
1/2 cup crushed potato chips

Combine chicken, evaporated milk, noodles and soups in bowl; mix well. Spoon into greased casserole. Top with potato chips. Bake for 30 minutes. One cup chicken, turkey or tuna may be substituted for canned chicken.

Nutritional information not available.

CHICKEN BREASTS PARMESAN

Yields: 4 servings *Pan Size: 9 x 13 inch* *Preheat: 350 degrees*

4 chicken breasts, split, skinned
1/2 cup Parmesan cheese
1 clove of garlic, minced
3 tablespoons flour
1 3/4 cups chicken broth
1/2 cup Sherry
1 (4-ounce) can mushroom pieces
1 teaspoon salt
1/4 teaspoon pepper
2 tablespoons minced parsley

Coat chicken with cheese. Brown in 1/2-inch oil in heavy skillet for 15 to 20 minutes. Remove from pan, reserving 3 tablespoons oil. Add garlic. Cook for several seconds. Stir in flour. Cook until frothy. Add broth. Cook until thickened, stirring constantly. Add Sherry, mushrooms with liquid and seasonings. Cook for several minutes, stirring constantly. Add chicken. Place in baking dish. Bake for 30 to 40 minutes or until tender. Sprinkle with parsley.

APPROX PER SERVING: Cal 311; Prot 41.0 gr; T Fat 7.5 gr; Chol 103.4 mg; Carbo 9.1 gr; Sod 1026.4 mg; Potas 542.5 mg.
Nutritional information does not include oil.

EASY CHICKEN PARMESAN

Yields: 6 servings *Pan Size: shallow glass* 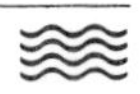

6 pieces chicken
1/2 cup butter
1 cup dry bread crumbs
1/2 cup Parmesan cheese
1/2 teaspoon garlic salt
1/4 teaspoon pepper
1 tablespoon parsley flakes
Paprika to taste

Wash chicken; pat dry. Microwave butter in glass dish for 1 minute or until melted. Combine the next 5 ingredients in plastic bag. Coat chicken with butter; shake in bag to coat evenly. Arrange in baking dish with thicker pieces toward the outside of dish. Sprinkle remaining crumbs and butter over top of chicken. Sprinkle with paprika to taste. Microwave on High for 17 to 20 minutes, turning twice. Let stand for 5 minutes before serving.

APPROX PER SERVING: Cal 320; Prot 19.8 gr; T Fat 20.9 gr; Chol 108.7 mg; Carbo 12.6 gr; Sod 598.5 mg; Potas 205.6 mg.

CHICKEN AND RICE CASSEROLE

Yields: 6 servings *Pan Size: 9 x 12 inch* *Preheat: 275 degrees*

1/2 cup margarine
6 meaty pieces chicken
1 1/4 cups rice
1 can cream of mushroom soup
1 can cream of chicken soup
1 can cream of celery soup
1 (4-ounce) can whole mushrooms

Melt margarine in baking dish. Coat chicken with margarine; set aside. Add mixture of rice, soups and mushrooms with liquid. Place chicken on top. Cover with foil. Bake for 2 hours. Remove foil. Bake for 30 minutes or until brown.

APPROX PER SERVING: Cal 489; Prot 19.7 gr; T Fat 26.2 gr; Chol 62.1 mg; Carbo 42.6 gr; Sod 1419.6 mg; Potas 319.1 mg.

TOMATO-STUFFED CHICKEN ROLLS

Yields: 4 servings *Pan Size: 6 x 10 inch* *Preheat: 350 degrees*

4 chicken breast filets
1 (1-ounce) slice Swiss cheese, cut into fourths
1 small tomato, peeled, seeded, chopped
1/2 teaspoon dried basil, crushed
1 tablespoon skim milk
1/4 cup fine dry bread crumbs
1 tablespoon Parmesan cheese
1 tablespoon snipped parsley

Place 1 chicken filet, boned side up, between 2 pieces clear plastic wrap. Pound with meat mallet to 1/4-inch thickness, working from center to edges. Repeat with remaining chicken. Place 1 piece Swiss cheese and tomato on each filet. Sprinkle with basil. Fold in sides of chicken; roll up to enclose filling, gently pressing all edges together to seal. Place chicken rolls in baking dish. Brush tops with milk. Combine bread crumbs, Parmesan cheese and parsley in bowl. Sprinkle over chicken. Bake, uncovered, for 40 to 45 minutes.

APPROX PER SERVING: Cal 238.8; Prot 36.9 gr; T Fat 6.4 gr; Chol 92.0 mg; Carbo 6.2 gr; Sod 177.5 mg; Potas 526.0 mg.

HOT CHICKEN SALAD

Yields: 6 servings | *Pan Size: 6 x 10 inch* | *Preheat: 350 degrees*

1 cup chopped cooked chicken
2 hard-boiled eggs, chopped
1/2 cup chopped celery
1 small pimento, chopped
1 can cream of chicken soup
3/4 cup mayonnaise
1/2 cup sliced almonds
1 cup cooked rice
1/2 teaspoon salt
2 1/4 tablespoons lemon juice
2 cups chow mein noodles

Combine chicken, eggs, celery and pimento in bowl. Add soup, mayonnaise, almonds, rice, salt and lemon juice; mix well. Place in casserole. Bake for 45 minutes. Top with noodles. Bake for 15 minutes longer.

APPROX PER SERVING: Cal 477; Prot 15.4 gr; T Fat 36.2 gr; Chol 127.6 mg; Carbo 23.8 gr; Sod 1073.5 mg; Potas 300.1 mg.

SWEET AND SOUR CHICKEN

Yields: 6 servings | *Pan Size: 8 x 13 inch* | *Preheat: 400 degrees*

3 tablespoons margarine
2 1/2 to 3 pounds chicken breasts, boned, cut into bite-sized pieces
1 egg
2 tablespoons water
1 cup bread crumbs
1/3 cup packed brown sugar
2 tablespoons cornstarch
1 (15 1/2-ounce) can pineapple
3 tablespoons vinegar
2 tablespoons catsup
2 tablespoons soy sauce
1 medium green bell pepper, chopped
1 small onion, chopped

Melt margarine; pour into baking pan. Dip chicken in mixture of egg and water; coat with crumbs. Place in baking pan. Bake for 25 to 30 minutes; turn. Bake for 15 minutes longer. Mix brown sugar and cornstarch in 3-quart saucepan. Drain pineapple, reserving syrup. Add enough water to syrup to make 1 2/3 cups. Add with vinegar, catsup and soy sauce to brown sugar. Cook over medium heat until thickened, stirring constantly. Stir in pineapple, green pepper and onion; reduce heat. Simmer for 5 to 7 minutes. Stir in chicken. Cook until heated through. Serve over hot rice.

APPROX PER SERVING: Cal 368; Prot 32.4 gr; T Fat 10.3 gr; Chol 116.0 mg; Carbo 36.6 gr; Sod 611.9 mg; Potas 694.9 mg.

CHICKEN SUPREME

Yields: 8 servings *Pan Size: 2½-quart casserole* *Preheat: 350 degrees*

Great for cooks with limited time.

- 2 cups chopped cooked chicken
- 2 cups macaroni
- 2 cans cream of mushroom soup
- 2 cups milk
- 2 medium onions, chopped
- 1/2 teaspoon salt
- 1/4 teaspoon pepper
- 3 tablespoons butter
- 1 cup sharp Cheddar cheese

Combine chicken, macaroni, soup, milk, onions, salt, pepper and butter in casserole. Sprinkle cheese over top. Refrigerate overnight. Bake for 1 1/2 hours.

Nutritional information not available.

TURKEY SAUSAGE

Yields: 4 servings *Pan Size: large skillet*

- 1 pound ground turkey
- 1/2 teaspoon salt
- 1/2 teaspoon pepper
- 1/2 teaspoon paprika
- 1 1/2 teaspoons sage
- 1/4 teaspoon onion powder
- 1/4 teaspoon sugar
- 1/4 cup dry bread crumbs
- 1 tablespoon oil
- Dash of cayenne pepper

Combine turkey, salt, pepper, paprika, sage, onion powder, sugar, bread crumbs, oil and a dash of cayenne pepper in bowl; mix well. Chill until firm. Shape into patties. Brown in additional oil in skillet.

APPROX PER SERVING: Cal 216; Prot 17.3 gr; T Fat 13.7 gr; Chol 64.6 mg; Carbo 4.6 gr; Sod 366.4 mg; Potas 211.7 mg.

BETTY CANFIELD'S BAKED SMALL-MOUTH BASS AMANDINE

Yields: 4 servings *Preheat: 350 degrees*

The favorite recipe of my husband, provided he has first caught the fish!

- 1 small-mouth bass
- Flour
- Oil
- Slivered almonds
- Juice of 1 lemon

Coat fish with flour. Brown in oil in skillet. Remove fish. Place on foil. Brown almonds in remaining oil. Pour lemon juice over almonds. Spoon mixture over fish. Seal foil. Bake for about 50 minutes.

Nutritional information not available.

MICROMEALS' CRISPY FISH FILLETS

Yields: 4 servings *Pan Size: baking dish* 

1/2 cup rich cracker crumbs
2 tablespoons finely chopped almonds
1 teaspoon parsley flakes
1/4 cup butter
1 pound fish fillets

Combine cracker crumbs, almonds and parsley flakes in dish. Microwave butter in glass baking dish until melted. Coat both sides of fish fillets with butter. Coat with crumb mixture. Arrange on microwave bacon rack with meatiest parts to outside of rack. Sprinkle with paprika to taste. Drizzle any remaining butter over fillets. Cover with waxed paper. Microwave on High for 5 to 7 minutes or until fish flakes easily, turning after 4 minutes.

APPROX PER SERVING: Cal 281; Prot 35.6 gr; T Fat 15.7 gr; Chol 85.5 mg; Carbo 9.1 gr; Sod 275.4 mg; Potas 46.1 mg.

PARMESAN FISH FILLETS

Yields: 4 servings *Pan Size: large skillet*

4 (4-ounce) fresh or frozen fish fillets
1 egg white, beaten
2 tablespoons water
1/2 cup finely crushed sodium-reduced wheat wafers
3 tablespoons Parmesan cheese
2 tablespoons finely snipped parsley

Pat fillets dry with paper towels. Combine egg white and water in dish. Combine cracker crumbs, Parmesan cheese and parsley. Dip fillets into egg white mixture; coat with crumbs. Spray large skillet with non-stick coating. Brown fish in hot skillet for 6 to 8 minutes or until fish flakes easily, turning once.

APPROX PER SERVING: Cal 138; Prot 36.8 gr; T Fat 2.8 gr; Chol 123.5 mg; Carbo 0.2 gr; Sod 135.7 mg; Potas 458.6 mg.

ORANGE ROUGHY WITH TOMATO AND BASIL

Yields: 4 servings *Pan Size: 10-inch glass pie plate*

1/2 cup chopped peeled seeded tomato
1/2 cup chopped fresh basil
1 tablespoon butter
1/4 teaspoon fresh ground pepper
1 pound orange roughy fillets
Juice of 1/2 lemon
1/4 cup fine dry bread crumbs

Combine tomato, basil, butter and pepper in glass pie plate. Microwave on High for 2 minutes or until butter is softened. Arrange fillets around edge of plate with thickest portion to outside, tucking under thinnest part of fillets for more even cooking. Squeeze lemon juice over fish. Cover loosely with waxed paper. Microwave on High for 3 1/2 to 4 1/2 minutes or just until firm to the touch. Remove fillets to serving plate. Add half the bread crumbs to tomato mixture; mix lightly. Spoon tomato mixture on top of fillets. Sprinkle with remaining bread crumbs.

APPROX PER SERVING: Cal 319;
Prot 38.0 gr; T Fat 12.8 gr; Chol 92.7 mg;
Carbo 23.1 gr; Sod 682.6 mg;
Potas 2885.6 mg.

BAKED SALMON SUPREME

Yields: 6 servings *Pan Size: 9 inch* *Preheat: 425 degrees*

1 (10-ounce) package frozen asparagus spears
1/4 cup chopped onion
2 tablespoons butter
3 eggs, slightly beaten
1/2 cup milk
2 tablespoons minced parsley
1/4 teaspoon sweet basil
1/2 teaspoon salt
1 (1-pound) can Pillar Rock Salmon, flaked
1 unbaked (9-inch) pie shell

Cook asparagus using package directions; drain. Saute onion in butter in skillet. Combine eggs, milk, herbs, salt and sauteed onion. Fold in flaked salmon. Reserve 6 asparagus spears; arrange remaining spears in pie shell. Pour in salmon mixture. Top with reserved asparagus spears. Bake for 35 to 40 minutes or until set.

APPROX PER SERVING: Cal 381;
Prot 22.8 gr; T Fat 24.6 gr; Chol 167.5 mg;
Carbo 16.7 gr; Sod 845.1 mg;
Potas 461.9 mg.

CRAB BISQUE

Yields: 4 servings *Pan Size: saucepan*

- 3 tablespoons butter
- 1/4 cup flour
- 1 teaspoon salt
- 1/8 teaspoon pepper
- 3 cups milk
- 1 cup chicken bouillon
- 1 (6 1/2-ounce) can crab meat
- 1 onion, sliced
- 1 sprig of parsley
- 1/2 cup milk

Melt butter in saucepan. Stir in flour, salt and pepper. Add milk and bouillon. Cook until thickened, stirring constantly. Add crab meat, onion and parsley. Simmer, covered, for 10 minutes. Add milk.

APPROX PER SERVING: Cal 306; Prot 17.0 gr; T Fat 17.4 gr; Chol 102.7 mg; Carbo 20.7 gr; Sod 1439.2 mg; Potas 434.6 mg.

STIR-FRIED SHRIMP

Yields: 4 servings *Pan Size: wok* *Preheat: 325 degrees*

Have everything else for meal ready before beginning to cook.

- 1 pound frozen shelled medium shrimp
- 6 tablespoons peanut oil
- 1 or 2 cloves of garlic, pressed
- 1 teaspoon tarragon
- 2 teaspoons Worcestershire sauce
- 2 tablespoon peanut oil
- 2 stalks celery, sliced
- 1/2 green bell pepper, chopped
- 8 ounces fresh mushrooms, sliced

Marinate partially thawed shrimp in mixture of peanut oil, pressed garlic, tarragon and Worcestershire sauce in bowl for 20 minutes. Pour 2 tablespoons peanut oil into heated wok. Add celery and green pepper. Stir-fry for 2 minutes, lowering heat to prevent browning. Add mushrooms. Stir-fry for 1 minute. Push vegetables to side; return heat to 325 degrees. Add shrimp. Stir-fry for about 3 minutes or until pink. Serve over rice or linguine.

APPROX PER SERVING: Cal 337; Prot 29.4 gr; T Fat 21.9 gr; Chol 170.1 mg; Carbo 5.4 gr; Sod 218.4 mg; Potas 488.9 mg.

Vegetables & Side Dishes

CHICKADEE

WESTERN BEANS

Yields: 4 servings *Pan Size: 2 quart* *Preheat: 350 degrees*

1 pound ground beef
1/2 cup chopped onion
2 (16-ounce) cans pork and beans
1 (16-ounce) can kidney beans
1 cup catsup
2 tablespoons mustard
2 teaspoons vinegar
1/4 cup packed brown sugar

Brown ground beef in skillet, stirring frequently; drain. Combine with onion, beans, catsup, mustard, vinegar and brown sugar in casserole. Bake for 30 to 40 minutes. May cook in Crock·Pot on Low for 4 hours.

APPROX PER SERVING: Cal 783; Prot 44.9 gr; T Fat 18.9 gr; Chol 76.6 mg; Carbo 110.5 gr; Sod 1639.4 mg; Potas 1551.7 mg.

FAVORITE BROCCOLI CASSEROLE

Yields: 6 servings *Pan Size: 2 quart* *Preheat: 325 degrees*

1/4 cup chopped onion
1/4 cup butter
2 tablespoons flour
1 teaspoon salt
1/2 cup water
1 (8-ounce) jar Cheez Whiz
2 (10-ounce) packages frozen chopped broccoli
3 eggs, beaten
3/4 cup sliced water chestnuts
1/2 cup buttered cracker crumbs

Saute onion in butter in skillet. Add flour and salt. Stir in water. Add Cheeze Whiz. Add broccoli, eggs and water chestnuts. Brown cracker crumbs in margarine in skillet. Pour broccoli mixture into casserole. Top with buttered crumbs. Bake for 45 minutes.

APPROX PER SERVING: Cal 265; Prot 11.5 gr; T Fat 18.4 gr; Chol 141.8 mg; Carbo 14.9 gr; Sod 909.2 mg; Potas 304.7 mg.

COLLEEN HAWKINSON'S BROCCOLI CASSEROLE

Yields: 10 servings *Pan Size: 2 quart* *Preheat: 350 degrees*

1 (24-ounce) package frozen broccoli, thawed
1 1/3 cups minute rice
1 (16-ounce) jar Cheez Whiz
1/2 cup chopped onion
1 can cream of celery soup
1/2 cup melted margarine

Combine broccoli, rice, Cheez Whiz, onion, soup and margarine in large bowl; mix well. Pour into casserole. Bake for 40 to 45 minutes.

APPROX PER SERVING: Cal 319; Prot 12.7 gr; T Fat 21.6 gr; Chol 34.4 mg; Carbo 19.9 gr; Sod 1085.8 mg; Potas 310.9 mg.

BROCCOLI AND RICE CASSEROLE

Yields: 10 servings *Pan Size: 9 x 13 inch* *Preheat: 375 degrees*

1/2 cup chopped onion
1/2 cup chopped celery
3 tablespoons butter
1 (8-ounce) jar Cheez Whiz
1 can mushroom soup
1/4 teaspoon each thyme, marjoram and rosemary
2 (10-ounce) packages frozen chopped broccoli, cooked
1 cup rice, cooked

Saute onion and celery in butter in saucepan. Add Cheez Whiz, soup and herbs. Add broccoli; mix well. Press rice in baking dish to form crust. Pour broccoli into pan. Sprinkle with paprika to taste. Bake for 10 to 15 minutes.

APPROX PER SERVING: Cal 225; Prot 8.3 gr; T Fat 11.5 gr; Chol 29.4 mg; Carbo 22.9 gr; Sod 659.9 mg; Potas 265.1 mg.

CARROT CASSEROLE

Yields: 6 servings *Pan Size: 1½ quart* *Preheat: 350 degrees*

2 pounds carrots
1/3 cup packed brown sugar
1/2 cup margarine
4 ounces Velveeta cheese
12 Ritz crackers, crushed

Cook carrots in boiling water in saucepan for 10 minutes; drain. Pour into baking dish. Sprinkle with brown sugar. Melt margarine in saucepan. Pour over carrots. Top with cracker crumbs. Bake for 30 minutes.

APPROX PER SERVING: Cal 717; Prot 11.9 gr; T Fat 36.3 gr; Chol 13.6 mg; Carbo 87.7 gr; Sod 1553.5 mg; Potas 703.6 mg.

ORANGE CARROTS

Yields: 6 servings *Pan Size: 1½ quart* *Preheat: 350 degrees*

1 cup frozen orange juice concentrate
2 tablespoons cornstarch
1/2 cup sugar
1 (16-ounce) can carrot nuggets

Combine orange juice concentrate, cornstarch and sugar in saucepan. Cook until clear, stirring constantly. Add carrots and nutmeg to taste. Pour into casserole. Bake for 30 minutes.

APPROX PER SERVING: Cal 168; Prot 1.6 gr; T Fat 0.2 gr; Chol 0.0 mg; Carbo 41.2 gr; Sod 123.0 mg; Potas 387.4 mg.

TERRY INGRASSIA'S CHEESY CAULIFLOWER SOUP

Yields: 6 servings *Pan Size: saucepan*

1 cup chopped onion
1 cup chopped celery
1 cup chopped carrots
6 tablespoons butter
3 (10-ounce) cans chicken broth
3 cups milk
3 tablespoons flour
3 (10-ounce) packages frozen cauliflower, cooked
1 pound Velveeta cheese, cubed
1/2 cup shredded mozzarella cheese

Cook onion, celery and carrots in water to cover in saucepan until tender; drain. Melt butter in large saucepan. Add chicken broth. Cook until heated through. Shake milk and flour together in jar until blended. Stir into stock. Add cooked vegetables, cauliflower, Velveeta cheese and salt and pepper to taste. Cook until cheese is melted, stirring constantly. May serve topped with mozzarella cheese.

APPROX PER SERVING: Cal 550; Prot 29.6 gr; T Fat 36.8 gr; Chol 134.7 mg; Carbo 28.2 gr; Sod 2395.8 mg; Potas 1018.6 mg.

DIFFERENT SCALLOPED CORN

Yields: 10 servings — *Pan Size: 9 x 13 inch* — *Preheat: 300 degrees*

- 1 (16-ounce) can cream-style corn
- 1 (16-ounce) can whole kernel corn, drained
- 2 cups sour cream
- 1/2 cup melted butter
- 1 (8-ounce) package corn muffin mix

Combine all ingredients in bowl; mix well. Pour into greased baking pan. Bake for 1 hour.

APPROX PER SERVING: Cal 382; Prot 5.8 gr; T Fat 22.3 gr; Chol 48.6 mg; Carbo 44.2 gr; Sod 592.2 mg; Potas 211.7 mg.

POTATOES AU GRATIN

Yields: 12 servings — *Pan Size: 9 x 13 inch* — *Preheat: 350 degrees*

- 3 pounds frozen hashed brown potatoes
- 2 cups half and half
- 1 cup butter
- 1 pound process cheese
- 8 ounces sharp Cheddar cheese, shredded

Place potatoes in baking pan. Combine half and half, butter and cheese in saucepan. Heat until cheese melts. Pour over potatoes. Let stand for 1 hour. Bake for 1 hour.

APPROX PER SERVING: Cal 469; Prot 14.9 gr; T Fat 35.2 gr; Chol 110.4 mg; Carbo 24.7 gr; Sod 949.5 mg; Potas 350.7 mg.

MARILYN'S POTATOES DELUXE

Yields: 10 servings — *Pan Size: 9 x 13 inch* — *Preheat: 375 degrees*

- 2 pounds frozen hashed brown potatoes, thawed
- 1 cup chopped onion
- 1 can cream of chicken soup
- 2 cups sour cream
- 1/2 cup melted margarine
- 8 ounces sharp cheese, shredded
- 1 cup cornflakes

Combine potatoes, onion, soup, sour cream, margarine, cheese and salt and pepper to taste in bowl; mix well. Spoon into baking pan. Sprinkle with cornflakes. Bake for 1 hour.

APPROX PER SERVING: Cal 475; Prot 10.9 gr; T Fat 37.3 gr; Chol 65.2 mg; Carbo 25.9 gr; Sod 594.2 mg; Potas 357.2 mg.

DILLED POTATOES

Yields: 6 servings *Pan Size: 1½ quart* *Preheat: 350 degrees*

5 unpeeled potatoes
2 tablespoons margarine
2 tablespoons flour
1 cup milk
1/2 cup mayonnaise
1/4 teaspoon dillweed
2 tablespoons chopped onion
1/4 teaspoon pepper

Cook potatoes in water in saucepan until tender. Peel and slice. Cool. Melt margarine in saucepan. Add flour. Cook until bubbly. Add milk. Cook until thickened, stirring constantly; remove from heat. Add mayonnaise, dillweed, chopped onion and pepper; mix well. Pour over potatoes; mix well. Pour into buttered casserole. Bake, covered, for 30 minutes.

APPROX PER SERVING: Cal 349; Prot 5.9 gr; T Fat 20.4 gr; Chol 18.8 mg; Carbo 36.9 gr; Sod 184.2 mg; Potas 840.2 mg.

SOUR CREAM POTATOES

Yields: 10 servings *Pan Size: 9 x 13 inch* *Preheat: 350 degrees*

2 pounds frozen chopped hashed brown potatoes, thawed
1/2 cup melted margarine
1/2 cup chopped onion
1 teaspoon salt
Pepper to taste
1 can cream of chicken soup
2 cups sour cream
2 cups grated mild Cheddar cheese
1/4 cup melted margarine
2 cups crushed cornflakes

Combine potatoes, 1/2 cup margarine, onion, salt, pepper to taste, soup, sour cream and cheese in bowl; mix well. Spoon into greased baking pan. Sprinkle mixture of 1/4 cup margarine and cornflakes over top. Bake for 45 minutes.

APPROX PER SERVING: Cal 470; Prot 10.5 gr; T Fat 32.2 gr; Chol 45.0 mg; Carbo 35.5 gr; Sod 984.0 mg; Potas 296.3 mg.

WHIPPOORWILL DINING HALL
AT CAMP MEDILL McCORMICK

SWEET AND SPICY SWEET POTATO CASSEROLE

Yields: 6 servings | *Pan Size: 2 quart* | *Preheat: 325 degrees*

- 4 cups hot mashed sweet potatoes
- 1/3 cup butter
- 2 tablespoons sugar
- 2 eggs, beaten
- 1/2 cup milk
- 1/3 cup chopped pecans
- 1/3 cup flaked coconut
- 1/3 cup packed brown sugar
- 2 tablespoons flour
- 2 tablespoons melted butter

Mix sweet potatoes, butter and sugar in bowl. Beat eggs and milk in bowl. Add to sweet potatoes; mix well. Pour mixture into casserole. Combine pecans, coconut, brown sugar and flour in bowl. Stir in 2 tablespoons melted butter. Sprinkle mixture over potatoes. Bake for 1 hour.

APPROX PER SERVING: Cal 992; Prot 7.2 gr; T Fat 80.3 gr; Chol 307.6 mg; Carbo 65.6 gr; Sod 930.4 mg; Potas 573.8 mg.

ZUCCHINI CASSEROLE

Yields: 10 servings | *Pan Size: 9 x 13 inch* | *Preheat: 350 degrees*

- 5 cups cubed unpeeled zucchini
- 1 medium onion, chopped
- 1 can cream of chicken soup
- 1 cup sour cream
- 1 cup shredded carrots
- 1 (8-ounce) package minus 2 cups herb-seasoned stuffing mix
- 1 cup melted butter
- 1 pound Cheddar cheese, shredded

Steam zucchini and onion in saucepan for 5 minutes; drain. Combine soup, sour cream and carrots in bowl. Fold in zucchini gently. Toss stuffing with butter in bowl. Layer 1/2 of the stuffing mixture in baking pan. Top with vegetable mixture, cheese and remaining stuffing mixture. Bake for 25 to 30 minutes.

APPROX PER SERVING: Cal 593; Prot 19.5 gr; T Fat 40.9 gr; Chol 115.7 mg; Carbo 39.3 gr; Sod 1360.5 mg; Potas 362.8 mg.

EASY VEGETABLE CASSEROLE

Yields: 6 servings *Pan Size: casserole* *Preheat: 350 degrees*

1 (16-ounce) bag frozen mixed vegetables
1 can cream of celery soup
1 cup cubed Velveeta cheese
1 cup croutons

Cook vegetables, using package directions; drain. Add soup, cheese and 1/2 cup croutons; mix well. Spoon into casserole. Top with remaining 1/2 cup croutons. Bake for 1 hour.

Nutritional information not available.

VEGETABLES IMPERIAL

Yields: 10 servings *Pan Size: saucepan*

Great for potlucks!

1 medium head cauliflower
1 bunch broccoli
8 ounces baby carrots
1 small onion, chopped
3 tablespoons bacon drippings
3 tablespoons packed brown sugar
3 tablespoons cider vinegar
1 teaspoon salt
1/4 teaspoon pepper
6 slices bacon, crisp-cooked, crumbled

Cook whole cauliflower, covered, in lightly salted water in saucepan for 25 minutes or until tender-crisp. Drain. Cut broccoli flowerettes from stems; cut stems into thin lengthwise slices. Cook flowerettes and stems, covered, in lightly salted water in saucepan for 10 minutes or until tender-crisp; drain. Slice carrots diagonally. Cook in lightly salted water in saucepan for about 10 minutes; drain. Saute onion in bacon drippings in skillet until soft. Stir in brown sugar, vinegar and seasonings. Simmer for 3 minutes. Spoon half the broccoli and carrots into heated serving dish; place whole cauliflower on top. Arrange remaining broccoli and carrots in ring around edges. Pour hot dressing over vegetables. Top with bacon.

APPROX PER SERVING: Cal 108; Prot 6.6 gr; T Fat 3.3 gr; Chol 5.0 mg; Carbo 16.1 gr; Sod 351.3 mg; Potas 603.6 mg.

VEGETABLE MEDLEY

Yields: 6 servings | *Pan Size: 1-quart casserole*

- 1 (16-ounce) bag frozen broccoli, carrots and cauliflower combination, thawed, drained
- 1/2 cup shredded Cheddar cheese
- 1 can cream mushroom soup
- 1/3 cup sour cream
- 1/4 teaspoon pepper
- 1 (1-ounce) jar chopped pimento, drained
- 1/2 (3-ounce) can French-fried onions
- 1/2 cup shredded Cheddar cheese
- 1/2 can French-fried onions

Combine vegetables, 1/2 cup cheese, soup, sour cream, pepper, pimento and 1/2 can onions in bowl; mix well. Spoon into casserole. Microwave, covered, on High for 8 minutes, turning once. Top with remaining cheese and onions. Microwave, uncovered, on High for 1 minute or until cheese melts.

APPROX PER SERVING: Cal 175; Prot 7.8 gr; T Fat 11.8 gr; Chol 20.8 mg; Carbo 11.3 gr; Sod 559.5 mg; Potas 245.1 mg.

BACON-SPINACH QUICHE

Yields: 8 servings | *Pan Size: 10 inch* | *Preheat: 375 degrees*

- 3 ounces cream cheese, softened
- 1/2 cup butter
- 1 cup flour
- 3 tablespoons chopped onion
- 3 tablespoons butter
- 1 (10-ounce) package frozen spinach, thawed, squeezed dry
- 8 ounces bacon, crisp-fried, crumbled
- 1 cup mixed shredded Cheddar cheese and Swiss cheese
- 5 eggs, beaten
- 1 1/2 cups half and half

Combine cream cheese, butter and flour in bowl. Mix just until dough forms soft ball. Press into quiche dish; flute edge. Chill for 10 minutes. Saute onion in butter in skillet. Add spinach, bacon and cheeses. Spread in pie shell. Beat eggs and cream in bowl. Pour over spinach mixture. Bake for 40 to 50 minutes or until set. Let stand for 5 minutes before serving.

Nutritional information not available.

SPINACH QUICHE

Yields: 6 servings *Pan Size: 9-inch pie plate* *Preheat: 350 degrees*

My own version of a Martha Stewart recipe, modified to cut down on fat and cholesterol.

- 1 medium yellow onion, chopped
- 2 tablespoons margarine
- 1 (10-ounce) package frozen chopped spinach, thawed, drained
- 3 eggs
- 1 cup evaporated milk
- 1 cup shredded mozzarella cheese
- 1 baked 9-inch pie shell

Saute onion in margarine in skillet. Add spinach. Cook on high for 2 minutes. Combine eggs and evaporated milk in bowl. Add to spinach mixture. Sprinkle cheese in bottom of pie shell. Add spinach mixture. Season with salt, pepper and nutmeg to taste. Bake for 40 minutes.

APPROX PER SERVING: Cal 364; Prot 14.0 gr; T Fat 24.8 gr; Chol 156.0 mg; Carbo 22.2 gr; Sod 417.9 mg; Potas 401.6 mg.

PEANUT SOUP

Yields: 10 servings *Pan Size: large saucepan*

Early settlers in the 1700's brought peanuts here from Brazil and after the Civil War peanuts began to be used in recipes.

- 1 medium onion, chopped
- 2 stalks celery, chopped
- 1/4 cup butter
- 3 tablespoons flour
- 8 cups chicken stock
- 2 cups smooth peanut butter
- 1 3/4 cups light cream
- 1/4 cup peanuts, chopped

Saute onion and celery in butter in saucepan until soft but not brown. Stir in flour. Add chicken stock. Bring to a boil, stirring constantly. Remove from heat. Puree in blender. Add peanut butter and cream. Process until blended. Return to saucepan. Heat over low heat until hot. Do not boil. Serve hot or cold. Garnish with peanuts.

APPROX PER SERVING: Cal 523; Prot 18.2 gr; T Fat 45.4 gr; Chol 72.1 mg; Carbo 17.1 gr; Sod 985.7 mg; Potas 549.3 mg.

PUMPKIN SOUP

Yields: 6 cups *Pan Size: saucepan*

Nutritious with a "winter" taste.

2 medium onions, chopped
1 tablespoon oil
4 cups milk
1 pound pumpkin puree
3 egg yolks, beaten
2 tablespoons butter

Saute onions in oil in skillet until soft. Combine milk, onions and pumpkin in saucepan. Simmer for 30 minutes. Stir a small amount of soup mixture into egg yolks; stir remaining soup into egg yolks. Add egg mixture to soup gradually, stirring briskly. Add 2 tablespoons butter and salt and pepper to taste. Serve hot with bread.

APPROX PER CUP: Cal 243; Prot 8.7 gr; T Fat 14.4 gr; Chol 160.4 mg; Carbo 19.4 gr; Sod 139.8 mg; Potas 528.6 mg.

MY OWN CREAM OF SPINACH SOUP

Yields: 4 servings *Pan Size: 1 quart saucepan*

1 (10-ounce) package frozen chopped spinach
1/4 cup chopped onion
1 tablespoon margarine
1 can cream of mushroom soup
1 cup evaporated milk
1/4 teaspoon basil
1/4 teaspoon tarragon
1/4 teaspoon parsley

Thaw spinach; drain well. Saute onion in margarine in saucepan until golden. Add spinach. Cook until heated through. Stir in soup, milk and herbs. Add salt and pepper to taste. Bring to a simmer. Serve immediately.

Nutritional information not available.

NIGHT HAWK

CHEESE SOUP

Yields: 4 servings *Pan Size: saucepan*

3 cups chicken stock
White part of 1 leek, sliced
1 stalk celery, chopped
1/2 medium onion, chopped
2 teaspoons cornstarch
2 tablespoons water
1 cup shredded sharp Cheddar cheese
1/8 teaspoon white pepper
1/2 teaspoon nutmeg
1 egg yolk
1/2 cup heavy cream
1/4 cup white wine

Combine stock, leek, celery and onion in saucepan. Simmer for 1 hour. Stir in mixture of cornstarch and water. Cook until slightly thickened, stirring constantly. Add cheese. Cook until cheese melts. Add white pepper and nutmeg. Combine egg yolk and cream; mix well. Stir into 1/2 cup hot soup; mix well. Stir egg mixture into soup. Cook for 2 minutes; do not boil.

APPROX PER SERVING: Cal 302; Prot 12.6 gr; T Fat 21.7 gr; Chol 141.2 mg; Carbo 14.1 gr; Sod 774.9 mg; Potas 358.6 mg.

Side Dishes

THREE-CHEESE CASSEROLE

Yields: 8 servings *Pan Size: 9 x 13 inch* *Preheat: 350 degrees*

1/2 cup butter, softened
20 slices bread, crusts trimmed
2 cups shredded Cheddar cheese
2 cups sliced Swiss cheese
12 ounces whipped cream cheese
4 eggs
2 cups milk
1 teaspoon salt
1/4 cup Sherry
1/8 teaspoon pepper
1 teaspoon dried onion
1 teaspoon dry mustard

Grease bottom and sides of glass casserole. Spread butter on each side of bread. Alternate layers of bread, shredded cheese, bread, Swiss cheese and whipped cream cheese in prepared casserole. Combine paprika to taste, eggs, milk, salt, Sherry, pepper, onion and mustard in bowl; mix well. Pour over layers. Cover with foil. Chill overnight. Bake for 1 hour.

APPROX PER SERVING: Cal 758.4; Prot 29.8 gr; T Fat 51.4 gr; Chol 270.6 mg; Carbo 41.5 gr; Sod 1307.5 mg; Potas 288.3 mg.

CHEESE SOUFFLE

Yields: 3 servings *Pan Size: 7½ inch* *Preheat: 350 degrees*

Souffle is done when puffed and center is set. Good for lunch or supper with soup and fruit salad. Leftovers good reheated in microwave.

3 tablespoons butter
3 tablespoons flour
1 cup milk
3 eggs, separated
1/2 cup Parmesan cheese
1/2 cup shredded Cheddar cheese
2 tablespoons Parmesan cheese

Melt butter in small saucepan. Add flour. Cook over low heat for 2 minutes, stirring constantly. Stir in milk gradually. Cook until smooth and thick, stirring constantly. Cool for 2 minutes. Stir in lightly beaten egg yolks, 1/2 cup Parmesan cheese and Cheddar cheese. Beat egg whites in bowl until stiff peaks form. Stir a small amount of egg whites into cheese mixture. Fold in remaining egg whites gently. Butter side and bottom of straight-sided souffle dish. Sprinkle with 2 tablespoons Parmesan cheese. Add souffle mixture. Bake for 25 to 30 minutes or until puffed and browned.

Nutritional information not available.

LOUISE TRULL'S OYSTER STUFFING

Yields: 10 servings *Pan Size: large bowl*

This comes from Mobile, Alabama, where oysters are the best. It is a must for Thanksgiving and Christmas at our house!

3/4 cup chopped onion
1/2 cup butter
1 pint oysters
1 1/2 cups (about) milk
1 (24-ounce) loaf bread, torn
4 eggs, beaten
2 teaspoons salt
1/2 teaspoon pepper
1 teaspoon sage

Saute onion in butter in skillet; set aside. Drain oysters, reserving liquid. Add enough milk to reserved liquid to measure 2 cups. Combine with bread in bowl, mashing bread to mix well. Add additional milk to make very moist mixture, if necessary. Add onion; mix well. Add oysters, eggs and seasonings; mix well. Use as stuffing for turkey or other poultry.

APPROX PER SERVING: Cal 358; Prot 14.1 gr; T Fat 15.8 gr; Chol 160.7 mg; Carbo 39.1 gr; Sod 962.5 mg; Potas 230.8 mg.

FIESTA RICE

Yields: 8 servings *Pan Size: 2-quart casserole* *Preheat: 275 degrees*

Good with chicken or with enchiladas and tacos.

1/2 cup chopped celery
1/2 cup chopped green bell pepper
1 bunch green onions, chopped
1/2 cup margarine
1 1/2 cups rice
1 can cream of chicken soup
1 can cream of celery soup
1 (2-ounce) jar pimento, chopped
1 (4-ounce) can mushrooms

Saute celery, green pepper and green onions in margarine in skillet. Add rice, soups, pimento and mushrooms. Spoon into casserole. Cover with foil. Bake for 1 1/2 hours.

APPROX PER SERVING: Cal 300; Prot 4.4 gr; T Fat 15.1 gr; Chol 5.2 mg; Carbo 36.6 gr; Sod 753.1 mg; Potas 198.2 mg.

BACON-FRIED RICE

Yields: 10 servings *Pan Size: 2-quart saucepan*

Other cooked meats could be substituted for bacon (pork, chicken or ham).

1 1/3 cups rice
2 2/3 cups cold water
8 ounces bacon
3 eggs, beaten
1/4 cup oil
1/4 cup soy sauce
1/2 teaspoon salt
1/2 cup chopped green onions

Place rice in strainer; rinse with cold running water. Drain. Combine rice and water in saucepan. Bring to a boil over high heat; reduce heat. Simmer, covered, for 20 minutes or until liquid is absorbed. Turn off heat. Let rice stand for 20 minutes. Stir rice. Chill in refrigerator. Cut bacon into 1/4-inch pieces. Brown in skillet. Drain on paper towel. Scramble eggs in 1 tablespoon oil in skillet; set aside. Heat remaining 3 tablespoons oil in wok. Add rice; mix well. Blend in soy sauce and salt. Add eggs, green onions and bacon; mix well. Serve immediately.

APPROX PER SERVING: Cal 211; Prot 6.0 gr; T Fat 11.3 gr; Chol 82.5 mg; Carbo 20.8 gr; Sod 730.4 mg; Potas 96.7 mg.

Breads

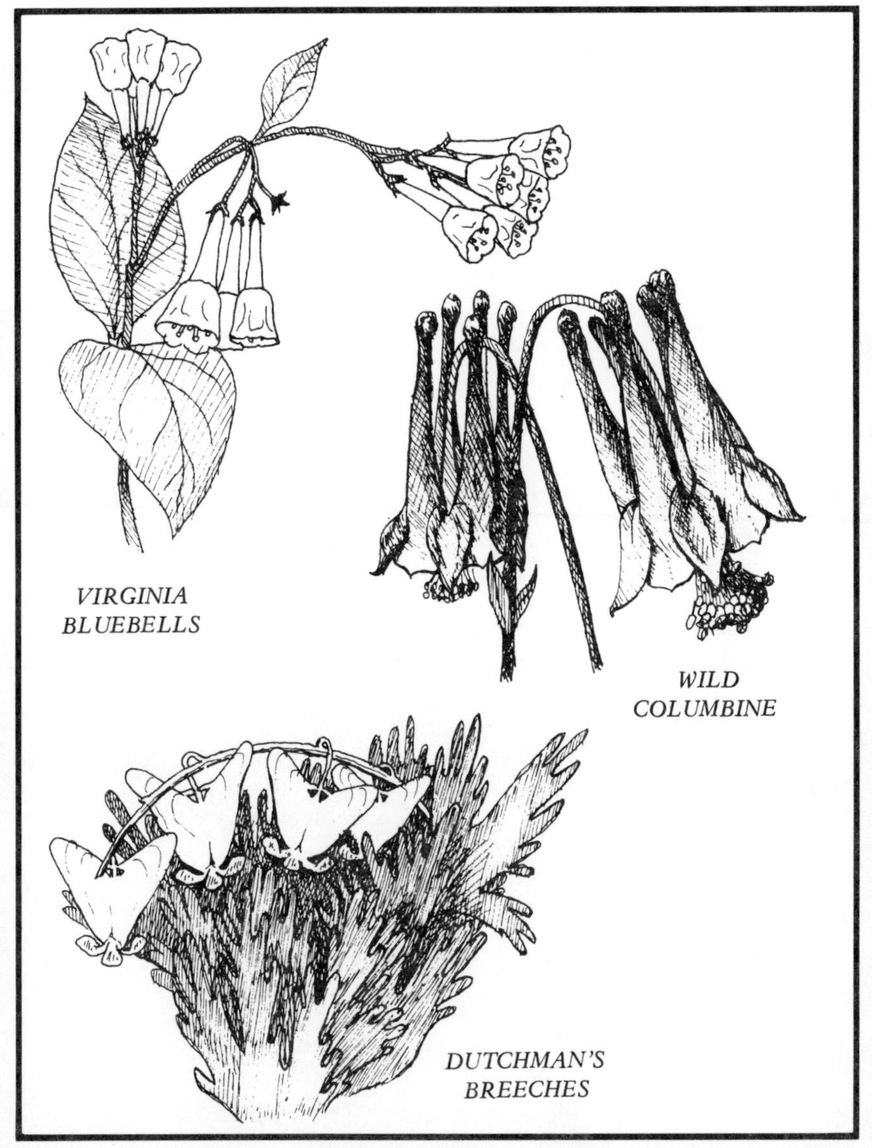

MAMA SCHEFFLER'S COFFEE CAKE

Yields: 20 slices *Pan Size: tube pan* *Preheat: 350 degrees*

1 (2-layer) package yellow cake mix
1 (4-ounce) package vanilla instant pudding mix
1 cup sour cream
1/2 cup oil
4 eggs
1/2 cup sugar
1/2 cup chopped pecans
1 tablespoon flour
1 tablespoon cinnamon

Combine cake mix, pudding mix, sour cream, oil and eggs in large mixer bowl. Beat at high speed for 10 minutes. Combine sugar, pecans, flour and cinnamon in small bowl. Sprinkle bottom and side of well-greased pan with mixture. Pour in half the cake batter. Sprinkle with half the remaining pecan mixture; cut with knife to marbleize. Add remaining batter and pecan mixture; marbleize. Bake for 55 to 60 minutes or until coffee cake tests done. Cool completely. Invert onto serving plate.

APPROX PER SLICE: Cal 261;
Prot 3.4 gr; T Fat 13.0 gr; Chol 55.6 mg;
Carbo 33.1 gr; Sod 286.6 mg;
Potas 53.2 mg.

PATRICK CURRAN'S APPLE FRITTERS

Yields: 3 servings *Pan Size: skillet*

1 cup whole wheat flour
1/2 cup wheat germ
1 tablespoon baking powder
1/2 teaspoon cinnamon
Dash of nutmeg
1 1/2 cups milk
2 tablespoons oil
1/4 cup honey
2 Granny Smith apples, peeled, sliced
Oil for deep frying

Combine first 8 ingredients in bowl; mix well. Dip apple slices into batter. Fry in oil in skillet over medium heat until golden brown. Serve with butter, maple syrup and cinnamon.

APPROX PER SERVING: Cal 505;
Prot 14.7 gr; T Fat 16.8 gr; Chol 17.1 mg;
Carbo 86.7 gr; Sod 392.5 mg;
Potas 637.9 mg.
Nutritional information does not include oil for deep frying.

APPLESAUCE HEIRLOOM BREAD

Yields: 24 slices *Pan Size: two 5 x 9 inch* *Preheat: 350 degrees*

2 cups sugar
1 cup shortening
4 eggs
1 teaspoon lemon extract
1 teaspoon vanilla extract
2 cups canned applesauce
4 cups flour
2 teaspoons baking powder
1 1/2 teaspoons soda
2 teaspoons salt
2 teaspoons cinnamon
1/2 teaspoon nutmeg
1/2 teaspoon cloves

Cream sugar and shortening in bowl until fluffy. Beat in eggs, flavorings and applesauce. Add remaining ingredients; blend well. Pour into greased loaf pans. Bake for 55 to 60 minutes or until loaves test done. Cool for 4 hours before slicing.

APPROX PER SLICE: Cal 237; Prot 3.3 gr; T Fat 10.5 gr; Chol 42.1 mg; Carbo 32.6 gr; Sod 267.1 mg; Potas 31.5 mg.

GRANDMOTHER'S BANANA BREAD

Yields: 12 slices *Pan Size: 5 x 9 inch* *Preheat: 325 degrees*

1 cup sugar
1/2 cup shortening
2 eggs, slightly beaten
3 bananas, mashed
1/8 teaspoon salt
1 teaspoon soda
1/2 teaspoon baking powder
1 3/4 cups flour

Cream sugar and shortening in bowl until light and fluffy. Add eggs and bananas; mix well. Add mixture of salt, soda, baking powder and unsifted flour; mix well. Pour into greased loaf pan. Bake for 45 minutes to 1 hour or until bread tests done.

APPROX PER SLICE: Cal 252; Prot 3.0 gr; T Fat 10.5 gr; Chol 42.1 mg; Carbo 36.6 gr; Sod 115.0 mg; Potas 138.8 mg.

STRAWBERRY-BANANA BREAD

Yields: 24 slices *Pan Size: two 5 x 9 inch* *Preheat: 350 degrees*

This recipe was made up one day after pureeing too many strawberries for making jam!

1 cup shortening
2 cups sugar
4 eggs
1 1/2 cups mashed bananas
1 1/2 cups pureed strawberries
4 cups all-purpose flour
1/2 cup whole wheat flour
2 teaspoons soda

Cream shortening and sugar in bowl. Add eggs; mix well. Mix in bananas and strawberries. Add mixture of flours and soda; mix well. Pour into greased loaf pans. Bake for 1 hour.

APPROX PER SLICE: Cal 265; Prot 3.9 gr; T Fat 10.7 gr; Chol 42.1 mg; Carbo 39.3 gr; Sod 79.7 mg; Potas 130.2 mg.

BREAKFAST BREAD

Yields: 12 servings *Pan Size: 9 x 13 inch* *Preheat: 350 degrees*

1 1/2 cups cornflakes
2 cups self-rising flour
1/3 cup margarine
1/3 cup sugar
2 eggs
2 teaspoons grated orange rind
1 cup orange juice
1 cup chopped pecans
1/2 cup seedless raisins

Measure cornflakes into bowl; crush to 3/4 cup. Stir in flour. Beat margarine and sugar in large bowl until light and fluffy. Add eggs; beat well. Stir in orange rind and juice. Add cornflake mixture; mix well. Stir in pecans and raisins. Spread in well-greased pan. Bake for 50 minutes. Cool in pan for 10 minutes. Remove to wire rack to cool completely.

APPROX PER SERVING: Cal 583; Prot 4.5 gr; T Fat 13.8 gr; Chol 42.1 mg; Carbo 115.0 gr; Sod 44.4 mg; Potas 196.6 mg.

AUNT MARIE'S DATE-PECAN BREAD

Yields: 48 slices *Pan Size: six 16-ounce cans* *Preheat: 325 degrees*

6 ounces cream cheese, softened
1 teaspoon vanilla extract
1/2 cup confectioners' sugar
1 egg
1 pound dates
2 teaspoons soda
2 cups boiling water
1 1/2 cups sugar
1/4 cup shortening
2 eggs
4 cups flour
2 teaspoons vanilla extract
1 teaspoon salt
1 cup chopped pecans

Combine cream cheese, 1 teaspoon vanilla, confectioners' sugar and 1 egg in bowl. Beat until light and fluffy. Chill for several hours. Combine dates, soda and boiling water in bowl. Cool. Drain dates, reserving liquid. Cream sugar, shortening and 2 eggs in bowl until light and fluffy. Add flour, liquid from dates, 2 teaspoons vanilla, salt and pecans. Fold in dates. Fill greased cans 1/2 full. Bake for 1 hour. Serve with cream cheese spread.

APPROX PER SLICE: Cal 153;
Prot 3.0 gr; T Fat 4.7 gr; Chol 19.7 mg;
Carbo 48.6 gr; Sod 92.6 mg;
Potas 321.6 mg.

PUMPKIN BREAD

Yields: 12 slices *Pan Size: 5 x 9 inch* *Preheat: 325 degrees*

1 1/2 cups sugar
1 teaspoon soda
1/4 teaspoon cloves
3/4 teaspoon salt
1/4 teaspoon baking powder
1/2 teaspoon cinnamon
1/2 teaspoon nutmeg
1 1/3 cups flour
1/2 cup oil
1 cup canned pumpkin
2 eggs
1/2 cup water
1/2 cup chopped pecans

Combine all ingredients in medium bowl; mix well. Pour into greased loaf pan. Bake for 1 hour and 30 minutes or until bread tests done.

APPROX PER SLICE: Cal 279;
Prot 3.0 gr; T Fat 13.7 gr; Chol 42.1 mg;
Carbo 37.0 gr; Sod 219.2 mg;
Potas 54.2 mg.

POPPY SEED BREAD

Yields: 24 slices *Pan Size: two 5 x 9 inch* *Preheat: 350 degrees*

2 eggs
1 1/2 cups milk
1 cup oil
3 cups flour
2 1/2 cups sugar
1 1/2 teaspoons salt
1 1/2 teaspoons baking powder
1 1/2 teaspoons butter flavoring
1 1/2 teaspoons vanilla extract
1 1/2 teaspoons almond extract
2 tablespoons poppy seed
3/4 cup sugar
1/4 cup lemon juice
1/2 teaspoon butter flavoring
1/2 teaspoon vanilla extract
1/2 teaspoon almond extract

Combine eggs, milk and oil in bowl. Beat until blended. Add flour, 2 1/2 cups sugar, salt, baking powder, 1 1/2 teaspoons each flavoring and poppy seed; mix well. Pour into greased and floured loaf pans. Bake for 1 hour. Pierce loaves with skewer. Spoon mixture of 3/4 cup sugar, lemon juice and 1/2 teaspoon of each flavoring over hot loaves. Cool in pans.

APPROX PER SLICE: Cal 259; Prot 2.7 gr; T Fat 10.2 gr; Chol 23.2 mg; Carbo 39.9 gr; Sod 167.1 mg; Potas 46.9 mg.

APPLE-RAISIN MUFFINS

Yields: 12 large muffins *Pan Size: 12-cup muffin pan* *Preheat: 400 degrees*

2 cups flour
1 cup sugar
1 teaspoon baking powder
1/2 teaspoon soda
1/2 teaspoon salt
1 egg, well beaten
1/3 cup orange juice
1/3 cup oil
3/4 cup raisins
1 cup chopped peeled apple
1/4 cup chopped pecans

Combine flour, sugar, baking powder, soda and salt in bowl. Add egg, juice and oil; mix well. Add raisins, apple and pecans; mix well. Mixture will be stiff. Fill greased muffin cups 2/3 full. Bake for 20 to 25 minutes or until golden brown.

Nutritional information not available.

RAISIN BRAN MUFFINS

Yields: 48 muffins *Pan Size: four 12-cup muffin pans* *Preheat: 400 degrees*

1 (15-ounce) box Raisin Bran cereal
3 cups sugar
5 cups flour
5 teaspoons soda
2 teaspoons salt
4 teaspoons cinnamon
4 eggs, slightly beaten
1 cup oil
4 cups buttermilk

Combine cereal, sugar, flour, soda, salt and cinnamon in large bowl; mix well. Add eggs, oil and buttermilk. Stir until completely moistened. Batter is very thick. Fill greased muffin cups 2/3 full. Bake for 10 to 15 minutes or until golden. May store batter in refrigerator for 6 weeks.

Nutritional information not available.

GERMAN POTATO PANCAKES

Yields: 6 servings *Pan Size: large skillet*

3 pounds potatoes
3 eggs
2 teaspoons salt
1 teaspoon pepper
2 tablespoons flour
1/4 cup milk
Solid shortening for frying

Peel and grate potatoes coarsely. Combine with eggs, salt, pepper, flour and milk in large bowl; mix well. Melt shortening in skillet. Do not use oil. Spoon heaping tablespoonfuls of potato mixture into skillet. Press flat with pancake turner. Brown slowly on both sides over low heat. Serve with applesauce, butter and sugar, or sour cream.

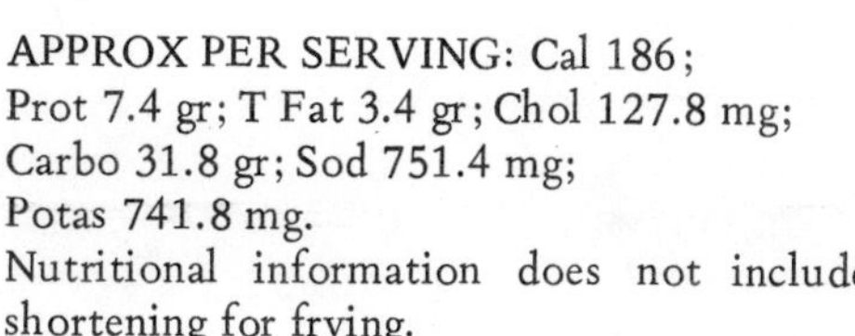
APPROX PER SERVING: Cal 186; Prot 7.4 gr; T Fat 3.4 gr; Chol 127.8 mg; Carbo 31.8 gr; Sod 751.4 mg; Potas 741.8 mg.
Nutritional information does not include shortening for frying.

TURKEY VULTURE

GERMAN PANCAKES WITH APPLESAUCE

Yields: 2 servings *Pan Size: two 9-inch pie plates* *Preheat: 400 degrees*

We love them for dinner.

4 eggs
1 tablespoon sugar
1/2 to 1 teaspoon cinnamon
2/3 cup flour
2/3 cup milk
2 tablespoons butter
1 1/2 cups applesauce
1/4 cup sugar

Butter pie plates. Place eggs in blender container. Process on High until light yellow. Add 1 tablespoon sugar, cinnamon, flour, milk and butter. Process on High until smooth. Pour into prepared pans. Bake for 15 minutes. Reduce temperature to 350 degrees. Bake for 5 minutes longer. Slide onto plates. Combine applesauce, cinnamon to taste and 1/4 cup sugar in saucepan. Bring to a boil. Pour sauce over pancakes.

APPROX PER SERVING: Cal 657;
Prot 20.3 gr; T Fat 26.3 gr; Chol 552.6 mg;
Carbo 85.7 gr; Sod 304.6 mg;
Potas 346.1 mg.

POLKA-DOT OVEN PANCAKE

Yields: 4 servings *Pan Size: 7 x 11 inch* *Preheat: 375 degrees*

1 (8-ounce) package brown and serve sausage links
1 cup flour
2 tablespoons sugar
2 teaspoons baking powder
1/4 teaspoon salt
1 egg, beaten
3/4 cup milk
3 tablespoons melted butter

Cut sausage into 1/2-inch slices. Brown in skillet; drain. Combine flour, sugar, baking powder and salt in bowl. Add mixture of egg, milk and butter. Mix just until moistened; batter will be lumpy. Pour into greased pan; sprinkle sausage over batter. Bake for 25 minutes or until golden. Cut into squares.

APPROX PER SERVING: Cal 410;
Prot 12.2 gr; T Fat 24.8 gr; Chol 126.5 mg;
Carbo 33.8 gr; Sod 849.2 mg;
Potas 208.1 mg.

ATWOOD PARK, SEPTEMBER 1982

THIN SWEDISH PANCAKES

Yields: 2 servings *Pan Size: griddle* *Preheat: medium hot*

Recipe used by cooks at old-time Stockholm Inn.

4 eggs, well beaten
1/4 cup sugar
1/8 teaspoon salt
1/2 cup flour
1 cup milk
1/3 cup melted butter

Combine eggs, sugar, salt, flour, milk and butter in bowl in order given; beat well. Batter will be thin. Drop by spoonfuls onto griddle. Bake until brown. Serve with warm syrup with cinnamon or berries or jelly.

APPROX PER SERVING: Cal 722; Prot 20.7 gr; T Fat 46.6 gr; Chol 616.8 mg; Carbo 55.7 gr; Sod 688.9 mg; Potas 344.2 mg.

CINNAMON SYRUP

Yields: 1/2 cup

1/2 cup sugar
1/4 teaspoon cinnamon
1 tablespoon flour
1/8 teaspoon salt
1/3 cup water
1 1/2 tablespoons butter

Combine sugar, cinnamon, flour and salt in saucepan. Add water; mix well. Bring to a boil. Cook for 3 minutes. Stir in butter.

APPROX PER 1/2 CUP: Cal 141; Prot 0.2 gr; T Fat 4.3 gr; Chol 13.3 mg; Carbo 26.3 gr; Sod 119.5 mg; Potas 3.8 mg.

MAGGIE'S COLD OVEN POPOVERS

Yields: 12 popovers *Pan Size: 12-cup muffin pan*

3 eggs
1 cup milk
1 cup flour
1/2 teaspoon salt

Combine eggs, milk, flour and salt in order listed in blender container. Process on High for 1 minute, scraping down sides with rubber spatula if necessary. Fill greased muffin cups 2/3 full. Place in cold oven; turn oven to 450 degrees. Bake for 30 minutes. Do not open oven door.

APPROX PER POPOVER: Cal 72; Prot 3.4 gr; T Fat 2.3 gr; Chol 66.0 mg; Carbo 9.0 gr; Sod 114.5 mg; Potas 55.4 mg.

ENGLISH MUFFIN BREAD

Yields: 24 slices *Pan Size: two 4 x 8 inch* *Preheat: 350 degrees*

Makes great toast for breakfast. Also good with creamed eggs, tuna, chicken, etc.

2 packages dry yeast
6 cups flour
1 tablespoon sugar
2 teaspoons salt
1/4 teaspoon soda
2 cups milk
1/2 cup water
1 tablespoon cornmeal

Combine yeast, 3 cups flour, sugar, salt and soda in bowl. Heat mixture of milk and water to 120 degrees in saucepan. Add to dry mixture; mix thoroughly. Stir in remaining flour to make a stiff batter. Sprinkle greased loaf pans with cornmeal. Place dough in prepared pans. Sprinkle cornmeal over top. Let rise in warm place for 45 minutes. Bake for 25 minutes. Remove from pans immediately; cool.

APPROX PER SLICE: Cal 131;
Prot 4.2 gr; T Fat 1.0 gr; Chol 2.8 mg;
Carbo 25.5 gr; Sod 197.3 mg;
Potas 70.7 mg.

MARY LUCAS WHITE BREAD

Yields: 24 slices *Pan Size: two 5 x 9 inch* *Preheat: 325 degrees*

1/2 cup sugar
1/2 cup oil
1 package dry yeast
2 cups milk
2 cups flour
1/2 teaspoon soda
1/2 teaspoon salt
1/2 teaspoon baking powder
6 cups flour

Mix sugar, oil, yeast, milk and 2 cups flour in bowl. Let stand, covered, in warm place until doubled in bulk. Add soda, salt, baking powder and enough remaining flour to make stiff dough. Let rise until doubled in bulk. Shape into 2 loaves; place in greased loaf pans. Let rise until doubled in bulk. Bake for 30 minutes or until bread tests done. Let stand for 10 minutes. Cool on wire rack.

APPROX PER SLICE: Cal 222;
Prot 5.2 gr; T Fat 5.7 gr; Chol 2.8 mg;
Carbo 37.0 gr; Sod 103.5 mg;
Potas 75.0 mg.

ELEPHANT EARS

Yields: 18 rolls *Pan Size: baking sheet* *Preheat: 400 degrees*

1 package dry yeast
1/4 cup lukewarm water
2 cups sifted flour
1 1/2 tablespoons sugar
1/2 teaspoon salt
1/2 cup butter
1/2 cup scalded milk, cooled
1 egg yolk
1/2 cup butter, softened
2 1/2 cups sugar
3 1/2 teaspoons cinnamon

Dissolve yeast in water in bowl. Mix flour, 1 1/2 tablespoons sugar and salt in bowl. Cut in 1/2 cup butter until crumbly. Add mixture of milk, egg yolk and yeast; mix well. Chill, covered, for 2 hours. Punch dough down. Turn onto floured surface. Let rest, covered, for 10 minutes. Roll into 10 x 18-inch rectangle. Spread with softened butter. Sprinkle with half the mixture of 2 1/2 cups sugar and cinnamon. Roll as for jelly roll from long edge. Cut into 1-inch slices. Sprinkle remaining cinnamon mixture on foil-lined surface. Roll each slice to 5-inch circle on prepared foil. Brush with butter. Coat with cinnamon mixture. Place on baking sheet. Bake for 12 minutes.

APPROX PER ROLL: Cal 299; Prot 1.8 gr; T Fat 15.7 gr; Chol 32.5 mg; Carbo 38.9 gr; Sod 250.2 mg; Potas 34.9 mg.

MONKEY BREAD

Yields: 16 servings *Pan Size: bundt pan* *Preheat: 400 degrees*

2 loaves frozen bread dough, thawed
2 tablespoons cinnamon
1/2 cup sugar
1/2 cup melted butter
1 cup pecans

Shape bread dough into small balls. Roll in mixture of cinnamon and sugar. Coat with mixture of butter and remaining cinnamon-sugar. Alternate layers of dough and pecans in greased pan. Bake for 20 to 25 minutes.

APPROX PER SERVING: Cal 231; Prot 5.6 gr; T Fat 7.4 gr; Chol 2.8 mg; Carbo 35.9 gr; Sod 291.9 mg; Potas 104.3 mg.

MINIATURE PECAN ROLLS

Yields: 24 rolls *Pan Size: 2 miniature muffin pans*

Like they used to have at Connie's Tea Room.

1 (8-count) package refrigerator crescent rolls
1/4 cup butter, softened
1/4 cup packed brown sugar
1/4 cup butter
1/4 cup chopped pecans

Unroll dough to form rectangles. Spread with butter; roll up. Cut into 3/4-inch slices. Butter muffin cups. Place 1/2 teaspoon brown sugar, 1/2 teaspoon butter and several pecans in each cup. Place 1 roll on top. Bake according to roll package directions. Invert onto serving plate immediately. May frost with confectioners' sugar frosting if desired.

APPROX PER ROLL: Cal 51;
Prot 0.1 gr; T Fat 4.7 gr; Chol 11.8 mg;
Carbo 2.4 gr; Sod 47.4 mg;
Potas 16.4 mg.
Nutritional information does not include crescent rolls.

LEFSE RECIPE

Original poet unknown.

Yew take yust ten big potatoes
    Den yew boil dem till dar done
Yew add to dis some sveet cream
    An' by cups it measures vun
Den yew steal t'ree ounce of butter
    An' vit two fingers steal some salt
Yew beat dis wery lightly
    If it ain't gude it iss your fault
Den yew roll dis tin vit flour
    An' light brown on stove, yew bake
Now call in all Scandihuvians
    Tew try da fine Lefse yew make.

Desserts

HAIRY WOODPECKER

RED-BREASTED NUTHATCH

BANANA SPLIT DESSERT

Yields: 15 servings *Pan Size: 9 x 13 inch*

- 2 cups graham cracker crumbs
- 1/4 cup sugar
- 1/2 cup melted butter
- 2 cups confectioners' sugar
- 2 eggs
- 1 cup butter, softened
- 4 bananas, sliced
- 1 (16-ounce) can crushed pineapple
- 8 ounces whipped topping
- 1 cup chopped pecans
- 1/2 cup maraschino cherries, chopped

Combine graham cracker crumbs, sugar and 1/2 cup melted butter in bowl. Press into baking pan. Combine confectioners' sugar, eggs and 1 cup butter in mixer bowl. Beat for 15 minutes. Pour into prepared pan. Layer bananas over egg mixture; top with pineapple. Spread with whipped topping; sprinkle with pecans and cherries. Chill in refrigerator. Garnish with confectioners' sugar.

APPROX PER SERVING: Cal 463; Prot 3.5 gr; T Fat 30.0 gr; Chol 90.5 mg; Carbo 49.8 gr; Sod 330.8 mg; Potas 268.4 mg.

CHOCOLATE ECLAIR DESSERT

Yields: 10 servings *Pan Size: 9 x 13 inch*

- 2 (3-ounce) packages French vanilla instant pudding mix
- 3 cups milk
- 12 ounces whipped topping
- 1 (1-pound) package graham crackers
- 3 tablespoons butter, softened
- 1 1/2 cups confectioners' sugar
- 3 tablespoons milk
- 1 tablespoon vanilla extract
- 2 envelopes liquid Choco-bake
- 2 teaspoons light corn syrup

Prepare pudding mix according to package directions, using only 3 cups milk. Fold in whipped topping. Layer whole graham crackers and pudding mixture in pan, beginning and ending with crackers. Combine butter, confectioners' sugar, 3 tablespoons milk, vanilla, Choco-bake and corn syrup in bowl; beat until smooth and of spreading consistency. Spread over crackers. Refrigerate for 12 hours.

APPROX PER SERVING: Cal 838; Prot 9.8 gr; T Fat 24.3 gr; Chol 20.9 mg; Carbo 159.4 gr; Sod 729.7 mg; Potas 369.8 mg.

FOUR-LAYER CHOCOLATE DESSERT

Yields: 15 servings *Pan Size: 9 x 13 inch*

- 1 1/2 (6-ounce) packages graham crackers, crushed
- 3/4 cup melted margarine
- 8 ounces cream cheese, softened
- 1 cup confectioners' sugar
- 4 ounces whipped topping
- 2 (3 1/2-ounce) packages chocolate instant pudding mix
- 3 cups milk
- 4 ounces whipped topping
- 2 graham crackers, crushed
- 2 (2-ounce) Hershey bars

Combine 1 1/2 packages crushed graham crackers and margarine in bowl; mix well. Press evenly in baking dish. Freeze for 30 minutes. Mix cream cheese, confectioners' sugar and 4 ounces whipped topping in bowl. Beat with spoon until fluffy. Spread over crust. Freeze for 45 to 60 minutes. Mix pudding mix and milk in bowl. Beat until thickened. Spread over frozen cream cheese layer. Freeze for 1 hour. Layer 4 ounces whipped topping and 2 crushed graham crackers over top. Break chocolate bars into very small chips. Sprinkle over top. Freeze until 1 hour before serving time.

APPROX PER SERVING: Cal 400; Prot 5.1 gr; T Fat 24.5 gr; Chol 25.1 mg; Carbo 43.4 gr; Sod 318.4 mg; Potas 165.2 mg.

HEATH BAR DESSERT

Yields: 12 servings *Pan Size: 8 x 11 inch* *Preheat: 350 degrees*

- 60 Ritz crackers, crushed
- 1/3 cup melted margarine
- 1 (4-ounce) package butterscotch instant pudding mix
- 1 (4-ounce) package vanilla instant pudding mix
- 1 1/2 cups milk
- 1 quart vanilla ice cream
- 16 ounces whipped topping
- 2 large Heath bars, crushed

Combine cracker crumbs and margarine in bowl; mix well. Press into baking pan. Bake for 10 minutes. Combine pudding mixes and milk in bowl; mix well. Add ice cream; beat well. Pour into crust. Chill until set. Top with whipped topping and Heath bars.

APPROX PER SERVING: Cal 340; Prot 4.3 gr; T Fat 18.5 gr; Chol 32.4 mg; Carbo 41.9 gr; Sod 361.2 mg; Potas 129.8 mg.
Nutritional information does not include Heath bars.

DIRT CAKE

Yields: 10 servings *Pan Size: 8-inch flower pot*

1/4 cup butter, softened
8 ounces cream cheese, softened
1 cup confectioners' sugar
3 cups milk
2 (3 1/2-ounce) packages instant vanilla pudding mix
12 ounces whipped topping
1 (20-ounce) package Oreo cookies, crushed

Cream butter, cream cheese and confectioners' sugar in mixer bowl. Mix milk, pudding mix and whipped topping in bowl. Fold into creamed mixture. Layer 1/3 of the cookie crumbs in bottom of foil-lined flower pot. Layer pudding mixture and remaining cookie crumbs 1/2 at a time over first layer. Chill overnight. Garnish with flowers and gummy worms. Serve with garden trowel.

APPROX PER SERVING: Cal 688; Prot 87.2 gr; T Fat 37.4 gr; Chol 71.7 mg; Carbo 83.8 gr; Sod 532.8 mg; Potas 172.9 mg.

WHITE CHOCOLATE MOUSSE

Yields: 28 servings *Pan Size: 4-quart serving dish*

2 cups sugar
1 cup water
8 egg whites
2 pounds white chocolate, cubed
4 cups whipping cream, whipped, chilled
2 pints fresh strawberries

Heat sugar and water in saucepan to 238 degrees on candy thermometer, soft-ball stage. Beat egg whites until soft peaks form. Do not overbeat. Add hot syrup to egg whites in a slow steady stream, beating constantly. Beat on high for 3 minutes. Add chocolate. Beat for 1 minute. Not all chocolate will melt. Fold in chilled whipped cream. Pour into serving dish. Chill, tightly covered, for 2 hours to 3 days. Top with strawberries.

APPROX PER SERVING: Cal 84; Prot 1.7 gr; T Fat 0.1 gr; Chol 0.0 mg; Carbo 19.9 gr; Sod 43.9 mg; Potas 156.7 mg.
Nutritional information does not include white chocolate.

MOUSSE AU CHOCOLAT

Yields: 12 servings *Pan Size: Champagne glasses*

Real chocolate mousse – no whipped cream! Keep servings small. Perfect way to end perfect meal.

16 ounces semisweet chocolate
9 egg yolks
1/2 cup unsalted butter
12 egg whites
1 tablespoon sugar
1/8 teaspoon salt
1 tablespoon vanilla extract

Melt chocolate in double boiler. Pour into large bowl. Add egg yolks and butter. Stir until smooth. Beat egg whites in bowl until soft peaks form. Add sugar and salt gradually, beating until stiff peaks form. Fold egg yolk mixture into egg whites by spoonfuls. Fold in vanilla. Pour into shallow Champagne glasses. Chill for several hours.

APPROX PER SERVING: Cal 324; Prot 7.3 gr; T Fat 25.1 gr; Chol 212.4 mg; Carbo 22.9 gr; Sod 78.7 mg; Potas 183.4 mg.

HOMEMADE MARSHMALLOWS

Yields: 216 marshmallows *Pan Size: 12 x 18 inch*

3 tablespoons unflavored gelatin
1/2 cup warm water
2 1/2 cups sugar
1/2 cup water
1 1/2 cups Nulomoline liquid invert sugar
3/4 cups light corn syrup
1 teaspoon vanilla extract
Confectioners' sugar

Soften gelatin in 1/2 cup warm water in bowl for 1 hour. Combine sugar, 1/2 cup water and Nulomoline in saucepan. Cook until heated through. Stir in gelatin until dissolved. Pour into large mixer bowl. Add corn syrup and vanilla gradually, beating constantly. Beat at high speed until doubled in volume. Pour into buttered dish. Sprinkle with confectioners' sugar. Let stand for several hours. Cut into 1-inch squares with wet scissors. Place in bag with additional confectioners' sugar; shake until coated. For Amaretto marshmallows, substitute 6 tablespoons Amaretto for 6 tablespoons water.

Nutritional information not available.

CREAMY FUDGE

Yields: 64 squares *Pan Size: 8 x 8 inch*

This recipe won first place at the DeKalb County Fair 5 years in a row.

9 ounces semisweet chocolate chips
9 ounces milk chocolate chips
1 (14-ounce) can sweetened condensed milk
1 1/2 teaspoons vanilla extract
1/2 cup chopped pecans

Melt chips in condensed milk in saucepan over low heat; remove from heat. Stir in vanilla and pecans. Spread evenly into plastic wrap-lined dish. Chill for 2 to 3 hours. Cut into squares.

APPROX PER SQUARE: Cal 80; Prot 1.2 gr; T Fat 4.9 gr; Chol 2.8 mg; Carbo 9.4 gr; Sod 9.5 mg; Potas 63.5 mg.

CHOCOLATE CASHEW FUDGE

Yields: 36 ounces

2 1/4 cups sugar
1/2 cup margarine
3/4 cup evaporated milk
6 ounces chocolate chips
1 teaspoon vanilla extract
1 cup chopped cashews

Combine sugar, margarine and milk in saucepan. Bring to a boil. Cook for 10 minutes; remove from heat. Stir in chocolate chips and vanilla. Beat with electric mixer until creamy. Add cashews. Pour into buttered dish. Let stand until firm. Cut into squares.

APPROX PER OUNCE: Cal 124; Prot 1.3 gr; T Fat 6.4 gr; Chol 1.6 mg; Carbo 16.8 gr; Sod 38.1 mg; Potas 50.4 mg.

MR. PEEPLES' PECAN PRALINES

Yields: 30 pralines *Pan Size: 2 to 3 quart*

2 cups sugar
3/4 cup evaporated milk
1/8 teaspoon soda
1/4 cup light corn syrup
1/4 cup margarine
2 cups chopped pecans

Combine sugar, evaporated milk, soda, syrup, margarine and pecans in saucepan. Cook over medium heat to 234 degrees on candy thermometer, soft-ball stage. Remove from heat. Beat with wooden spoon until mixture starts to lose its luster. Drop by teaspoonfuls onto waxed paper.

Nutritional information not available.

BARB'S NO-BAKE CHEESECAKE

Yields: 15 servings *Pan Size: 9 x 13 inch*

I won G. S. cooking contest with this recipe when I was 13 years old.

1 cup boiling water
1 (3-ounce) package gelatin
1 can Milnot, chilled
1/2 cup sugar
12 ounces cream cheese, softened
1 tablespoon vanilla extract
1 3/4 cups graham cracker crumbs
1/2 cup sugar
1 tablespoon cinnamon
1/2 cup melted butter

Combine water and gelatin, stirring to dissolve. Chill until partially set. Beat until fluffy. Beat Milnot until doubled in bulk. Add 1/2 cup sugar, gelatin, cream cheese and vanilla. Combine graham cracker crumbs, 1/2 cup sugar, cinnamon and butter in bowl; mix well. Reserve 1/2 cup for topping. Spread remaining crumb mixture in buttered dish. Pour in cream cheese mixture. Top with reserved crumbs. Chill for several hours.

APPROX PER SERVING: Cal 244; Prot 3.0 gr; T Fat 15.8 gr; Chol 44.1 mg; Carbo 24.4 gr; Sod 219.7 mg; Potas 69.9 mg.

LAFAYETTE PARISH CHEESECAKE

Yields: 15 servings *Pan Size: 9 x 13 inch* *Preheat: 300 degrees*

My sister Janet cooked desserts at a Chicago restaurant and this was very popular!

1 (16-ounce) package graham crackers, crushed
1/2 cup sugar
1/4 cup butter, softened
24 ounces cream cheese, softened
5 eggs
1 cup sugar
1 1/2 teaspoons vanilla extract
3 cups sour cream
1 1/2 tablespoons lemon juice
1/2 cup sugar

Combine first 3 ingredients in bowl; mix well. Press into baking pan. Beat cream cheese in bowl until soft. Add eggs, 1 cup sugar and vanilla; beat until smooth. Pour over crumbs. Bake for 1 hour. Mix sour cream, lemon juice and 1/2 cup sugar in bowl until smooth. Pour over cooled layers. Bake for 5 minutes. Chill for several hours before serving.

APPROX PER SERVING: Cal 550; Prot 9.3 gr; T Fat 35.2 gr; Chol 164.3 mg; Carbo 52.9 gr; Sod 348.2 mg; Potas 206.8 mg.

MOON CAKE

Yields: 15 servings | *Pan Size: 9 x 13 inch* | *Preheat: 400 degrees*

Tastes like cream puffs and everyone loves it!

1 cup water
1/2 cup margarine
1 cup flour
4 eggs
1 (6-ounce) package vanilla instant pudding mix
8 ounces cream cheese, softened
16 ounces whipped topping
8 ounces chocolate syrup

Bring water and margarine to a boil in saucepan. Stir in flour. Add eggs 1 at a time, mixing well after each addition. Spread in baking pan. Bake for 25 to 30 minutes. Cool. Prepare pudding mix using package directions. Beat cream cheese in bowl until fluffy. Add pudding; mix well. Spread over baked layer. Top with whipped topping and chocolate syrup.

APPROX PER SERVING: Cal 278; Prot 5.8 gr; T Fat 16.0 gr; Chol 88.8 mg; Carbo 30.2 gr; Sod 205.5 mg; Potas 139.0 mg.

AUSTRALIAN PAVLOVA

Yields: 8 servings | *Pan Size: cookie sheet* | *Preheat: 350 degrees*

This recipe was discovered during Quota International Convention in Sydney in 1980.

8 egg whites
2 cups sifted sugar
2 tablespoons cornstarch
2 teaspoons vinegar

Beat egg whites in bowl until stiff peaks form. Add sugar very gradually, beating until very stiff and glossy. Fold in cornstarch and vinegar. Fold 30 inches aluminum foil in half lengthwise. Make circle of foil; secure with straight pins. Place on thickly cornstarched baking sheet. Spoon meringue into foil; level with knife. Bake for 1 minute. Reduce temperature to 250 degrees. Bake for 1 hour and 15 minutes. Turn off oven. Let stand in closed oven until cool.

APPROX PER SERVING: Cal 213; Prot 3.6 gr; T Fat 0.0 gr; Chol 0.0 mg; Carbo 51.0 gr; Sod 48.7 mg; Potas 48.6 mg.

ELLA JO'S QUICK FRUIT COBBLER

Yields: 8 servings *Pan Size: 9 x 13 inch* *Preheat: 425 degrees*

It has been a favorite in our family for the past 30 years.

1 (28-ounce) can peaches
1/2 cup margarine
1/2 teaspoon salt
1 cup flour
1 cup sugar
1 teaspoon baking powder
1 cup milk

Heat peaches in saucepan just to the boiling point. Melt margarine in baking pan in oven. Combine salt, flour, sugar, baking powder and milk in small mixing bowl; mix well. Pour batter into melted margarine; do not stir. Spoon hot fruit over batter; pour hot fruit juice over all. Do not stir. Bake for 30 to 35 minutes or until crust is golden brown.

APPROX PER SERVING: Cal 376; Prot 3.3 gr; T Fat 12.9 gr; Chol 4.3 mg; Carbo 64.2 gr; Sod 332.8 mg; Potas 229.8 mg.

LEMON LOVE NOTES

Yields: 12 servings *Pan Size: 9 x 9 inch* *Preheat: 350 degrees*

1/2 cup butter
1/4 cup confectioners' sugar
1 cup flour
3 eggs
1/4 cup lemon juice
1 cup sugar
2 tablespoons flour

Combine butter, confectioners' sugar and 1 cup flour in bowl; mix well. Pat into baking dish. Bake for 20 minutes. Combine eggs, lemon juice, sugar and 2 tablespoons flour in mixer bowl. Beat with mixer. Pour over baked crust. Bake for 20 to 30 minutes or until set. Sprinkle with additional confectioners' sugar. Cool. Cut into squares.

APPROX PER SERVING: Cal 206; Prot 2.9 gr; T Fat 9.2 gr; Chol 86.9 mg; Carbo 28.5 gr; Sod 109.2 mg; Potas 37.2 mg.

BENNETT'S DESSERT

Yields: 12 servings *Pan Size: 9 x 12 inch*

3/4 large angel food cake
2 (4-ounce) packages vanilla instant pudding mix
8 ounces cream cheese, softened, whipped
1 (16-ounce) can crushed pineapple, drained
8 ounces whipped topping

Tear cake into small pieces. Place in dish. Prepare pudding mix using package directions. Add pudding to cream cheese gradually, beating until smooth. Pour half the pudding over cake. Layer pineapple and remaining pudding mix on top. Spread whipped topping over all. Garnish with ground nuts and cherry halves. Chill for 24 hours.

APPROX PER SERVING: Cal 358; Prot 5.7 gr; T Fat 12.3 gr; Chol 21.0 mg; Carbo 59.3 gr; Sod 265.2 mg; Potas 115.7 mg.

PINA COLADA WEDGES

Yields: 8 servings *Pan Size: 8-inch round*

8 ounces cream cheese, softened
1/3 cup sugar
2 tablespoons rum
2 cups whipped topping
1 (8-ounce) can crushed pineapple in syrup
2 2/3 cups coconut
1 1/2 cups whipped topping

Beat cream cheese with sugar and rum in bowl until smooth. Fold in 2 cups whipped topping, pineapple with syrup and 2 cups coconut. Spread in layer pan lined with plastic wrap. Invert pan onto serving plate; remove pan and plastic wrap. Spread with remaining coconut. Frost with 1 1/2 cups whipped topping. Freeze for 2 hours or until firm. Cut into wedges. Garnish with pineapple and cherries, if desired.

APPROX PER SERVING: Cal 418; Prot 3.7 gr; T Fat 29.5 gr; Chol 31.5 mg; Carbo 34.7 gr; Sod 140.2 mg; Potas 148.7 mg.

PEEK-A-BOO CAKE

Yields: 15 bars *Pan Size: 9 x 13 inch* *Preheat: 350 degrees*

1 1/2 cups dry oatmeal
2 cups flour
1 cup packed brown sugar
3/4 cup melted butter
4 cups pie filling

Combine oatmeal, flour, brown sugar and butter in bowl; mix well. Pat half the crumb mixture into baking pan. Pour pie filling over mixture. Top with remaining crumb mixture. Bake for 15 to 20 minutes. Serve with whipped cream or ice cream.

APPROX PER BAR: Cal 314;
Prot 3.0 gr; T Fat 10.0 gr; Chol 28.4 mg;
Carbo 54.1 gr; Sod 117.0 mg;
Potas 97.1 mg.

HOLLAND RUSK PUDDING

Yields: 15 servings *Pan Size: 9 x 13 inch* *Preheat: 375 degrees*

This recipe was handed down from my great-grandmother to my grandmother to my mom and to me. It's at least 80 years old.

1/4 cup sugar
1/3 cup melted margarine
2 packages rusk, ground
6 egg yolks
2 1/2 cups milk
2/3 cup sugar
1 teaspoon vanilla extract
1/2 cup milk
1/4 cup cornstarch
6 egg whites
1 tablespoon sugar

Combine 1/2 cup sugar, margarine and rusk crumbs in bowl; mix well. Press half the mixture into greased baking dish. Combine egg yolks, 2 1/2 cups milk, 2/3 cup sugar and vanilla in saucepan; mix well. Add 1/2 cup milk and cornstarch gradually; mix well. Cook over low heat until thickened, stirring constantly. Cool slightly. Pour over crust. Beat egg whites in bowl until soft peaks form. Add 1 tablespoon sugar gradually, beating until stiff peaks form. Spread over pudding. Sprinkle with remaining rusk mixture. Bake for 15 minutes or until golden. Store in refrigerator.

APPROX PER SERVING: Cal 124;
Prot 4.3 gr; T Fat 7.9 gr; Chol 107.5 mg;
Carbo 9.1 gr; Sod 97.1 mg;
Potas 96.6 mg.
Nutritional information does not include rusk.

AUNT LUCILLE'S BREAD PUDDING

Yields: 6 servings *Pan Size: 10-inch square* *Preheat: 350 degrees*

6 slices lightly toasted bread, cubed
2 cups milk, scalded
1/2 cup sugar
1/2 teaspoon vanilla extract
2 eggs, beaten
1/2 cup seedless raisins
1/2 cup butter, softened
1 1/2 tablespoons flour
1/2 cup sugar
1 cup boiling water
6 tablespoons butter
1 tablespoon vanilla extract
1/4 teaspoon lemon extract

Combine bread, milk, 1/2 cup sugar, vanilla, eggs and raisins in bowl; mix well. Pour into casserole. Spread butter over top. Bake until set. Mix flour and sugar in saucepan. Add water; mix well. Cook until thickened. Add butter. Remove from heat. Add flavorings. Serve over pudding.

APPROX PER SERVING: Cal 324; Prot 4.8 gr; T Fat 19.5 gr; Chol 107.6 mg; Carbo 33.6 gr; Sod 319.9 mg; Potas 123.7 mg.

PERSIMMON PUDDING

Yields: 15 servings *Pan Size: 9 x 13 inch* *Preheat: 350 degrees*

An old Indiana recipe from my husband's family. Any persimmons are good, but Indiana persimmons are best.

2 eggs
1 1/2 cups sugar
2 1/4 cups milk
3 cups persimmon pulp
2 cups flour
1 teaspoon baking powder
1/2 teaspoon soda
1/8 teaspoon salt
1/3 cup melted butter

Blend eggs and sugar in mixer bowl. Add milk and persimmon pulp; mix well. Add dry ingredients gradually; mix well. Add butter gradually; mix well. Pour into baking pan sprayed with nonstick cooking spray. Bake for 45 to 60 minutes or until dark brown and thick, stirring every 10 minutes during baking.

APPROX PER SERVING: Cal 209; Prot 3.9 gr; T Fat 6.3 gr; Chol 38.8 mg; Carbo 34.5 gr; Sod 143.8 mg; Potas 29.2 mg.
Nutritional information does not include persimmons.

RAISIN-RICE PUDDING

Yields: 4 servings | *Pan Size: 1 quart* | *Preheat: 325 degrees*

1/2 cup rice
2 1/2 cups milk
1/2 teaspoon salt
1/2 cup sugar
1 teaspoon vanilla extract
1/2 cup raisins
1/2 teaspoon cinnamon

Combine uncooked rice, milk and salt in greased casserole; mix well. Bake for 45 minutes, stirring occasionally. Add sugar, vanilla, raisins and cinnamon. Bake for 40 minutes longer or until milk is absorbed, stirring occasionally.

Nutritional information not available.

SCHNORR'S PUMPKIN TORTURE

Yields: 15 servings | *Pan Size: 9 x 13 inch* | *Preheat: 350 degrees*

This is really called Pumpkin Torte, but our 7 children renamed it years ago because it was torture to have to wait for it.

1 (2-layer) package yellow cake mix
1/2 cup margarine, softened
1 egg
1 (28-ounce) can pumpkin
2 eggs
2/3 cup evaporated milk
1 1/2 cups sugar
1 1/2 teaspoons pumpkin pie spice
1/4 cup packed brown sugar
1 teaspoon cinnamon
1/4 cup melted margarine

Reserve 1 cup cake mix. Combine remaining cake mix, 1/2 cup margarine and 1 egg in bowl; mix well. Pat into greased baking pan. Blend pumpkin, 2 eggs, evaporated milk, sugar and pumpkin pie spice in bowl. Pour into prepared pan. Sprinkle with mixture of brown sugar, cinnamon, 1/4 cup melted margarine and reserved 1 cup cake mix. Bake for 1 hour. Serve warm or cool. Garnish with whipped cream.

APPROX PER SERVING: Cal 367; Prot 4.3 gr; T Fat 13.8 gr; Chol 54.1 mg; Carbo 57.2 gr; Sod 597.0 mg; Potas 200.1 mg.

STRAWBERRY MILLE FEUILLE

Yields: 8 servings *Pan Size: baking sheet* *Preheat: 425 degrees*

1 sheet frozen puff pastry, thawed
1 pint strawberries
1/4 cup confectioners' sugar
1 1/2 cups whipping cream, whipped
1/4 cup chopped toasted almonds
1/4 cup raspberry jam
2 teaspoons water

Cut pastry into thirds. Roll each into 5 x 12-inch rectangle. Place on baking sheets; prick well. Chill for 15 minutes. Bake for 10 to 12 minutes or until golden brown. Cool on wire rack. Trim edges to make even; crumble trimmings. Chop half the strawberries coarsely. Slice remaining strawberries. Fold chopped strawberries and confectioners' sugar into whipped cream. Spread strawberry mixture between pastry rectangles. Combine crumbled pastry trimmings with almonds. Press against sides. Heat jam with water in saucepan. Brush glaze over top pastry layer. Arrange sliced strawberries on top. Brush with remaining glaze.

APPROX PER SERVING: Cal 234;
Prot 2.0 gr; T Fat 18.9 gr; Chol 59.4 mg;
Carbo 15.9 gr; Sod 16.0 mg;
Potas 137.5 mg.
Nutritional information does not include puff pastry.

COFFEE CUSTARD

Yields: 4 servings *Pan Size: double boiler*

6 egg yolks, slightly beaten
1/2 cup sugar
1/2 cup coffee
1 tablespoon flour
1 cup butter, at room temperature

Mix egg yolks, sugar, coffee and flour together in double boiler. Cook until thickened, stirring constantly. Cool. Add butter, 1 tablespoon at a time, beating well after each addition. Pour into dessert dishes.

APPROX PER SERVING: Cal 598;
Prot 4.6 gr; T Fat 53.8 gr; Chol 519.4 mg;
Carbo 26.7 gr; Sod 574.2 mg;
Potas 40.6 mg.

CHOCO-PEPPERMINT CAKE ROLL

Yields: 10 servings *Pan Size: jelly roll pan* *Preheat: 375 degrees*

4 eggs
1 teaspoon vanilla extract
3/4 cup sugar
3/4 cup sifted flour
1/4 teaspoon soda
2 (1-ounce) squares unsweetened chocolate, melted
1/4 teaspoon soda
2 tablespoons sugar
3 tablespoons water
1/4 cup confectioners' sugar
1 cup heavy cream
1 cup crushed peppermint stick candy
1/2 cup semisweet chocolate chips
2 tablespoons butter
2 tablespoons honey

Beat eggs and vanilla in mixer bowl until thick and lemon-colored. Add 3/4 cup sugar, 2 tablespoons at a time, beating well after each addition. Combine flour and 1/4 teaspoon soda. Fold gently into egg mixture. Combine unsweetened chocolate, 1/4 teaspoon soda, 2 tablespoons sugar and water in bowl. Fold gently into batter. Grease pan; line with waxed paper, then grease again and flour. Spread batter evenly in prepared pan. Bake for 14 to 16 minutes or until cake tests done. Invert immediately onto towel sprinkled with confectioners' sugar; remove waxed paper. Roll in towel as for jelly roll; cool. Beat cream until stiff peaks form. Fold crushed candy gently into cream. Unroll cake. Spread with cream; reroll. Melt chocolate chips, butter and honey in saucepan, stirring until smooth. Drizzle over cake roll. Chill for several hours before serving.

APPROX PER SERVING: Cal 366; Prot 5.0 gr; T Fat 19.7 gr; Chol 139.9 mg; Carbo 46.8 gr; Sod 102.2 mg; Potas 133.6 mg.

YOGURT POPSICLES

Yields: 6 servings *Pan Size: popsicle molds*

2 cups unflavored yogurt
1 (6-ounce) can frozen orange juice concentrate, thawed
1 teaspoon vanilla extract

Combine yogurt, orange juice concentrate and vanilla in blender container. Process until smooth. Pour into molds. Freeze until firm. Unmold onto serving plates.

APPROX PER SERVING: Cal 111; Prot 3.3 gr; T Fat 2.8 gr; Chol 6.5 mg; Carbo 18.5 gr; Sod 39.1 mg; Potas 357.7 mg.

BITTER CHOCOLATE TORTE

Yields: 6 servings *Pan Size: 9-inch springform* *Preheat: 350 degrees*

1/2 cup plus 1 tablespoon unsalted butter, softened
3/4 cup sugar
7 egg yolks
8 ounces bittersweet chocolate, melted
7 egg whites
1/4 cup raspberry preserves

Cream butter and sugar in mixer bowl until fluffy. Add egg yolks. Beat until thoroughly mixed. Add chocolate. Beat until smooth. Beat egg whites until stiff peaks form. Fold gently into chocolate mixture. Pour batter into buttered and floured springform pan. Bake for 40 minutes or until center springs back when lightly touched. Place pan on rack; remove side. Cool to room temperature. Spread preserves on top. Serve with whipped cream.

APPROX PER SERVING: Cal 565; Prot 9.2 gr; T Fat 36.8 gr; Chol 346.8 mg; Carbo 56.3 gr; Sod 71.3 mg; Potas 213.2 mg.

HAZEL NUT TORTE

Yields: 12 servings *Pan Size: three 8 inch* *Preheat: 350 degrees*

6 egg yolks
1 1/2 cups sugar
3 tablespoons flour
1 teaspoon salt
1 teaspoon baking powder
2 tablespoons rum
3 cups ground filberts
6 egg whites
1 cup whipping cream, whipped
2 tablespoons confectioners' sugar
1 teaspoon rum
1 cup milk chocolate chips, melted
1/2 cup sour cream

Beat egg yolks until thick and light. Beat in 1 cup sugar gradually. Add flour, salt, baking powder and 2 tablespoons rum. Fold in filberts. Beat egg whites until stiff peaks form. Beat in remaining 1/2 cup sugar until mixture is glossy and holds soft peaks. Fold into egg yolk mixture. Line cake pans with buttered waxed paper. Spoon batter into pans. Bake for 25 minutes or until tops are shiny and layers test done. Remove from pans. Cool thoroughly. Spread mixture of whipped cream, confectioners' sugar and 1 teaspoon rum between layers. Frost with mixture of melted chocolate and sour cream.

APPROX PER SERVING: Cal 499; Prot 8.3 gr; T Fat 35.1 gr; Chol 186.4 mg; Carbo 41.8 gr; Sod 246.2 mg; Potas 314.3 mg.

COFFEE MERINGUE TORTE

Yields: 16 servings *Pan Size: baking sheet* *Preheat: 250 degrees*

6 egg whites, at room temperature
1/4 teaspoon cream of tartar
1 cup sugar
1 teaspoon almond extract
1/4 teaspoon allspice
1/4 teaspoon ground mace
Coffee Butter Cream

Beat egg whites in bowl until foamy. Add cream of tartar. Beat until stiff peaks form. Add sugar gradually, beating well after each addition. Add flavorings. Beat for 2 minutes longer. Cut four 8-inch circles from parchment. Pipe meringue into 4 equal circles; spread evenly with spatula. Place on baking sheets. Bake for 1 hour and 15 minutes. Cool. Remove parchment. Spread Coffee Butter Cream between layers. Garnish top and side with whipped cream and dusting of cocoa over top. Serve within 2 hours.

Coffee Butter Cream

2 3/4 cups sugar
1 1/4 cups water
1/2 teaspoon cream of tartar
5 eggs, at room temperature
4 egg yolks, at room temperature
4 cups unsalted butter, sliced
1 1/2 teaspoons instant coffee
3/4 teaspoon water

Combine sugar, water and cream of tartar in heavy saucepan; mix well. Cover. Bring to a boil over high heat. Cook for about 5 minutes. Uncover. Wash down side of pan. Cook to 248 degrees on candy thermometer. Beat eggs and egg yolks in bowl until doubled in volume and very light. Pour hot syrup into egg mixture in thin stream. Beat over ice water bath until cool. Beat in butter gradually. Add mixture of coffee and water.

APPROX PER SERVING: Cal 634; Prot 4.4 gr; T Fat 49.1 gr; Chol 283.9 mg; Carbo 47.2 gr; Sod 55.2 mg; Potas 63.8 mg.

HEAVENLY TORTE

Yields: 16 servings *Pan Size: two 9 inch* *Preheat: 275 degrees*

Elegant to look at and to taste!

6 egg whites, at room temperature
2 teaspoons vanilla extract
1/2 teaspoon cream of tartar
1/8 teaspoon salt
2 cups sugar
6 (3/4-ounce) chocolate-coated toffee bars, chilled, crushed
1/8 teaspoon salt
2 cups whipping cream, whipped

Beat egg whites with vanilla, cream of tartar and 1/8 teaspoon salt in bowl until soft peaks form. Add sugar gradually, beating until stiff peaks form. Spread in waxed paper-lined pie plates. Bake for 1 hour. Turn off heat. Let stand in closed oven for 2 hours. Fold candy and 1/8 teaspoon salt into whipped cream. Spread between meringue layers and over top and side of torte. Chill for 8 hours. Garnish with additional crushed toffee bars.

APPROX PER SERVING: Cal 207; Prot 2.0 gr; T Fat 11.2 gr; Chol 39.6 mg; Carbo 25.9 gr; Sod 57.5 mg; Potas 0.0 mg.
Nutritional information does not include toffee bars.

MANDARIN TORTE

Yields: 16 servings *Pan Size: 10 inch torte pan*

1 angel food cake
2 (8-ounce) cans mandarin oranges, drained
1 (6-ounce) package orange gelatin
2 cups boiling water
1 pint orange sherbet
2 cups whipping cream, whipped

Tear cake into small pieces. Place in bottom of torte pan. Top with oranges. Dissolve gelatin in boiling water in bowl. Add sherbet; stir until dissolved. Chill until slightly thick. Fold in whipped cream. Pour over cake. Chill overnight. Remove from pan to serve. May garnish torte with mandarin orange slices, if desired.

APPROX PER SERVING: Cal 231; Prot 3.3 gr; T Fat 2.6 gr; Chol 0.0 mg; Carbo 48.9 gr; Sod 365.6 mg; Potas 149.3 mg.

LEMON RIBBON TORTE

Yields: 10 servings *Pan Size: baking sheet* *Preheat: 375 degrees*

2 cups pastry flour
1/4 teaspoon salt
1 cup butter
4 to 6 tablespoons ice water
3 tablespoons sugar
1/4 cup cornstarch
1/8 teaspoon salt
1 1/2 cups sugar
1 1/2 cups water
4 egg yolks, slightly beaten
6 tablespoons fresh lemon juice
2 teaspoons grated lemon rind
3 tablespoons butter

Combine flour and salt in bowl. Cut in butter until crumbly. Add ice water 1 tablespoon at a time, mixing with fork after each addition. Shape into ball. Chill for 30 minutes. Divide into 6 portions. Roll each into circle on 9-inch baking parchment round. Place on baking sheet. Bake for 5 to 7 minutes or until light brown. Cool. Combine cornstarch, salt and 1 1/2 cups sugar in saucepan. Add water, egg yolks and lemon juice. Cook over medium heat until thickened, stirring constantly. Add lemon rind and 3 tablespoons butter. Cool. Spread between pastry layers, ending with custard. Garnish with whipped cream and chopped almonds.

APPROX PER SERVING: Cal 440; Prot 2.9 gr; T Fat 24.1 gr; Chol 12.6 mg; Carbo 34.5 gr; Sod 350.6 mg; Potas 47.5 mg.

RHUBARB MERINGUE TORTE

Yields: 15 servings *Pan Size: 9 x 13 inch* *Preheat: 350 degrees*

1 cup melted margarine, cooled
2 cups flour
2 egg yolks
1/8 teaspoon salt
5 cups finely chopped rhubarb
2 1/2 cups sugar
4 egg yolks
1/4 cup flour
6 egg whites
1 cup sugar

Combine margarine, 2 cups flour, 2 egg yolks and salt in bowl; mix well. Pat into baking pan. Bake for 10 minutes or until light brown. Combine rhubarb, 2 1/2 cups sugar, 4 egg yolks and 1/4 cup flour. Pour over baked crust. Bake for 35 minutes. Beat egg whites in bowl until stiff peaks form. Add 1 cup sugar, beating until stiff and glossy. Spread over rhubarb. Bake until brown.

APPROX PER SERVING: Cal 394; Prot 4.8 gr; T Fat 14.6 gr; Chol 100.6 mg; Carbo 62.4 gr; Sod 191.7 mg; Potas 149.8 mg.

Cakes

STRAWBERRY ANGEL CAKE

Yields: 12 servings | *Pan Size: angel food cake pan* | *Preheat: 325 degrees*

A delicious "special occasion" cake.

1 (13-ounce) package angel food cake mix
1 (3-ounce) package strawberry gelatin
1 cup hot water
1 1/3 cups sliced fresh strawberries
2 cups heavy cream
1 tablespoon sugar

Prepare cake mix using package directions; cool. Dissolve gelatin in hot water; cool slightly. Add strawberries. Chill until partially set. Beat 1 cup cream until stiff. Fold gently into strawberry mixture. Chill until thick. Cut cake crosswise into 3 layers. Spread strawberry mixture between layers on cake plate, stacking carefully. Chill until firm. Beat remaining 1 cup cream and sugar in bowl until thick. Swirl over top of cake. Garnish with whole strawberries.

APPROX PER SERVING: Cal 336; Prot 5.9 gr; T Fat 15.1 gr; Chol 52.8 mg; Carbo 45.7 gr; Sod 204.2 mg; Potas 129.2 mg.

FANNY VOGLE'S CHERRY CAKE

Yields: 15 servings | *Pan Size: 9 x 13 inch* | *Preheat: 350 degrees*

This recipe is approximately 100 years old.

1 cup fresh pie cherries, drained
Flour
1 1/4 cups sugar
3/4 cup margarine
2 eggs
1 teaspoon soda
1 cup buttermilk
2 cups flour
1 teaspoon cinnamon

Coat cherries with a small amount of flour. Cream sugar and margarine in bowl until light and fluffy. Add eggs; mix well. Add soda to buttermilk; stir well. Add to creamed mixture; mix well. Stir in flour and cinnamon; mix well. Fold in floured cherries. Pour into greased baking pan. Bake for 30 minutes or until cake tests done.

APPROX PER SERVING: Cal 229; Prot 3.4 gr; T Fat 10.2 gr; Chol 34.0 mg; Carbo 31.7 gr; Sod 197.0 mg; Potas 70.2 mg.

CREME DE MENTHE CAKE

Yields: 15 servings *Pan Size: 9 x 13 inch* *Preheat: 350 degrees*

- 1 (2-layer) package white cake mix
- 1/2 cup Creme de Menthe liqueur
- 1 (16-ounce) can chocolate syrup
- 1 (12-ounce) container Cool Whip

Prepare cake mix according to package directions, using 1/4 cup less water. Add 1/4 cup Creme de Menthe to batter. Bake as directed. Cool. Spread chocolate syrup over top of cake. Top with Cool Whip mixed with remaining 1/4 cup Creme de Menthe. Chill.

Nutritional information not available.

ONE HUNDRED DOLLAR DEVIL'S FOOD CAKE

Yields: 15 servings *Pan Size: 9 x 13 inch* *Preheat: 350 degrees*

This recipe is 40 years old. No one can remember why it's called one hundred dollar cake, but when tasted, it is worth that much!

- 2 cups sifted flour
- 1 cup sugar
- 1 1/2 teaspoon soda
- 1/4 cup unsweetened baking cocoa
- 1 cup cold water
- 1 cup mayonnaise-type salad dressing
- 1/4 teaspoon vanilla extract
- 1/4 cup unsweetened baking cocoa
- 1 cup sugar
- 1/4 teaspoon butter
- 1/4 cup milk
- 1/8 teaspoon salt
- 1/8 teaspoon vanilla extract

Sift together flour, 1 cup sugar, soda and 1/4 cup cocoa in mixing bowl. Add water, salad dressing and 1/4 teaspoon vanilla, stirring just enough to mix. Pour into greased baking pan. Bake for 30 minutes or until cake tests done. Cool. Combine 1/4 cup cocoa, 1 cup sugar, butter, milk, salt and 1/8 teaspoon vanilla in saucepan. Cook over medium heat for 1 minute. Spread over cooled cake.

APPROX PER SERVING: Cal 239; Prot 2.4 gr; T Fat 7.7 gr; Chol 8.8 mg; Carbo 42.2 gr; Sod 197.2 mg; Potas 66.5 mg.

MRS. CURTIS' TEXAS SHEET CAKE

Yields: 20 servings | *Pan Size: jelly roll pan* | *Preheat: 375 degrees*

2 cups flour
2 cups sugar
1 teaspoon salt
1 cup margarine
1/4 cup unsweetened baking cocoa
1 cup water
2 eggs
1/2 cup buttermilk
1 teaspoon soda
1 teaspoon vanilla extract
1/2 cup margarine
1/4 cup unsweetened baking cocoa
2 cups confectioners' sugar
1 teaspoon vanilla extract
1 cup chopped pecans

Combine flour, sugar and salt in bowl. Combine 1 cup margarine, 1/4 cup cocoa and water in saucepan. Bring to a boil. Cook until smooth. Pour over flour mixture; mix well. Add eggs, buttermilk, soda and 1 teaspoon vanilla; mix well. Pour into greased and floured pan. Bake for 20 to 22 minutes or until cake tests done. Cool. Combine 1/2 cup margarine and 1/4 cup cocoa in saucepan. Cook over medium heat until margarine is melted; remove from heat. Stir in confectioners' sugar, 1 teaspoon vanilla and pecans. Spread over warm cake.

APPROX PER SERVING: Cal 348; Prot 3.2 gr; T Fat 19.1 gr; Chol 25.4 mg; Carbo 43.8 gr; Sod 330.6 mg; Potas 100.3 mg.

FAMILY FAVORITE CAKE

Yields: 12 servings | *Pan Size: 9 x 13 inch* | *Preheat: 325 degrees*

2 cups flour
2 cups sugar
2 teaspoons soda
1 teaspoon salt
2 eggs
2 (8-ounce) cans mandarin oranges, drained
1 teaspoon vanilla extract
3/4 cup firmly packed brown sugar
3 tablespoons butter
3 tablespoons milk

Sift flour, sugar, soda and salt into large bowl. Add eggs, mandarin oranges and vanilla; mix well. Pour into lightly greased baking pan. Bake for 35 to 40 minutes or until cake tests done. Combine brown sugar, butter and milk in saucepan. Bring to a boil. Cook for 30 seconds, stirring constantly. Spoon over hot cake. Serve with dollops of Cool Whip.

APPROX PER SERVING: Cal 310; Prot 3.6 gr; T Fat 4.2 gr; Chol 51.5 mg; Carbo 65.9 gr; Sod 367.1 mg; Potas 121.3 mg.

FRAN ARTMAN'S OATMEAL CAKE

Yields: 15 servings *Pan Size: 9 x 13 inch* *Preheat: 350 degrees*

1 cup quick-cooking dry oatmeal
1 1/2 cups boiling water
1/2 cup margarine
1 cup sugar
1 cup firmly packed brown sugar
2 eggs, slightly beaten
1 teaspoon cinnamon
1 teaspoon vanilla extract
1 1/2 cups flour
1 teaspoon soda
3 tablespoons margarine
2 tablespoons cream
2 cups firmly packed brown sugar
1 cup coconut
1 cup chopped pecans

Combine oatmeal and boiling water in bowl. Let stand for 20 minutes. Cream 1/2 cup margarine, sugar and 1 cup brown sugar in mixer bowl until light and fluffy. Add eggs, cinnamon and vanilla; mix well. Add oatmeal, flour and soda; mix well. Pour into greased and floured baking pan. Bake for 30 minutes. Combine 3 tablespoons margarine, cream, 2 cups brown sugar, coconut and pecans; mix well. Spread evenly over hot cake. Place under broiler until golden and bubbly.

APPROX PER SERVING: Cal 453; Prot 3.9 gr; T Fat 17.8 gr; Chol 36.5 mg; Carbo 72.2 gr; Sod 191.8 mg; Potas 260.6 mg.

GRACE KAMPMEIER'S RHUBARB CAKE

Yields: 12 servings *Pan Size: 9-inch square* *Preheat: 350 degrees*

1/4 cup butter
2/3 cup sugar
1 egg
1 cup plus 2 tablespoons flour
1/4 teaspoon salt
1 1/2 teaspoons baking powder
1/2 cup milk
1/2 teaspoon vanilla extract
1 1/2 cups chopped fresh rhubarb
1/2 teaspoon cinnamon
3 tablespoons sugar

Cream butter and 2/3 cup sugar in bowl until light and fluffy. Add egg; mix well. Sift flour, salt and baking powder; add to creamed mixture. Add milk and vanilla; beat until smooth. Fold in rhubarb. Pour batter evenly into greased cake pan. Combine cinnamon and 3 tablespoons sugar in small bowl. Sprinkle over cake batter. Bake for 45 minutes or until cake tests done. Cool.

APPROX PER SERVING: Cal 148; Prot 2.2 gr; T Fat 4.8 gr; Chol 34.3 mg; Carbo 24.4 gr; Sod 143.1 mg; Potas 71.5 mg.

PINEAPPLE-CARROT CAKE

Yields: 15 servings *Pan Size: 9 x 13 inch* *Preheat: 350 degrees*

2 cups sifted flour
2 teaspoons soda
1 teaspoon baking powder
1 teaspoon salt
1 teaspoon ground cinnamon
1 3/4 cups sugar
1 cup vegetable oil
3 eggs
1 teaspoon vanilla extract
2 cups shredded carrots
1 cup flaked coconut
1 cup chopped walnuts
1 (8 1/2-ounce) can crushed pineapple
3 ounces cream cheese, softened
1/4 cup margarine, softened
2 cups confectioners' sugar
1/3 cup coconut (optional)
1/2 teaspoon vanilla extract

Sift flour, soda, baking powder, salt and cinnamon into large bowl. Make a well in center. Add in order listed, sugar, oil, eggs and 1 teaspoon vanilla. Beat with wooden spoon until smooth. Stir in carrots, 1 cup coconut, walnuts and pineapple until well blended. Pour into greased and floured baking pan. Bake for 45 minutes or until cake tests done. Cool completely in pan on wire rack. Combine cream cheese, margarine, confectioners' sugar, 1/3 cup coconut and 1/2 teaspoon vanilla in bowl; mix well. Add enough milk to make of spreading consistency. Spread over cooled cake. Store in refrigerator.

APPROX PER SERVING: Cal 500; Prot 5.0 gr; T Fat 28.4 gr; Chol 57.0 mg; Carbo 59.1 gr; Sod 357.5 mg; Potas 136.1 mg.

UGLY DUCKLING CAKE

Yields: 12 servings *Pan Size: 9 x 13 inch* *Preheat: 325 degrees*

1 (2-layer) package yellow cake mix
1 (16-ounce) can fruit cocktail
1 cup flaked coconut
2 eggs
1/2 cup packed brown sugar
1/2 cup margarine
1/2 cup sugar
1/3 cup milk
1 1/3 cups flaked coconut

Combine cake mix, fruit cocktail with juice, 1 cup coconut and eggs in mixing bowl; beat for 2 minutes. Pour into greased baking pan. Sprinkle with brown sugar. Bake for 45 minutes. Combine margarine, sugar, milk and 1 1/3 cups coconut in saucepan. Bring to a boil. Cook until thickened, stirring constantly. Spoon over hot cake.

APPROX PER SERVING: Cal 435; Prot 4.1 gr; T Fat 16.9 gr; Chol 43.1 mg; Carbo 67.0 gr; Sod 550.1 mg; Potas 174.9 mg.

CREAM CHEESE POUND CAKE

Yields: 12 servings *Pan Size: loaf pan* *Preheat: 350 degrees*

3 cups all-purpose flour
1/2 teaspoon salt
2 teaspoons baking powder
1 cup butter
8 ounces cream cheese, softened
2 cups sugar
5 eggs
2 teaspoons vanilla extract

Sift together flour, salt and baking powder; set aside. Blend butter, cream cheese, sugar, eggs and vanilla in bowl. Combine flour mixture with moist ingredients; mix well. Pour batter into well-greased pan. Bake for 1 hour and 30 minutes. Cool in pan for 10 minutes. Remove to wire rack to cool completely. Garnish with confectioners' sugar.

APPROX PER SERVING: Cal 483; Prot 7.6 gr; T Fat 25.2 gr; Chol 173.6 mg; Carbo 57.8 gr; Sod 404.2 mg; Potas 76.7 mg.

MOM STARKE'S WAR CAKES

Yields: 24 servings *Pan Size: 2 loaf pans* *Preheat: 325 degrees*

Given to my mother from her mother. Ingredients are those that were available or inexpensive during World War I.

2 cups sugar
2 cups water
2 teaspoons cinnamon
2 tablespoons shortening
1 (15-ounce) box seedless raisins
1/2 teaspoon salt
3 cups sifted flour
1 teaspoon soda

Combine sugar, water, cinnamon, shortening, raisins and salt in large saucepan. Bring to a boil. Cook for 5 minutes, stirring constantly. Cool. Add flour and soda; mix well. Pour into greased pans. Bake for 1 hour and 30 minutes. Cool on wire rack. Serve sliced with butter or cream cheese.

APPROX PER SERVING: Cal 173; Prot 1.9 gr; T Fat 1.3 gr; Chol 0.0 mg; Carbo 40.0 gr; Sod 83.4 mg; Potas 137.2 mg.

ALMOND BUTTER CREAM

Yields: 10 tablespoons *Pan Size: medium bowl*

6 tablespoons butter
1/2 cup sugar
1 egg yolk
1 cup ground almonds
1/2 cup cream

Cream butter and sugar until light and fluffy. Add egg yolk, almonds and cream; beat until smooth.

APPROX PER TABLESPOON: Cal 54; Prot 0.7 gr; T Fat 4.5 gr; Chol 15.6 mg; Carbo 3.2 grp. Sod 22.3 mg; Potas 25.9 mg.

BLACK FOREST FILLING

Yields: 32 tablespoons *Pan Size: medium saucepan*

1 (16 1/2-ounce) can black cherries
1 1/2 tablespoons cornstarch
3 tablespoons sugar
1 tablespoon lemon juice
2 tablespoons Kirschwasser or brandy

Combine black cherries, cornstarch, sugar and lemon juice in saucepan. Cook until thickened and clear. Add Kirschwasser; mix well. Cool.

APPROX PER TABLESPOON: Cal 19; Prot 0.1 gr; T Fat 0.0 gr; Chol 0.0 mg; Carbo 4.8 gr; Sod 0.2 mg; Potas 20.9 mg.
Nutritional information does not include Kirschwasser.

CHOCOLATE SOUR CREAM FROSTING

Yields: 24 tablespoons

1 cup chocolate chips
1/2 cup sour cream

Melt chocolate chips in saucepan, stirring constantly. Stir in sour cream slowly. Use immediately.

APPROX PER TABLESPOONS: Cal 46; Prot 0.5 gr; T Fat 3.5 gr; Chol 2.1 mg; Carbo 4.2 gr; Sod 2.7 mg; Potas 29.9 mg.

CREAM CHEESE FILLING

Yields: 8 cups *Pan Size: medium saucepan*

2 1/2 cups sugar
1 cup water
3 pounds cream cheese, softened
Juice of 1/2 lemon

Combine sugar and water in saucepan. Bring to a boil. Cook to 248 degrees on candy thermometer, washing down side of pan occasionally. Beat cream cheese until light and fluffy. Add sugar syrup slowly to taste, stirring constantly. Add lemon juice; mix well.

APPROX PER CUP: Cal 878;
Prot 13.6 gr; T Fat 64.1 gr; Chol 188.8 mg;
Carbo 66.0 gr; Sod 425.9 mg;
Potas 131.8 mg.

VANILLA FROSTING

Yields: 16 servings *Pan Size: mixer bowl*

1 cup cold milk
2 tablespoons cornstarch
1/2 cup margarine
1/3 cup shortening
1 teaspoon vanilla extract
1 cup sugar

Place milk in saucepan. Add cornstarch; mix well. Cook until thickened, stirring constantly. Remove from heat; cool to lukewarm. Combine margarine, shortening and vanilla in mixer bowl. Add sugar a small amount at a time, beating well after each addition. Add milk mixture; beat until smooth. Add food coloring, if desired.

APPROX PER SERVING: Cal 154;
Prot 0.6 gr; T Fat 10.9 gr; Chol 2.1 mg;
Carbo 14.1 gr; Sod 77.8 mg;
Potas 24.0 mg.

JOHN TERRANOVA'S GERMAN CHOCOLATE CAKE TOPPING

Yields: 16 servings *Pan Size: medium saucepan*

- 1 cup evaporated milk
- 1 cup sugar
- 3 egg yolks, slightly beaten
- 1/2 cup butter
- 1 teaspoon vanilla extract
- 2 cups flaked coconut
- 1 cup chopped pecans

Combine milk, sugar, egg yolks, butter and vanilla in saucepan. Cook over medium heat for 12 minutes or until thickened. Remove from heat. Add coconut and pecans; stir until of spreading consistency.

APPROX PER SERVING: Cal 228;
Prot 2.7 gr; T Fat 16.4 gr; Chol 69.8 mg;
Carbo 19.0 gr; Sod 112.5 mg;
Potas 130.9 mg.

Cookies

CHEESECAKE BARS

Yields: 48 bars *Pan Size: 9 x 13 inch* *Preheat: 350 degrees*

- 2 (8-count) packages refrigerator crescent rolls
- 19 ounces cream cheese
- 1 cup sugar
- 1 egg yolk, slightly beaten
- 1 teaspoon vanilla extract
- 1 tablespoon sugar

Line baking pan with 1 package crescent rolls. Combine cream cheese, 1 cup sugar, egg yolk and vanilla in bowl; mix well. Spread over rolls. Top with remaining package of rolls, pinching to seal perforations. Sprinkle 1 tablespoon sugar over top. Bake for 30 to 35 minutes. Cool. Cut into bars. Store in refrigerator.

APPROX PER BAR: Cal 59;
Prot 1.0 gr; T Fat 4.3 gr; Chol 17.7 mg;
Carbo 4.4 gr; Sod 28.3 mg;
Potas 8.8 mg.
Nutritional information does not include crescent roll dough.

THE TEPEES AT CAMP MEDILL McCORMICK

GIRL SCOUT BROWNIES

Yields: 48 squares | *Pan Size: two 10 x 14 inch* | *Preheat: 450 degrees*

- 4 (1-ounce) squares unsweetened baking chocolate
- 3/4 cup butter
- 6 eggs
- 3 cups sugar
- 2 cups flour
- 1/2 teaspoon salt
- 1/2 cup chopped pecans
- 2 teaspoons vanilla extract

Melt chocolate and butter in saucepan. Beat eggs in mixer bowl until light and fluffy. Add sugar and chocolate mixture; mix well. Add mixture of sifted flour and salt; mix well. Stir in pecans and vanilla. Spread into greased baking pans. Bake for 12 minutes. Cool. Cut into squares. Frost with chocolate frosting, if desired.

APPROX PER SQUARE: Cal 111;
Prot 1.5 gr; T Fat 4.5 gr; Chol 40.5 mg;
Carbo 16.7 gr; Sod 65.1 mg;
Potas 21.6 mg.

HOLIDAY SQUARES

Yields: 72 squares | *Pan Size: 11 x 17 inch* | *Preheat: 350 degrees*

- 1 cup margarine, softened
- 1 1/2 cups sugar
- 4 eggs
- 2 cups flour
- 1 tablespoon lemon juice
- 1 (21-ounce) can cherry pie filling
- 1 cup confectioners' sugar

Cream margarine and sugar in mixer bowl at medium speed until light and fluffy. Add eggs 1 at a time, beating well at low speed after each addition. Add flour and lemon juice; mix well. Spread evenly into greased baking pan. Score into squares. Drop pie filling by teaspoonfuls onto each square. Bake for 25 to 30 minutes. Sprinkle with confectioners' sugar while hot. Cut into squares.

APPROX PER SQUARE: Cal 50;
Prot 0.7 gr; T Fat 1.6 gr; Chol 14.0 mg;
Carbo 8.2 gr; Sod 19.1 mg;
Potas 7.7 mg.

GREAT-GRANDMOTHER'S FROSTED COFFEE BARS

Yields: 24 squares *Pan Size: 10 x 15 inch* *Preheat: 350 degrees*

A four generation family recipe!

1/4 cup shortening
1 cup packed brown sugar
1 egg
1 1/2 cups flour
1/2 teaspoon baking powder
1/2 teaspoon salt
1/2 teaspoon soda
1/2 teaspoon cinnamon
1/2 cup hot coffee
1/2 cup raisins
1/4 cup pecans

Cream shortening and brown sugar in mixer bowl until light and fluffy. Add egg; mix well. Add flour, baking powder, salt, soda, cinnamon and coffee; mix well. Stir in raisins and pecans. Spread on baking sheet. Bake for 15 minutes. Cool. Cut into squares.

APPROX PER SQUARE: Cal 104; Prot 1.3 gr; T Fat 3.5 gr; Chol 10.5 mg; Carbo 17.3 gr; Sod 74.6 mg; Potas 72.2 mg.

K-BARS

Yields: 48 bars *Pan Size: 9 x 13 inch*

1/2 cup sugar
1/2 cup corn syrup
1 teaspoon vanilla extract
3/4 cup peanut butter
3 cups Special-K cereal
1/2 (6-ounce) package chocolate chips
1 (6-ounce) package butterscotch chips

Combine sugar, corn syrup and vanilla in saucepan; mix well. Cook over low heat until bubbly, stirring occasionally; do not boil. Remove from heat. Add peanut butter and cereal; mix well. Spoon into buttered dish. Melt chocolate chips and butterscotch chips in saucepan over low heat, stirring constantly. Spread over cereal mixture. Cut into bars.

APPROX PER BAR: Cal 68; Prot 1.2 gr; T Fat 3.9 gr; Chol 0.0 mg; Carbo 8.4 gr; Sod 26.7 mg; Potas 42.6 mg.

SUGARED DATE-WALNUT SQUARES

Yields: 64 squares *Pan Size: 8-inch square*

3/4 cup butter
3/4 cup packed brown sugar
8 ounces dates, chopped
1 cup chopped walnuts
3 cups crisp rice cereal
1 teaspoon vanilla extract
1 cup confectioners' sugar

Combine butter, brown sugar and dates in saucepan. Cook over medium heat until almost smooth, stirring occasionally. Add walnuts, cereal and vanilla; mix well. Press into buttered dish. Cut into 1-inch squares. Coat each square with confectioners' sugar.

APPROX PER SQUARE: Cal 58; Prot 0.4 gr; T Fat 3.4 gr; Chol 6.7 mg; Carbo 7.3 gr; Sod 27.2 mg; Potas 36.7 mg.

WAVERLY WAFER BARS

Yields: 24 bars *Pan Size: 9 x 13 inch* *Preheat: 350 degrees*

These are quick and easy cookies to make for a cookie exchange.

1/4 package Waverly Wafer crackers
3/4 cup chopped pecans
1/2 pound butter
1/2 cup sugar

Line baking dish with crackers. Sprinkle pecans over top; set aside. Bring butter and sugar to a boil in saucepan. Boil for 2 minutes. Drizzle gradually over crackers. Bake for 5 minutes. Cool for 1 minute in baking dish. Remove to waxed paper to cool completely. Cut into bars.

APPROX PER BAR: Cal 124; Prot 0.6 gr; T Fat 10.9 gr; Chol 23.7 mg; Carbo 7.0 gr; Sod 129.9 mg; Potas 28.3 mg.

SHOOTING STAR

GINGERSNAPS

Yields: 60 cookies *Pan Size: cookie sheet* *Preheat: 350 degrees*

Was given to me as a bride in 1938 by Mrs. Robert Homer, who was treasurer on Girl Scout Board.

3/4 cup shortening
1 cup sugar
1 egg
1/4 cup molasses
2 tablespoons soda
2 cups flour
2 teaspoons ginger
1/2 teaspoon cloves
2 teaspoons cinnamon
1/4 teaspoon salt
1 teaspoon vanilla extract

Combine shortening, sugar, egg, molasses, soda, flour, spices, salt and vanilla in mixing bowl in order given; mix well. Chill for several hours to overnight. Shape by teaspoonfuls into balls. Dip one side of each ball into additional sugar. Place on greased cookie sheet. Bake for 15 minutes.

APPROX PER COOKIE: Cal 58;
Prot 0.5 gr; T Fat 2.9 gr; Chol 4.2 mg;
Carbo 7.4 gr; Sod 37.6 mg;
Potas 17.7 mg.

RAMONA GRAUPNER'S SUGAR COOKIES

Yields: 60 cookies *Pan Size: cookie sheet* *Preheat: 350 degrees*

This recipe helped 24 RRV Girl Scouts get to the Cabana in 1982! We made and sold these cookies at Christmas time at the mall.

3 cups flour
1/2 teaspoon salt
1 teaspoon cream of tartar
1/4 teaspoon soda
1 cup margarine, softened
1 cup sugar
3 tablespoons milk
2 eggs
1 teaspoon vanilla extract

Combine flour, salt, cream of tartar and soda in bowl. Add margarine and sugar; mix well. Add mixture of milk, eggs and vanilla; mix well. Chill in refrigerator. Divide into 4 portions. Roll each portion 1/2 inch thick on floured surface. Cut with cookie cutter. Place on cookie sheet. Bake for 7 minutes or until lightly browned around edges. Cool on wire rack.

APPROX PER COOKIE: Cal 90;
Prot 2.9 gr; T Fat 5.0 gr; Chol 18.7 mg;
Carbo 8.1 gr; Sod 65.3 mg;
Potas 30.7 mg.

CHOCOLATE SHOT COOKIES

Yields: 36 cookies *Pan Size: cookie sheet* *Preheat: 325 degrees*

1 cup butter, softened
1 cup confectioners' sugar
2 teaspoons vanilla extract
1 cup dry oatmeal
1 1/2 cups sifted flour
1/2 teaspoon soda
1/2 cup chocolate shot

Cream butter and confectioners' sugar in mixer bowl until fluffy. Stir in vanilla. Add oatmeal and mixture of sifted flour and soda; mix well. Chill for 1 hour. Shape into 1 1/2-inch rolls. Coat each roll with chocolate shot. Slice 3/8 inch thick. Place on ungreased cookie sheet. Bake for 20 to 25 minutes. Cool on wire rack.

APPROX PER COOKIE: Cal 94;
Prot 1.0 gr; T Fat 6.2 gr; Chol 15.8 mg;
Carbo 9.3 gr; Sod 73.9;
Potas 21.6 mg.

EASY CHOCOLATE CHIP COOKIES

Yields: 21 cookies *Pan Size: cookie sheet* *Preheat: 350 degrees*

1/2 cup shortening
1/2 cup sugar
1/2 cup packed brown sugar
1 egg
1/2 teaspoon salt
1/2 teaspoon soda
1 1/2 cups flour
2 1/2 tablespoons water
6 ounces chocolate chips

Cream shortening and sugars together in mixer bowl until light and fluffy. Beat in egg. Add salt, soda, flour and water; mix well. Stir in chocolate chips. Drop by heaping tablespoonfuls onto ungreased cookie sheet. Bake for 11 minutes or until light brown. Cool on cookie sheet.

APPROX PER COOKIE: Cal 163;
Prot 1.6 gr; T Fat 8.6 gr; Chol 12.0 mg;
Carbo 21.2 gr; Sod 75.2 mg;
Potas 56.1 mg.

DATE PINWHEEL COOKIES

Yields: 48 cookies *Pan Size: cookie sheet* *Preheat: 375 degrees*

16 ounces pitted dates, chopped
1/2 cup water
1/2 cup sugar
1 cup chopped pecans
2 cups sifted flour
1/2 teaspoon soda
1/2 teaspoon salt
1/2 cup margarine, softened
1/2 cup packed brown sugar
1/2 cup sugar
1 egg, well beaten
1/2 teaspoon vanilla extract

Combine dates, water and 1/2 cup sugar in saucepan. Cook until thickened, stirring constantly. Cool. Stir in pecans; set aside. Sift flour with soda and salt; set aside. Cream margarine with brown sugar and 1/2 cup sugar in mixer bowl until light and fluffy. Add egg; beat until fluffy. Stir in vanilla. Add flour mixture; mix until smooth. Chill until easy to handle. Divide into 2 equal portions. Roll 1 portion into rectangle on lightly floured surface. Spread half the date mixture evenly on dough. Roll as for jelly roll. Wrap in waxed paper. Repeat process with remaining portion. Chill overnight. Cut crosswise into 1/4-inch slices. Place on cookie sheet. Bake for 10 to 12 minutes or until lightly browned.

APPROX PER COOKIE: Cal 79; Prot 0.9 gr; T Fat 3.8 gr; Chol 5.3 mg; Carbo 10.7 gr; Sod 56.2 mg; Potas 29.7 mg.

S'MORES

Yields: 1 serving *Pan Size: paper napkin*

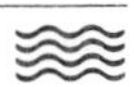

2 graham cracker squares
4 ounces milk chocolate candy
1 large marshmallow

Place 1 graham cracker square on paper napkin. Top with chocolate and marshmallow. Microwave on High for 15 to 20 seconds or until marshmallow puffs. Place remaining graham cracker over top.

APPROX PER SERVING: Cal 225; Prot 3.5 gr; T Fat 10.5 gr; Chol 5.7 mg; Carbo 32.3 gr; Sod 124.6 mg; Potas 163.8 mg.

BROWN-EYED SUSANS

Yields: 36 cookies *Pan Size: cookie sheet* *Preheat: 400 degrees*

1 cup margarine, softened
3 tablespoons sugar
1 teaspoon vanilla extract
2 cups flour
1/2 teaspoon salt
1 cup sifted confectioners' sugar
2 tablespoons unsweetened baking cocoa
2 tablespoons water
1/2 teaspoon vanilla extract
36 pecan halves

Cream margarine and sugar in bowl until light and fluffy. Add vanilla, flour and salt; mix well. Shape by level tablesoonfuls into balls. Place on greased cookie sheet; flatten slightly. Bake for 10 to 12 minutes. Cool on wire rack. Combine confectioners' sugar and cocoa in bowl. Add water and vanilla; mix well. Frost each cookie with 1/2 teaspoonful of frosting. Place pecan half in center of each.

APPROX PER COOKIE: Cal 97; Prot 1.0 gr; T Fat 6.4 gr; Chol 0.0 mg; Carbo 9.5 gr; Sod 92.1 mg; Potas 22.6 mg.

CAPE COD OATMEAL COOKIES

Yields: 60 cookies *Pan Size: cookie sheet* *Preheat: 350 degrees*

1 egg, beaten
1/2 cup melted butter
1/2 cup melted shortening
1 tablespoon molasses
1 1/2 cups flour
1/2 teaspoon soda
1 teaspoon cinnamon
1/2 teaspoon salt
1/4 cup milk
1 3/4 cups dry oatmeal
1 cup raisins
1 cup pecans

Combine egg, butter, shortening and molasses in mixer bowl; mix well. Add mixture of flour, soda, cinnamon and salt; mix well. Add milk alternately with oatmeal, mixing well after each addition. Stir in raisins and pecans. Drop by teaspoonfuls onto greased cookie sheet. Bake for 10 to 12 minutes. Cool on wire rack.

APPROX PER COOKIE: Cal 87; Prot 1.1 gr; T Fat 5.1 gr; Chol 9.1 mg; Carbo 9.7 gr; Sod 46.4 mg; Potas 94.6 mg.

ITALIAN BISCOTTI COOKIES

Yields: 48 cookies *Pan Size: cookie sheet* *Preheat: 350 degrees*

3 cups flour
1/4 teaspoon salt
1 cup sugar
3 tablespoons baking powder
1 cup unsweetened baking cocoa
1/4 teaspoon cinnamon
1/4 teaspoon nutmeg
1/4 teaspoon ground cloves
3 eggs
1 teaspoon vanilla extract
3/4 cup margarine, softened
1 cup confectioners' sugar

Combine flour, salt, sugar, baking powder, cocoa, spices, eggs, vanilla and margarine in mixer bowl; mix well. Add a small amount of milk, if needed. Drop by teaspoonfuls onto greased cookie sheet. Bake for 12 minutes or until firm. Cool on wire rack. Drizzle mixture of confectioners' sugar and enough water to make a glaze over cookies. May add chocolate chips and nuts to batter before baking.

APPROX PER COOKIE: Cal 90; Prot 1.6 gr; T Fat 3.7 gr; Chol 15.8 mg; Carbo 13.6 gr; Sod 70.8 mg; Potas 40.2 mg.

MOM'S MONSTER COOKIES

Yields: 16 cookies *Pan Size: cookie sheet* *Preheat: 350 degrees*

1 1/4 cups margarine, softened
1 cup packed brown sugar
1 cup sugar
3 eggs
2 tablespoons vanilla extract
1 teaspoon salt
1 teaspoon soda
1 teaspoon baking powder
3 3/4 cups flour
1 1/2 cups chocolate chips
48 M and M's

Cream margarine and sugars in bowl until light and fluffy. Add eggs and vanilla; mix well. Add mixture of salt, soda, baking powder and flour; mix well. Stir in chocolate chips. Spray cookie sheet with nonstick cooking spray. Spoon 1/3 cup batter per cookie onto cookie sheet. Spread slightly with spatula. Bake for 8 to 10 minutes. Decorate with M and M's.

APPROX PER COOKIE: Cal 344; Prot 5.2 gr; T Fat 10.6 gr; Chol 47.8 mg; Carbo 59.8 gr; Sod 259.3 mg; Potas 145.4 mg.

Pies

APPLE PIE

Yields: 6 servings | *Pan Size: 9-inch pie plate* | *Preheat: 350 degrees*

2 cups sifted flour
1 teaspoon salt
1 cup shortening
1/4 to 1/2 cup ice water
8 apples, peeled, sliced
1 cup sugar
3 tablespoons flour
1 teaspoon cinnamon
1/2 teaspoon allspice
or nutmeg

Sift 2 cups flour and salt together into large bowl; reserve 1/3 cup. Cut in shortening until crumbly. Add mixture of 1/3 cup reserved flour mixture and ice water; mix well. Divide into 2 portions. Roll each portion 1/4 to 1/8 inch thick on floured surface. Line pie plate with pastry. Add sliced apples. Sprinkle mixture of sugar, 3 tablespoons flour and spices over apples. Cover with remaining pastry; seal edge. Slash and prick upper crust. Sprinkle lightly with additional sugar. Bake for 1 hour or until crust is light brown.

APPROX PER SERVING: Cal 776; Prot 5.0 gr; T Fat 39.4 gr; Chol 40 mg; Carbo 106.2 gr; Sod 359.3 mg; Potas 351.5 mg.

BIRD'S NEST PIE

Yields: 6 servings | *Pan Size: 9-inch pie plate* | *Preheat: 350 degrees*

Handed down from my husband's great grandmother.

2 cups chopped fresh
rhubarb
1/2 cup sugar
1 egg
3/4 cup milk
1 1/2 cups flour
1 cup sugar
1 1/2 teaspoons baking
powder

Place rhubarb in pie plate. Sprinkle 1/2 cup sugar over top. Combine egg, milk, flour, 1 cup sugar and baking powder in bowl; mix well. Pour over rhubarb. Bake for 30 to 40 minutes. Invert onto serving plate.

APPROX PER SERVING: Cal 347; Prot 5.7 gr; T Fat 2.4 gr; Chol 46.4 mg; Carbo 76.8 gr; Sod 109.5 mg; Potas 189.1 mg.

FLUFFY FUDGE PIE

Yields: 6 servings | *Pan Size: 9-inch pie plate* | *Preheat: 375 degrees*

Most people tell me this is better than "French Silk" pie!

- 1 1/4 cups graham cracker crumbs
- 1/4 cup sugar
- 6 tablespoons melted margarine
- 1 cup margarine, softened
- 1 cup confectioners' sugar
- 1 teaspoon vanilla extract
- 3 eggs
- 2 (1-ounce) squares unsweetened baking chocolate, melted

Combine graham cracker crumbs, sugar and 6 tablespoons margarine in bowl; mix well. Reserve 2 tablespoons mixture. Press on bottom and up side of pie plate. Bake for 6 to 8 minutes. Cool. Cream 1 cup margarine and confectioners' sugar together in mixer bowl. Add vanilla; mix well. Add eggs 1 at a time, beating thoroughly after each addition. Stir in melted chocolate; mix well. Pour into pie shell; smooth top with spatula. Garnish with reserved crumbs. Refrigerate overnight.

APPROX PER SERVING: Cal 581; Prot 4.8 gr; T Fat 51.1 gr; Chol 128.4 mg; Carbo 31.1 gr; Sod 555.3 mg; Potas 132.6 mg.

MINT TEA PIE

Yields: 6 servings | *Pan Size: 9-inch pie plate* | *Preheat: 325 degrees*

Girl Scout cookies become even more wonderful.

- 14 chocolate mint Girl Scout cookies, chilled
- 3 egg whites
- 1/8 teaspoon salt
- 3/4 cup sugar
- 1/2 cup chopped pecans
- 1/2 teaspoon vanilla extract

Place cookies between folds of waxed paper. Crumble with rolling pin. Beat egg whites and salt in glass bowl until soft peaks form. Add sugar gradually, beating until stiff peaks form. Stir in cookie crumbs, pecans and vanilla. Spread in buttered pie plate. Bake for 35 minutes. Cool. Chill for 3 to 4 hours. Garnish with whipped topping and unsweetened chocolate curls.

Nutritional information not available.

LEMON MERINGUE PIE

Yields: 6 servings | *Pan Size: 9-inch pie plate* | *Preheat: 350 degrees*

Firm enough to hold shape when cut.

1 1/2 cups sugar
3 tablespoons cornstarch
3 tablespoons flour
1/8 teaspoon salt
1 1/2 cups hot water
3 egg yolks, slightly beaten
2 tablespoons butter
1/2 teaspoon grated lemon rind
1/3 cup lemon juice
1 baked 9-inch pie shell
1 recipe meringue

Combine sugar, cornstarch, flour and salt in saucepan; mix well. Add hot water gradually, stirring constantly. Cook over high heat until mixture comes to a boil, stirring constantly. Reduce heat. Simmer for 2 minutes, stirring constantly. Stir a small amount of hot mixture into egg yolks; stir egg yolks into hot mixture. Bring to a boil. Cook for 2 minutes, stirring constantly. Add butter and lemon rind. Add lemon juice, mixing well. Pour gradually into pie shell. Spread meringue over filling, sealing to edge. Bake for 12 to 15 minutes or until light brown.

APPROX PER SERVING: Cal 497; Prot 5.6 gr; T Fat 16.8 gr; Chol 138.2 mg; Carbo 83.1 gr; Sod 305.9 mg; Potas 73.2 mg.

CHILLED STRAWBERRY PIE

Yields: 6 servings | *Pan Size: 9-inch pie plate*

1 cup water
1 cup sugar
3 tablespoons cornstarch
2 tablespoons light corn syrup
3 tablespoons dry strawberry gelatin
1 tablespoon butter
1 quart strawberries
1 baked 9-inch pie shell

Combine water, sugar, cornstarch and corn syrup in saucepan; mix well. Cook for 5 minutes or until clear, stirring constantly. Stir in gelatin until dissolved. Add butter, stirring until melted. Cool. Add strawberries, stirring to coat well. Pour into pie shell. Chill for 1 hour. Garnish with whipped cream.

APPROX PER SERVING: Cal 390; Prot 3.9 gr; T Fat 12.4 gr; Chol 5.9 mg; Carbo 70.6 gr; Sod 253.0 mg; Potas 209.2 mg.
Nutritional information does not include light corn syrup.

MRS. LOWRY'S TARTS

Yields: 12 tarts *Pan Size: medium muffin pan* *Preheat: 450 degrees*

1 recipe pie pastry
1 cup dark corn syrup
3 eggs, slightly beaten
1 cup packed brown sugar
1 teaspoon nutmeg
1/8 teaspoon salt
1 tablespoon melted butter
12 whole pecan halves

Roll pie pastry on floured surface. Cut into 5-inch circles to fit muffin cups. Flute edges. Combine corn syrup, eggs, brown sugar, nutmeg, salt and butter in mixer bowl. Beat at high speed until well mixed. Fill tart shells 3/4 full. Bake for 5 minutes. Reduce oven temperature to 350 degrees. Bake for 15 minutes. Place pecan halves on top of each tart. Bake for 1 to 5 minutes longer or until set.

APPROX PER TART: Cal 146;
Prot 3.5 gr; T Fat 5.6 gr; Chol 129.4 mg;
Carbo 21.1 gr; Sod 83.1 mg;
Potas 48.5 mg.

FLAKY PASTRY

Yields: one 2-crust pie *Pan Size: 9 inch*

2 cups sifted
  all-purpose flour
1/2 teaspoon salt
1 1/2 tablespoons butter
2/3 cup shortening
1/4 cup cold water

Combine flour and salt in mixing bowl. Cut in butter and shortening until crumbly. Add water 1 tablespoonful at a time, tossing after each addition. Shape into 1 large ball. Divide into 2 portions, 1 portion slightly larger than the other. Roll out larger portion first on floured surface. Fit into pie plate. Roll smaller portion to cover pie.

APPROX PER RECIPE: Cal 2386;
Prot 26.4 gr; T Fat 169.1 gr; Chol 53.2 mg;
Carbo 190.3 gr; Sod 1281.1 mg;
Potas 242.5 mg.

Potluck

BALTIMORE ORIOLE

POTLUCK SURVIVAL

or
How to survive a Potluck even though you
Work
Volunteer
Have 6 kids (or one that *seems* like six)
Are not a gourmet cook
Have closed your kitchen (by choice or request)
Nap in the afternoon
Goof-off (NOT the same as napping)
Or otherwise have a life to lead beyond the Potluck Circuit.

THE NO-POT ANSWER

One of the most thoughtful (and easiest) contributions is to offer to bring some of the following "extras." You can even afford to splurge on the plastic or paper products if you don't have to cook or buy food.

Napkins, plates and cups
Mustard and mayonnaise
Onions, pickles and relish
Sugar and cream
Salt and pepper
Bakery rolls and flavored butters
Ice and ice bucket

The purchases can be made on the way. Just add your own serving pieces and a pretty basket with a colorful napkin to hold your contributions. You can outshine even the professional gourmet cooks who spend all week in the kitchen.

THE POTLUCK TRAVELING SURVIVAL KIT

Hand-operated can opener
Church key (punch/bottle opener)
Plastic wrap
Napkins or handi-wipes

Store these items in a large zip-lock bag in the car. Use the can opener and church key to open purchases made on the way, the plastic wrap to wrap up messy utensils and the napkins to clean up *you.*

THE DRIVE-THRU SPECIAL

Bring a lovely bowl from home. Go through the drive-thru. Buy 1 pound coleslaw. Place in your dish. Refuse to give the recipe – it is a family secret! This technique may be used for many other salads, main dishes and some desserts.

COTTAGE CHEESE SALAD PRONTO

2 (1-pound) containers cottage cheese
1 (3-ounce) package flavored gelatin

Take a pretty bowl and a large serving spoon from home. Dash into the most convenient grocery store. Buy the cottage cheese and gelatin (black raspberry and grape do not work too well.) Combine cottage cheese and gelatin in bowl when you stop at the first long stop light. Mix well, keeping bowl neat. If time and traffic permit, you can add whipped topping, drained crushed pineapple and drained mandarin oranges.

POTLUCK POTATO SALAD

Yields: 8 servings *Pan Size: salad bowl*

2 (16-ounce) containers deli potato salad
Chopped celery to taste
Chopped onions to taste
Mustard to taste
Chopped cucumbers to taste

Combine potato salad, celery, onions, mustard and cucumbers in large salad bowl; mix well. Chill. Serve on bed of lettuce garnished with hard-boiled eggs or tomatoes.

BIRD NEST

POTLUCK CHICKEN SALAD

Yields: 7 servings *Pan Size: large salad bowl*

2 (16-ounce) containers deli chicken salad
Chopped celery
Olives
Grapes
Pineapple chunks
Chopped apples
Raisins
Nuts

Combine chicken salad with any combination of remaining ingredients in large bowl; mix well. Chill. Serve on bed of lettuce.

COLLEEN HAWKINSON'S BROCCOLI CASSEROLE

Yields: 8 to 10 servings *Pan Size: 2 quart* *Preheat: 350 degrees*

This casserole makes a great dish to pass. I have yet to bring any leftover home!

1 (16-ounce) package frozen broccoli
1 1/3 cups minute rice
1 jar Cheez Whiz
1/2 cup chopped onion
1 can cream of celery soup
1/2 cup melted margarine

Combine broccoli, rice, Cheez Whiz, onion, soup and margarine in large bowl; mix well. Pour into greased casserole. Bake for 1 hour. Serve hot.

FAST DESSERT

Instant pudding mix
Milk
Whipped topping
Maraschino cherries with stems

Combine pudding mix with correct amount of milk in container with tight-fitting lid (peanut butter jars with measurements marked are especially good). Shake until blended. Spoon into pretty paper cups. Top with whipped topping and maraschino cherry. These ingredients can be purchased and mixed on the way and served up at the party.

Outdoor Cooking

WHITE-FOOTED MOUSE

WOODCHUCK

RACCOON

Outdoor Cooking

Cooking outdoors is a big part of Girl Scout camping. Over the years, Girl Scouts have invented a wide variety of outdoor cooking techniques as well as unusual recipes.

The good news for campers and noncampers alike is that these outdoor recipes are fun and easy on your backyard charcoal grill, gas grill, or an old-fashioned wood fire.

If you're looking for something to amaze your barbecue guests, both young and old, try one of these recipes. Each one has been tested and mastered by literally hundreds of girls as young as 5 years old. Surely, they will work for you! Start with these fire starters. Remember that young cooks should always have adult supervision.

FIRE STARTERS I

Newspapers
String
Paraffin

Tear several sheets of newspaper into strips about 4 inches wide. Roll up each strip tightly. Tie with string leaving one end of the string about 4 inches long. Grasp the newspaper in the center of the roll and spiral out gently until roll is about 8 inches long. Melt paraffin in pan or metal can. Dip each roll in melted paraffin, holding by the string. The string will form a wick. Use for starting wet or dry wood or charcoal fires.

FIRE STARTERS II

Paper egg carton
Sawdust
String
Paraffin

Fill egg cartons with sawdust. Place 1 piece of string in each section for wick. Melt paraffin in saucepan. Pour over sawdust. Let stand until firm. Cut apart into individual chunks. Great for starting charcoal or wood fires (especially damp wood).

CHARCOAL GRILL STARTERS

Paraffin
Cardboard egg cartons
Charcoal briquets

Melt 2 cakes paraffin in aluminum pan or a clean can. Fill 2 cardboard egg cartons with 24 charcoal briquets. Pour melted paraffin over briquets; cool. Break off 3 "grill starters" (including carton) to start fire. Place in grill. Pile charcoal on top. Light "grill starters" with a match.

Foil Cooking

Cooking in aluminum foil is clean and easy, and there are no pots to carry or dishes to wash. Aluminum foil is used to broil, braise, fry, saute and steam foods. Steaming, the most common method, is done by sealing the food in foil so that moisture cannot escape.

TO WRAP FOODS IN FOIL

Place the food in the center of heavy-duty or two layers of foil, shiny side up. The shine reflects heat, so you want to keep the heat inside. Fold up opposite sides of the foil, and fold over both edges together twice. Fold the 2 remaining end edges together in the same way. This will ensure a complete seal and will keep the steam inside to help cook. It also prevents moisture and juices from escaping onto the coals to cause a flame.

Be patient when cooking in foil over coals. Allow the flames to die down until the coals are all gray. Spread the coals out to make a layer 1 coal deep; place food on coals. Cooking time will depend on how hot the fire is. (Coals are very hot, and you don't need a lot to cook a dinner completely.)

HOBO POPCORN

Yields: 4 servings *Preheat: coals*

1/4 cup popcorn
4 teaspoons oil

Place 1 tablespoon popcorn and 1 teaspoon oil on each of four 9-inch foil squares. Bring corners together; seal edges. Tie each pouch onto long-handled green stick. Place on hot coals. Shake until popped.

APPROX PER SERVING: Cal 86; Prot 1.5 gr; T Fat 5.0 gr; Chol 0.0 mg; Carbo 9.2 gr; Sod 0.4 mg; Potas 36.4 mg.

BUSY DAY FOIL DINNERS

Yields: 8 servings *Preheat: coals*

This recipe is mainly for the inexperienced or a troop with a very busy day. No peeling, cutting or cleaning up.

2 pounds lean ground beef
2 (29-ounce) cans mixed stew vegetables, drained
2 (10-ounce) cans mushrooms
Garlic powder to taste
1 envelope dry onion soup mix

Divide ground beef into serving portions. Break into small pieces. Place each portion in center of 15-inch piece heavy duty foil. Add vegetables, garlic powder and soup mix to taste. Fold longest sides over twice to seal. Fold over each end to make packet. Place in hot coals. Cook for 15 minutes on each side.

APPROX PER SERVING: Cal 352; Prot 31.6 gr; T Fat 10.9 gr; Chol 87.9 mg; Carbo 32.9 gr; Sod 537.4 mg; Potas 718.9 mg.

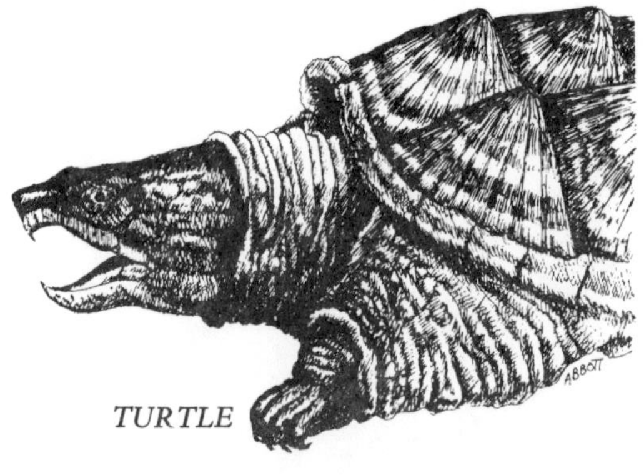

TURTLE

PICNIC PIZZA LOAVES

Yields: 6 servings *Preheat: coals*

1 pound ground beef
1/2 cup chopped onion
1 (8-ounce) can pizza sauce
1/2 teaspoon salt
1/2 teaspoon oregano
1/4 cup sliced stuffed olives
1 loaf French bread, split lengthwise
1 cup shredded Muenster cheese

Brown ground beef and onion in skillet, stirring frequently. Stir in pizza sauce, salt, oregano and olives. Place each bread half on foil. Spoon ground beef mixture over bread. Sprinkle with cheese. Seal foil. Cook over low coals for 15 minutes or until heated through.

APPROX PER SERVING: Cal 446; Prot 24.5 gr; T Fat 20.0 gr; Chol 71.8 mg; Carbo 40.5 gr; Sod 903.7 mg; Potas 251.5 mg.
Nutritional information does not include pizza sauce.

HEAVENLY HAM

Yields: variable *Preheat: coals*

Ham slices
Prepared mustard
Brown sugar
Pineapple juice

Spread each ham slice with mustard. Sprinkle with brown sugar. Moisten with pineapple juice. Wrap in foil. Cook over hot coals for 30 to 45 minutes or until ham is tender.

Nutritional information not available.

CHICKEN IN THE GARDEN

Yields: 1 serving *Pan Size: shallow baking pan* *Preheat: coals*

1 chicken breast
1 potato, sliced
1 tomato, sliced
1 onion, sliced
2 green bell pepper rings
2 tablespoons minute rice
1 teaspoon Worcestershire sauce
1 tablespoon butter

Layer chicken breast, potato, tomato, onion and green pepper on foil. Sprinkle with rice, Worcestershire sauce, salt, pepper and paprika to taste. Dot with butter. Seal foil. Place in shallow pan. Cook over hot coals for 1 hour and 15 minutes or until chicken is tender.

APPROX PER SERVING: Cal 565; Prot 42.4 gr; T Fat 15.7 gr; Chol 118.4 mg; Carbo 64.8 gr; Sod 285.7 mg; Potas 1851.8 mg.

POTATO SUPREME

Yields: 1 serving *Preheat: coals*

1 baking potato
1 smoky sausage link

Make hole through center of potato with apple corer. Place sausage link in hole. Wrap in foil. Bake in hot coals for 1 hour.

APPROX PER SERVING: Cal 266; Prot 8.6 gr; T Fat 11.7 gr; Chol 23.1 mg; Carbo 32.1 gr; Sod 254.7 mg; Potas 833.1 mg.

SCALLOPED POTATOES

Yields: 1 serving *Preheat: coals*

1 potato, sliced
1 (3-ounce) slice ham
1 small onion, chopped
1/4 cup milk
1 tablespoon flour

Combine potato, ham, onion, milk and flour in bowl; mix well. Spoon onto foil; seal. Bake in hot coals for 20 minutes.

Nutritional information not available.

CORN MUFFINS IN ORANGE SHELLS

Yields: 6 servings *Pan Size: orange cups* *Preheat: coals*

6 oranges
1 (7-ounce) package corn muffin mix
2 tablespoons butter

Cut off top 1/4 of each orange. Remove and discard pulp to make hollow shells. Mix muffin mix in plastic bag, according to package directions. Butter inside of orange shells lightly; do not butter lid. Pour enough muffin batter into shells to fill half full. Cover with orange lids. Wrap in foil. Bake on hot coals for 20 to 30 minutes. Remove foil. Eat with spoon or peel to free muffin.

APPROX PER SERVING: Cal 176; Prot 2.1 gr; T Fat 7.7 gr; Chol 11.8 mg; Carbo 24.4 gr; Sod 271.1 mg; Potas 26.9 mg.

APPLE DELIGHT

Yields: 12 servings | *Preheat: coals*

12 apples
1/4 cup sugar
1/2 cup raisins
3/4 cup buttermilk baking mix
3 tablespoons cinnamon

Peel, core and thinly slice apples. Combine apples, sugar, raisins, baking mix and cinnamon in bowl; mix well. Spoon onto double thick foil square. Seal, leaving room for steam. Cook in hot coals for 30 to 45 minutes or until apples are tender.

APPROX PER SERVING: Cal 188; Prot 1.2 gr; T Fat 2.2 gr; Chol 0.0 mg; Carbo 44.7 gr; Sod 101.3 mg; Potas 285.0 mg.

BAKED APPLES

Yields: variable | *Preheat: coals*

Juicy apples
Brown sugar or jelly
Cinnamon to taste
Raisins, nuts, coconut or dates to taste

Core apples, leaving 1/2-inch plug in bottom. Fill with brown sugar. Add cinnamon, raisins, nuts, coconut or dates to taste. Wrap in double thickness of foil. Place in hot coals. Cook for 10 minutes.

Nutritional information not available.

CAKE IN ORANGE

Yields: 10 servings | *Pan Size: orange cups* | *Preheat: coals*

1 (2-layer) package cake mix
10 oranges

Mix cake mix using package directions. Slice top 1/3 off oranges. Remove pulp leaving hollow shell. Reserve fruit for another purpose. Fill orange shells half full with batter. Place tops on oranges. Wrap in foil. Place upright in coals or in box oven. Bake for 10 to 15 minutes or until cake tests done.

APPROX PER SERVING: Cal 216; Prot 2.4 gr; T Fat 3.6 gr; Chol 0.0 mg; Carbo 42.0 gr; Sod 484.7 mg; Potas 0.0 mg.

Stick Cooking

Use a green wood stick, cooking fork, wire hanger (straightened out) or a skewer. Hangers work well for shish kabobs because the food slides on easily. Meats should be cut into thin strips and double-threaded onto the wire or stick. Heavy foods which aren't evenly balanced will swivel around on a hanger or skewer and only cook on one side. These foods are more successful on a real stick. Hold the sticks over the *coals* of a fire, but not too near. If the food is too near the coals, it will be done on the outside but raw in the middle. If the food requires a long time to cook, you may want to invent a way to suspend the stick over the coals. Turn the stick periodically to cook the food evenly.

SHISH KABOBS

Yields: 8 servings *Preheat: coals*

1/2 cup oil
1/4 cup vinegar
1/4 cup chopped onion
1 teaspoon salt
Dash of pepper
2 teaspoons Worcestershire sauce
2 pounds sirloin tip, cut into 1-inch cubes
Onion, zucchini, cucumber and green bell pepper chunks
Cherry tomatoes
Mushrooms
Bacon slices
Cheez Whiz
Rolls

Combine oil, vinegar, chopped onion, salt, pepper and Worcestershire sauce in bowl. Add steak. Marinate for 3 hours to overnight. Thread vegetables and steak onto skewer intertwining with bacon slices. Cook over hot coals. Spread Cheez Whiz on rolls. Serve shish kabobs on rolls.

Nutritional information not available.

MAD DOGS

Yields: 1 serving *Preheat: coals*

1 hot dog
1 slice American cheese
1 slice bacon
1 hot dog bun

Cut lengthwise slit in hot dog. Fill with cheese. Wrap bacon around hot dog. Fasten with toothpicks. Spear on stick at an angle. Toast carefully, cheese side down, over hot coals. Rotate hot dog. Cook until bacon is crisp. Garnish as desired. Serve with bun.

APPROX PER SERVING: Cal 437; Prot 18.1 gr; T Fat 26.0; Chol 58.4 mg; Carbo 31.3 gr; Sod 1319.4 mg; Potas 249.1 mg.

S'MORES

Yields: 1 serving *Preheat: coals*

1 marshmallow
1/2 ounce milk chocolate
2 graham crackers

Toast marshmallow on stick over hot coals. Place chocolate and marshmallow between crackers; press gently. Note: Use peanut butter, toasted peanuts, or chocolate-covered graham crackers for chocolate.

APPROX PER SERVING: Cal 151; Prot 2.4 gr; T Fat 5.9 gr; Chol 2.9 mg; Carbo 24.2 gr; Sod 111.2 mg; Potas 109.4 mg.

ANGELS ON HORSEBACK

Yields: 12 servings *Preheat: coals*

Mock Angel Food from Fran Liston's 1956 troop cookbook.

1 (16-ounce) loaf unsliced day-old bread
1 (14-ounce) can sweetened condensed milk
1 (7-ounce) package shredded coconut

Trim crusts from bread. Cut into 2-inch cubes. Dip each cube in condensed milk until well covered; roll in coconut. Toast on end of stick over hot coals until golden brown.

Nutritional information not available.

Box Oven Cooking

Baking in a box oven can be just like baking in your own oven. Any food that can be baked in an oven can be baked in a box oven. Cookies, biscuits, pizza, cakes and cobblers are some of the favorites. Meat can be broiled easily also. Baking time will vary depending on the number of coals used.

To make a box oven, you need:

1 heavy cardboard box with a lid
Heavy-duty aluminum foil
3 or 4 empty cans
6 to 8 white hot coals

Cut holes about 2 inches in diameter on two opposite sides of the box near the bottom. Line the entire inside of the box (top, sides and bottom) with two layers of foil. Leave the holes open to supply air for the fire. Place the box on a flat surface (patio, gravel, etc.) with the open lid at the top. Place the empty cans on the bottom of the box to support your pan or cookie sheet and keep it above the coals. Put the hot coals around the cans in the bottom of the box. Place pan or cookie sheet on top of the empty cans. Place food on pan. Close the lid. Bake food, checking occasionally to see how it is doing.

MINUTE PIZZA

Yields: 10 servings | *Pan Size: cookie sheet* | *Preheat: coals*

1 (10-count) can refrigerator biscuits
1 can pizza sauce
3 ounces sliced pepperoni
1 pound ground beef, cooked, drained
Olives, green bell peppers, onions, mushrooms, etc.
1 1/2 cups shredded mozzarella cheese

Flatten and spread individual biscuits into round shapes on cookie sheet. Spread with sauce, pepperoni, ground beef and other ingredients as desired. Top with cheese. Place in box oven. Bake for 10 to 15 minutes or until biscuits are done and cheese is melted.

Nutritional information not available.

HAMBURGER THRIFTY

Yields: 6 servings | *Pan Size: roaster* | *Preheat: coals*

Can be done in box oven at camp.

2 pounds ground beef
6 carrots, grated
4 potatoes, grated
3 medium onions, grated
1 can cream of tomato soup
1 soup can water
Pepper to taste

Combine ground beef, carrots, potatoes and onions in bowl; mix well. Shape into medium meatballs. Pour mixture of soup and water into roasting pan. Place meatballs in soup. Bake in covered pan in box oven for 1 hour.

APPROX PER SERVING: Cal 599; Prot 32.6 gr; T Fat 33.5 gr; Chol 102.8 mg; Carbo 42.2 gr; Sod 543.4 mg; Potas 1416.6 mg.

EASY BROWNIES

Yields: 24 brownies | *Pan Size: 9 x 13 inch* | *Preheat: coals*

1 1/2 cups flour
2 cups sugar
1/2 cup plus 2 tablespoons unsweetened cocoa
1 teaspoon vanilla extract
1 teaspoon salt
1 cup oil
4 eggs
1/2 cup pecans

Combine flour, sugar, cocoa, vanilla, salt, oil, eggs and pecans in bowl; mix well. Pour into cake pan. Bake in box oven for 30 to 40 minutes or just until edge pulls away from side of pan. Do not overbake.

APPROX PER SERVING: Cal 209; Prot 2.5 gr; T Fat 12.3 gr; Chol 42.1 mg; Carbo 24.1 gr; Sod 99.5 mg; Potas 67.8 mg.

DONNA JO WAIT'S DUMP CAKE

Yields: 15 servings | *Pan Size: 9 x 13 inch* | *Preheat: coals*

1 (29-ounce) can syrup-pack sliced peaches
1 (2-layer) package butter pecan cake mix
1/2 cup melted margarine
1/2 cup chopped pecans

Layer undrained peaches, cake mix, margarine and pecans in greased cake pan; do not stir. Bake in box oven for 45 minutes.

APPROX PER SERVING: Cal 272; Prot 2.3 gr; T Fat 11.4 gr; Chol 0.0 mg; Carbo 40.6 gr; Sod 399.1 mg; Potas 103.1 mg.

No Cooking

Not everything has to be cooked, of course. Some of the easiest, most delicious and most nutritious foods for camping out are just mixed together. Try some of the following easy suggestions.

PEPPERMINT-ORANGE SODA

Yields: 1 serving

1 orange
1 peppermint stick

Roll orange between hand and hard surface to make it juicy. Insert peppermint stick into orange. Drink orange by sucking through the peppermint stick straw. It takes a while to finish the orange. Guaranteed to keep a child involved for a little while.

Nutritional information not available.

WALKING LUNCHES

An ice cream cone is a perfect container for foods to eat on hikes. No mess, and no leftovers. Try filling cones with one of the following: gorp, chicken salad, tuna salad, mixed fruit, egg salad or instant pudding.

Nutritional information not available.

WALKING SALAD

Yields: 12 servings *Pan Size: mixing bowl*

12 apples
2 cups cottage cheese
1/2 cup raisins
1/2 cup pecans
2 tablespoons mayonnaise-style salad dressing

Cut off tops of apples. Core apples, leaving bottom skin over the hole. Scoop out pulp; chop. Combine with cottage cheese, raisins and pecans in bowl. Add salad dressing; mix well. Stuff mixture into apple shells. Replace tops. Eat while hiking.

APPROX PER SERVING: Cal 228; Prot 6.6 gr; T Fat 7.6 gr; Chol 9.0 mg; Carbo 37.6 gr; Sod 111.9 mg; Potas 343.4 mg.

CAMPER'S SALAD DRESSING

Yields: 64 tablespoons *Pan Size: mixing bowl*

This was a must in the 50's to take on a campout at McCormick.

1 cup sugar
1 cup cider vinegar
1/4 cup chili sauce
1/4 cup oil
1 green bell pepper, ground
1 (2-ounce) can chopped pimento
1 medium onion, ground
6 to 8 stalks celery, ground
4 medium carrots, ground

Combine sugar, vinegar, chili sauce and oil in bowl. Add green pepper, pimento, onion, celery and carrots; mix well. Serve over lettuce.

APPROX PER TABLESPOON: Cal 25; Prot 0.2 gr; T Fat 0.9 gr; Chol 0.0 mg; Carbo 4.5 gr; Sod 18.9 mg; Potas 48.3 mg.

EASY DOOZITS

Yields: 30 servings *Pan Size: mixing bowl*

1 1/4 cups graham cracker crumbs
1/4 cup sugar
1/2 teaspoon cinnamon
1/2 teaspoon nutmeg
1/2 cup peanut butter
1 1/3 cups corn syrup
1 cup confectioners' sugar

Combine graham cracker crumbs, sugar and spices in bowl. Stir in peanut butter and corn syrup. Roll into 1/2-inch balls. Chill in refrigerator. Roll in confectioners' sugar.

APPROX PER SERVING: Cal 98; Prot 1.4 gr; T Fat 2.6 gr; Chol 0.0 mg; Carbo 18.5 gr; Sod 55.5 mg; Potas 47.3 mg.

GORP

Yields: variable *Pan Size: large bowl*

M and M's
Skittles
Chocolate chips
Miniature marshmallows
Golden Grahams cereal
Oyster crackers
Miniature pretzels
Shoestring potatoes
Sunflower seeds
Raisins
Dates
Peanuts

Combine any or all ingredients in bowl; mix well. Serve in ice cream cones.

For Groups: Have each person bring her favorite ingredients. Mix together for the group's snack.

Nutritional information not available.

Outdoor Favorites

You should be ready to try your hand at outdoor cooking. These are some favorites of campers. Use some of the cooking techniques already explained or invent some of your own.

BAGS OF GOLD

Yields: 4 servings *Pan Size: saucepan* *Preheat: coals*

1 (10-count) can refrigerator biscuits
1/4 pound Velveeta cheese, cubed
1 can tomato soup
1 soup can milk

Shape biscuits into balls around cheese cubes. Drop balls into mixture of hot tomato soup and milk. Cook over low coals until cooked through.

APPROX PER SERVING: Cal 436; Prot 15.9 gr; T Fat 16.5 gr; Chol 69.2 mg; Carbo 55.8 gr; Sod 1852.9 mg; Potas 371.2 mg.

BAKED EGGS

Yields: 1 serving *Preheat: coals*

Chip off a bit of shell a little larger than a pin head from the larger end of the egg without puncturing the membrane. Make a hole about the size of two pin heads through both the shell and the membrane of the smaller end. Stand the egg in hot ashes, close enough to the fire for reflected heat for about 5 minutes.

Nutritional information not available.

HAMBURGER IN AN ORANGE

Yields: 2 servings *Preheat: coals*

1 orange
Ground beef

Cut orange in half. Scoop out pulp of orange. Fill with ground beef. Place in hot coals. Cook until hamburger is cooked through.
May substitute large onion for orange.

Nutritional information not available.

CHICKEN IN THE WOODS

Yields: 12 servings *Pan Size: saucepan* *Preheat: coals*

4 cups minute rice
3 cans cream of chicken soup

Prepare minute rice using package directions. Let stand for 5 minutes. Add soup; mix well. Cook over coals until heated through.

APPROX PER SERVING: Cal 177; Prot 4.2 gr; T Fat 3.6 gr; Chol 6.0 mg; Carbo 31.1 gr; Sod 603.0 mg; Potas 49.2 mg.

GOOEY GUNK

Yields: 12 servings *Pan Size: skillet* *Preheat: coals*

3 pounds ground beef
1 large onion, chopped
1 pound Velveeta cheese
1 can tomato soup
12 buns

Brown ground beef with onion in skillet over hot coals. Add cheese and soup. Cook until cheese melts. Serve on buns.

APPROX PER SERVING: Cal 532; Prot 32.8 gr; T Fat 28.0 gr; Chol 105.5 mg; Carbo 35.8 gr; Sod 1141.8 mg; Potas 437.0 mg.

HAZEL JOHANNES' GUMBOBURGERS

Yields: 8 servings *Pan Size: skillet* *Preheat: coals*

Hazel was active in our Council for over 30 years. She loved to cook outdoors and also loved to share her recipes and techniques.

1 pound ground beef
1 small onion, chopped
1 can chicken gumbo soup
2 tablespoons catsup
2 tablespoons mustard
8 hamburger buns

Brown ground beef with chopped onion in skillet until ground beef is no longer pink. Add soup, catsup, mustard and salt and pepper to taste. Simmer over low coals for 30 minutes. Serve on buns.

APPROX PER SERVING: Cal 298; Prot 16.2 gr; T Fat 10.8 gr; Chol 44.5 mg; Carbo 33.0 gr; Sod 693.7 mg; Potas 238.3 mg.

SHIPWRECK

Yields: 6 servings *Pan Size: kettle* *Preheat: coals*

Always requested by Girl Scouts when we went camping.

1 pound lean ground beef
1 large onion, chopped
4 large potatoes, peeled, sliced
2 cans tomato soup
2 soup cans water
1 (15-ounce) can kidney beans

Brown ground beef and chopped onion in large kettle over hot coals, stirring frequently. Add potatoes, soup, water, beans and salt and pepper to taste. Cook until potatoes are done, stirring frequently.

APPROX PER SERVING: Cal 411; Prot 22.7 gr; T Fat 13.7 gr; Chol 51.1 mg; Carbo 50.7 gr; Sod 846.6 mg; Potas 1116.0 mg.

CAMPFIRE STEW

Yields: 8 servings *Pan Size: skillet* *Preheat: coals*

2 pounds ground beef
1 large onion, chopped
2 cans vegetable soup

Shape ground beef into small balls. Sprinkle with salt and pepper to taste. Brown with onions in skillet over hot coals until onion is light brown and meatballs are well browned. Drain. Add soup and enough water to prevent sticking; cover. Cook over low coals until meatballs are cooked through.

APPROX PER SERVING: Cal 291; Prot 23.2 gr; T Fat 17.9 gr; Chol 91.1 mg; Carbo 7.9 gr; Sod 701.6 mg; Potas 354.1 mg.

DOODLEBUGS

Yields: 20 servings *Pan Size: saucepan* *Preheat: coals*

1 (12-ounce) package chocolate chips
1 (12-ounce) package butterscotch chips
2 (3-ounce) cans chow mein noodles

Melt chocolate and butterscotch chips in saucepan over low coals. Stir in noodles. Drop by spoonfuls onto waxed paper. Cool.

APPROX PER SERVING: Cal 214; Prot 2.6 gr; T Fat 14.1 gr; Chol 1.0 mg; Carbo 24.3 gr; Sod 85.7 mg; Potas 116.8 mg.

A PLATFORM TENT AT CAMP MEDILL McCORMICK

BANANA BOATS

Yields: 12 servings *Preheat: coals*

12 bananas
4 (1 1/2-ounce) Hershey bars, cut in thirds
2 cups miniature marshmallows
1/2 cup pecans

Peel back narrow strip in inside curve of bananas. Scoop out a small amount of banana. Add chocolate, marshmallows and pecans. Cover with banana skin. Wrap in foil. Place in coals. Cook until banana is hot.

APPROX PER SERVING: Cal 233; Prot 3.0 gr; T Fat 8.3 gr; Chol 2.9 mg; Carbo 41.4 gr; Sod 17.5 mg; Potas 524.8 mg.

FRUIT DUMPLINGS

Yields: 6 servings *Preheat: coals*

1 (21-ounce) can apple pie filling
1/2 cup water
1 egg
2 tablespoons oil
1/4 cup sugar
1/4 cup milk
1 cup pancake mix

Bring mixture of pie filling and water to a boil in saucepan over coals. Combine egg, oil, sugar, milk and pancake mix in bowl; mix well. Drop by spoonfuls into hot mixture. Cook, covered, for 10 minutes.

APPROX PER SERVING: Cal 273; Prot 3.5 gr; t Fat 6.3 gr; Chol 43.6 mg; Carbo 50.7 gr; Sod 337.8 mg; Potas 62.1 mg.

STICKY ICKYS

Yields: 40 servings *Pan Size: saucepan* *Preheat: coals*

Donna Jo Wait's (long-time Girl Scout outdoor trainer) recipe. Girls line up to dip their marshmallows or apple slices and get back in line to do another as they eat it.

1 (14-ounce) package caramels
1/2 cup margarine
1/2 can sweetened condensed milk
1 (10-ounce) package large marshmallows
Rice Krispies
Chopped nuts
Coconut

Melt caramels, margarine and condensed milk together in saucepan over low coals. Dip marshmallow into caramel mixture with toothpicks. Roll in cereal, nuts or coconut. May also use apples.

APPROX PER SERVING: Cal 118; Prot 1.2 gr; T Fat 3.9 gr; Chol 2.6 mg; Carbo 20.5 gr; Sod 62.4 mg; Potas 41.4 mg. Nutritional information does not include coating ingredients.

Magic Kitchen System

Submitted by Beth Galbreath

This special cooking system is more versatile, weatherproof, safe, cheap and portable than any other large charcoal or wood-burning stove. It's easily made and used by Brownies and Seniors, can be adapted for an individual or a whole troop, and cooks much faster than an open fire. And it's fun to make and use!

To make the "Magic Kitchen System" for a patrol or a troop, you will need these materials: (Figure A)

5 wide (18 to 24-inch) washtubs with bucket-type wire handles
6 (Number 10) juice cans
12 tuna cans
6 soup cans
2 (18 to 24-inch) hardware cloth circles (hardware cloth is galvanized steel netting, with squares 1/4 to 1/2 inch between the wires)
2 sets of kitchen tongs

And these materials:

Charcoal or wood
Fire starters
Matches
Pots and kitchen utensils

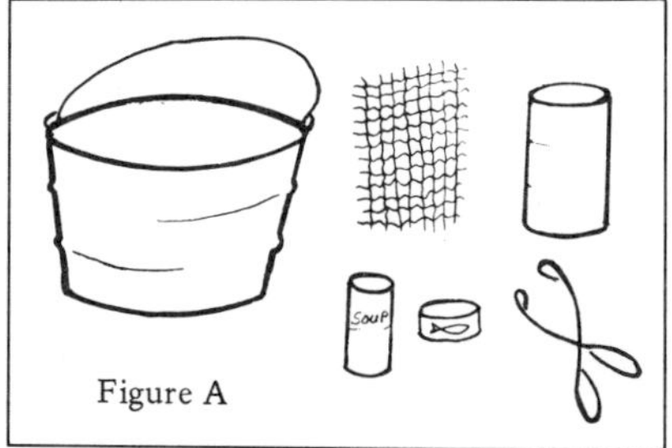

Figure A

And these tools:

Center punch(es)
Hammer(s)
Can openers
Punch-type can openers
Wire or metal cutters
Needlenose pliers
A patch of lawn

HOW TO MAKE IT:

1. Punch holes with the punch can opener about 2 to 3 inches apart on the *side* (not the bottom) around one end of each Number 10 juice can. Punch about 2 holes at the other end. Do this *before* you remove the ends.
2. Remove both tops and bottoms from all the juice cans, tuna cans and soup cans. Remove the paper wrappers. Have an adult or older girl use the pliers to turn under and flatten any exposed sharp points of metal left by the punch can openers. (Figure B)
3. A strong older girl or adult should cut 2 circles out of the hardware cloth. To measure the right size, set the soup cans inside a tub. The circles should be 1 inch less than the diameter of your washtubs at the top of the soup cans. (Figure C)

4. Turn 2 of the washtubs upside down. Hammer the center punch through the bottom of the tubs. Make holes about 2 to 3 inches apart all over the bottom of the tubs. (Figure D)

Figure B

HOW TO USE IT:

Your Magic Kitchen System includes 2 stoves, 3 water buckets/dishpans, 2 lighting chimneys and the spacing and fire support hardware (grids and cans) to make any combination of fires you need. You manipulate all these items with the tongs, especially when they're hot!

Figure C

Figure D

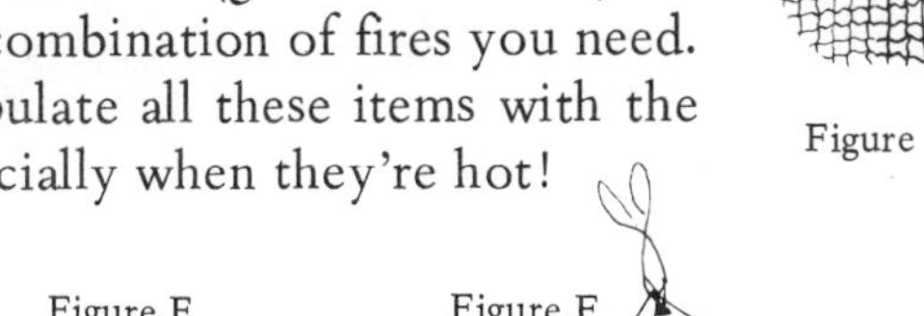

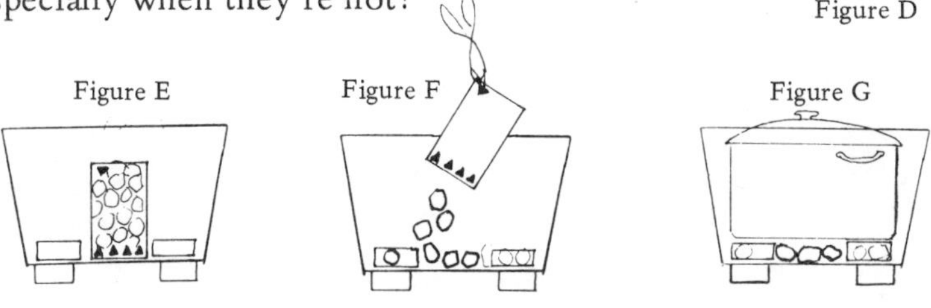

Figure E Figure F Figure G

1. Select a safe-fire area for the stoves and fill 2 of the water buckets with water. Put 3 tuna can rings on the ground in a triangle and set the stove on top. Set the lighting chimney and 3 tuna can rings in the stove. Put 1 egg carton-section fire starter in the chimney and fill the chimney with charcoal. Insert a lighted match through one of the punched holes on the bottom rim of the chimney and light the egg carton fire starter. Prepare the second stove the same way. Your coals are ready in 30 minutes or when heavy smoke stops. (Figure E)
2. Use the tongs to lift the chimney, gently shaking to dislodge the coals. Set aside in a safe place to cool. Spread the coals, with the tongs, around and in the tuna rings. (Figure F)
3. Set your pot in the stove on the tuna rings. Set one of the water buckets in the second stove to heat water for dishwashing while dinner is cooking. (Figure G)
4. When dinner is served, pour half of the wash water into the third water pail and set it in the cooking stove; now it will heat faster and you will have hot water for washing and rinsing. You can add a "glug" of bleach to the other pail of water (cold) for your final sanitizing rinse.
5. To put the fires out: Lift the stove by its bail and gently shake the stove; the loose ashes will fall out through the holes. (You can do

this right over the ash bucket and save work!) Use the tongs to drop the coals into 1 of the water buckets to soak (a quick dunk usually will not put them completely out). If a few tiny coals remain that escape the tongs, you can lift the stove and *carefully* lower it into the water; hold the bail to the side so you don't get steamed. Drain the water from the coals and dry in the stove or on the grids for re-use.

HOW TO USE YOUR STOVE FOR FRYING OR TOASTING:

When you need the fire up higher in the stove, start by setting the stove on 3 tuna rings as usual. Then place 3 soup can rings in the stove and lay a hardware cloth grid on the soup cans. Put your lighting chimney on the hardware cloth and start fire.

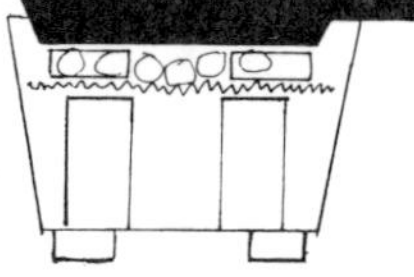
Figure H

Place 3 tuna rings among the lighted coals and set your frying pan or griddle on the rings, or bring out the marshmallow sticks and toast in comfort. You can also build a wood fire in the stove. (Figure H)

HOW IT WORKS:

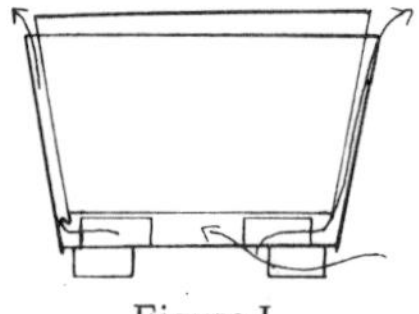
Figure I

Your pot will boil much faster than over an open fire or traditional charcoal grill. Why? Because this stove *wraps* your pot in heat instead of heating the bottom and letting the wind remove heat from the sides. (Figure I)

The stove and pot form a hollow chimney around your food. Air is drawn up through the holes in the stove and heated as it passes through the charcoal. The hot air rises around the pot. As long as the stove is *off* the ground, the pot is *off* the charcoal (resting on the tuna rings), and there is room between the pot and the stove wall, the charcoal will burn and provide steady heat even in wind or rain.

The bottom can get very hot, so *stir your food* regularly.

You can use the system in this configuration with a teakettle, a small Dutch oven, or any other pot. Do NOT cook directly in one of the galvanized water pails; this can poison food.

For the same reason, do not grill food directly on the grids; if you want to grill, use a cake cooler, small *oven* (not refrigerator) rack or charcoal grill rack designed for use with food.

The Magic Kitchen System was invented by Louis and Zillah Davis for use by their Girl Scout and Boy Scout troops, and has been used by troops in Philadelphia, Chicago, and Rock River Valley Council.

Potpourri

HAWK

COAL FLOWERS

1 chunk coal or charcoal briquette
6 tablespoons salt
6 tablespoons laundry bluing
6 tablespoons water
Household ammonia

Place coal in shallow glass dish. Pour mixture of salt, bluing, water and 1 tablespoon ammonia over coal. Let stand overnight. Add 1 teaspoon ammonia daily. May add a drop of food coloring to ammonia to tint flowerets as they form and grow. Changes appear daily.

PLAY DOUGH

1 cup water
Several drops of food coloring
2 tablespoons oil
1 cup flour
2 teaspoons cream of tartar
1/2 cup salt
1 or 2 drops of oil of peppermint

Combine water, food coloring and oil in saucepan. Stir in flour, cream of tartar, salt and oil of peppermint. Cook over medium heat until mixture forms ball, stirring constantly. Spoon onto waxed paper. Let stand until cool enough to handle. Knead until smooth. Store in plastic bag.

MODELING CLAY

1 cup cornstarch
2 cups soda
1 1/2 cups cold water
Food coloring
Shellac

Mix cornstarch and soda in saucepan. Stir in water and desired amount of food coloring. Cook over medium heat until thickened to consistency of dough, stirring constantly. Cover with damp cloth. Let stand until cool. Shape as desired. Paint finished objects with shellac.

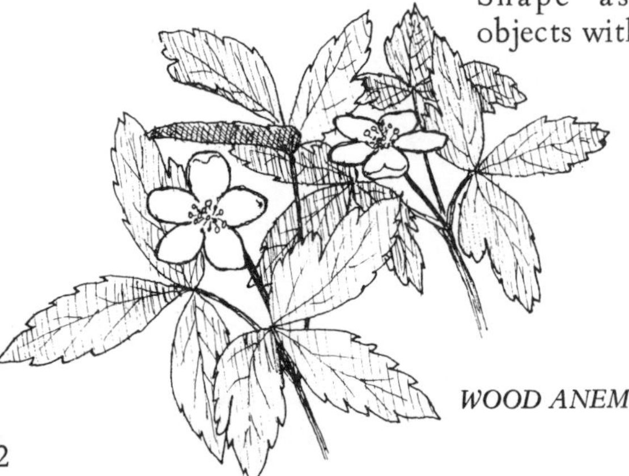

WOOD ANEMONE

CREPE PAPER MODELING PLASTER

1 package crepe paper
1 1/2 cups flour
1/4 cup salt

Cut crepe paper into narrow strips or small pieces; the smaller the pieces, the finer the texture. Place in large pan. Add enough water to cover. Let stand for 8 hours to overnight. Drain well but do not squeeze dry. Mix flour and salt together. Stir into crepe paper mixture gradually until mixture is consistency of thick dough. Knead until well blended. This is thicker and less messy than papier-mache. Mixture does not store; prepare enough for each project.

SOAP FLAKES PLASTER OR FINGER PAINT

2 cups soap flakes
2 cups liquid laundry starch
4 to 6 drops of food coloring

Mix soap flakes and starch in large bowl. Beat with electric mixer at high speed until consistency of whipped cream. Beat in food coloring. Use as finger paint or decorative plaster. Mixture does not store; prepare enough for each project.

POSTER PAINT

1/4 cup flour
1 1/2 cups water
3/4 cup dry poster paint powder
2 teaspoons colorless dishwashing detergent (optional)
2 teaspoons liquid starch (optional)

Place flour in small saucepan. Gradually stir in 1 cup water. Cook over medium heat until thickened, stirring constantly. Cool. Measure 1/4 cup mixture into each of 4 small clean jars. Add 2 tablespoons water to each jar; blend well. Add 3 tablespoons paint powder to each jar; blend well. Add 1/2 teaspoon dishwashing detergent to each jar if glossy finish is desired or add 1/2 teaspoon starch to each jar for matte finish. Store tightly covered. Mix well before using.

INVISIBLE INK

2 teaspoons cobalt chloride
2 teaspoons white dextrin
3 1/2 tablespoons glycerine

Combine all ingredients in small saucepan. Cook over low heat until well blended, stirring constantly. Cool completely. Store in tightly covered clean jar. Ink is pale pink on colored paper. Expose to heat or light bulb and writing turns blue.
Note: Cobalt chloride and dextrin may be purchased from a chemical supply house and glycerine from a drugstore.

INSTANT ERASE INK

3 tablespoons water
36 drops of tincture of iodine
1 tablespoon cornstarch

Mix water and iodine in small jar. Stir in cornstarch gradually. Store tightly covered. Ink is blue-black. Let dry completely. Wipe off with soft cloth.

MAGIC WRITING SURFACE

1/4 cup beeswax
9 tablespoons Venice turpentine
1/4 cup lard
2 tablespoons mineral oil
1 tablespoon carbon black
3 tablespoons powdered China clay
Cardboard or fiberboard
Waxed paper or transparent plastic

Combine beeswax, turpentine, lard and mineral oil in double boiler. Heat over hot water until well blended, stirring frequently. Stir in carbon and China clay. Paint uniform coat on cardboard. Cool. Place waxed paper over surface. Write or draw with sharpened stick, fingernail or other object that will mark without tearing waxed paper. Erase marks by lifting waxed paper.

NEWSPRINT TRANSFER

1/2 cup water
1/4 cup turpentine
2 tablespoons liquid dishwashing detergent

Combine all ingredients in tightly covered jar; shake vigorously to mix. Paint over any newspaper picture or story; blot gently with paper towel. Place clean white paper over newsprint. Rub evenly with small roller or back of spoon. Peel off paper carefully. Picture will appear in reverse on white paper.

Note: Use in well-ventilated room. Not for use by small children.

HUMIDITY INDICATOR

1/4 cup cobalt chloride
1/4 cup water

Paint mixture of cobalt chloride and water onto any paper, plastic or metal surface. Color changes will indicate bright blue for low humidity or pink for high humidity.

NATURAL EGG DYES

Place desired number of eggs and desired coloring material (see below) in saucepan. Add 1 teaspoon vinegar. Simmer in water to cover for 20 minutes. Polish with a small amount of oil on soft cloth to intensify color and add gloss. Adding a small amount of cream of tartar to water may deepen some shades.

- Fresh mint or oregano – beige
- Strong coffee – brown
- Spinach – grayish gold/pink
- Yellow Delicious apple peel – lavender
- Beet juice – reddish purple
- Red cabbage leaves – blue
- Walnut shells – buff
- Carrot tops – greenish yellow
- Onion skins – orange
- Cranberry juice – red

DOUBLE-STRENGTH BAKER'S VANILLA

1 vanilla bean
3 ounces vodka

Break vanilla bean into several pieces. Combine with vodka in tightly covered bottle. Store in dark place for 1 month, shaking occasionally. Strain before using. This is a thoughtful gift for a favorite cook.

FURNITURE SCRATCH REMOVER

1 tablespoon finely ground pecan meal
Mineral oil

Mix pecan meal with several drops of oil to make a paste consistency. Store in small tins. Rub paste into scratches with soft cloth.

LEMON FURNITURE POLISH

1 quart mineral oil
1 tablespoon lemon extract

Mix oil and extract in glass or plastic bottle. Pour or spray a small amount on wood furniture; polish with soft cloth. Do not spray on upholstery.

BLACKBOARD CLEANER

2 cups vinegar
1 cup detergent
1 gallon water

Mix all ingredients in pail. Use with cloth or sponge to clean board. Dry with squeegee or rinse with clean water.

MAKE YOUR OWN WINDOW CLEANER

2 cups water
1/2 cup rubbing alcohol
1 tablespoon household ammonia

Mix all ingredients in spray bottle. Makes 2 1/2 cups cleaner at a cost of 17 cents.

EFFERVESCENT BATH SALTS

9 tablespoons soda
7 1/2 tablespoons citric acid powder
2 tablespoons cornstarch
4 to 6 drops of cologne

Mix soda, citric acid and cornstarch in bowl. Add cologne; mix well. Store in tightly covered clean jar. Use about 2 tablespoons mixture for each bath.

POISON IVY LOTION

1/2 cup water
1/4 cup ammonium alum
1/2 cup white vinegar

Mix water and alum in small saucepan. Heat over low heat until alum dissolves, stirring constantly. Heat vinegar in medium saucepan over low heat. Stir alum mixture very gradually into vinegar; a white precipitate will form. Remove from heat. Let stand until precipitate settles to bottom. Decant clear liquid into clean bottle; discard precipitate. Store in tightly covered bottle. Wipe skin with rubbing alcohol. Place compress of clean cloth saturated with vinegar mixture on affected area. Let stand for 10 minutes. Remove compress. Allow lotion to dry on skin. Use 3 times a day.

MOSQUITO REPELLENT POWDER

2 tablespoons eucalyptus oil
1/4 cup talc
1 3/4 cups cornstarch

Stir oil into mixture of talc and cornstarch until oil is absorbed. Dust over clothing, outside of sleeping bag or wherever necessary.

NONTOXIC ANT EXTERMINATOR

1/2 cup molasses
1/4 cup sugar
1/4 cup dry yeast

Mix all ingredients in jar. Paint on small pieces of waxed paper and place on ant hill entrances and on ant runways.

CANVAS WATERPROOFING

3 cups soybean oil
1 1/2 cups turpentine

Mix oil and turpentine together. Paint or spray on canvas. Repeat as necessary if canvas is exposed to the weather for long periods.

CANVAS FIREPROOFING

1/2 cup ammonium phosphate
1 cup ammonium chloride
1 quart water

Combine all ingredients; mix until dissolved. Soak canvas in solution or paint or spray over surface. Repeat as necessary if canvas is exposed to rainy weather.

DOGGIE BISCUITS

Yields: 10 biscuits *Pan Size: cookie sheet* *Preheat: 350 degrees*

If your dog does not like the recipe, it is time for a visit to the veterinarian.

2 1/2 cups whole wheat flour
1/2 cup dry milk powder
1/2 teaspoon each salt, garlic powder
1 teaspoon brown sugar
6 tablespoons margarine, shortening or meat drippings
1 egg, beaten
1/2 cup ice water

Combine flour, milk powder, salt, garlic powder and brown sugar in bowl. Cut in shortening until mixture resembles cornmeal. Mix in egg. Add enough water so that mixture forms ball. Pat dough 1/2 inch thick with fingers on lightly oiled cookie sheet. Cut with doggie biscuit cutter and remove scraps. Pat out scraps and proceed as before. Bake for 25 to 30 minutes. Cool on wire rack.

Microwave Tips

- Always choose the minimum cooking time. Remember, food continues to cook after it is removed from the microwave.
- Keep your microwave clean. Built-up grease or spatters can slow cooking times.
- When poaching or frying an egg in a browning dish, always prick the center of the yolk with a fork to keep the egg from exploding.
- Do not try to hard-cook eggs in the shell in a microwave. They will build up pressure and burst.
- To prevent soggy rolls, elevate rolls on roasting rack or place on paper towels while heating.
- Do not use metal dishes or aluminum foil except as specifically recommended by the manufacturer of your microwave.
- Never use a foil tray over 3/4-inch deep in your microwave.
- When heating TV-style dinners, remove the foil cover, then place tray back in carton. Food will heat only from the top.
- Be sure to prick potatoes before baking to allow steam to escape.
- Cut a small slit in pouch-packed frozen foods before heating to allow steam to escape.
- When placing more than one food item in microwave, arrange foods in a circle near edges of oven.
- Cover foods that need to be steamed or tenderized.
- Do not try to pop popcorn unless you have a microwave-approved corn popper.

DID YOU KNOW YOU CAN . . .?

(Use High setting for the following unless otherwise indicated.)

- Use your microwave oven to melt chocolate, soften cream cheese and butter.
- Roast shelled nuts for 6 to 10 minutes, stirring frequently.
- Peel fruit or tomatoes. Place in 1 cup hot water. Microwave for 30 to 45 seconds; remove skins easily.
- Plump dried fruit by placing in a dish with 1 to 2 teaspoons water. Cover tightly with plastic wrap. Heat for 1/2 to 1 1/2 minutes.
- Precook barbecued ribs or chicken until almost done then place on the grill to sear and add a charcoal flavor.
- Soften brown sugar by placing in a dish with a slice of bread or apple. Heat for 30 to 45 seconds, stirring once.
- Dry bread for crumbs or croutons. Place cubed or crumbled bread on paper towels. Heat for 6 to 7 minutes, stirring occasionally.
- Warm baby food or bottles by removing metal lid and heating for 10 to 20 seconds.
- Freshen chips and crackers by heating for 15 to 30 seconds. Let stand for 2 to 3 minutes.
- Dry herbs by placing on paper towels and heating for 2 to 3 minutes or until dry.
- Ripen an avocado by heating on Low for 2 to 4 minutes.

Cheese Chart

HOW MUCH TO BUY

If a recipe calls for 2 1/2 cups of Cheddar cheese, how much do you buy? If the recipe calls for 3 cups of cottage cheese, will one carton be enough? Use this table when buying cheese for cooking.

BUY:	IF YOU NEED:			
	Cottage Cheese	Shredded	Grated	Crumbled
3/4 ounce			1/4 cup	
1 ounce		1/4 cup	1/3 cup	1/4 cup
1 1/2 ounces			1/2 cup	
2 ounces	1/4 cup	1/2 cup	2/3 cup	1/2 cup
2 1/4 ounces			3/4 cup	
3 ounces		3/4 cup	1 cup	3/4 cup
4 ounces	1/2 cup	1 cup	1 1/3 cups	1 cup
8 ounces	1 cup	2 cups	2 2/3 cups	2 cups
12 ounces	1 1/2 cups	3 cups	4 cups	3 cups
1 pound	2 cups	4 cups		4 cups

CHEESE CHART

NATURAL CHEESE	CHARACTERISTICS AND USES
Bel Paese	A soft cheese often used in cooking to replace mozzarella. Although it is an Italian cheese, there is a very good American version bearing the same name that is made in Wisconsin.
Blue	A crumbly and sharp-flavored soft dessert cheese that is white and contains blue mold. French blue cheese is referred to as "bleu cheese."
Brie	A soft, creamy dessert cheese ranked as one of the world's great cheeses. It should be served at room temperature. At room temperature, good Brie is almost always runny.
Camembert	A soft, creamy, rich dessert cheese that is another of the world's great cheeses. Camembert that is shrunken in appearance or smells like ammonia is past its prime.

Cheddar	A variety of hard cheese that is the most popular American cheese. Cheddar is sold as mild, mellow, or sharp cheese. Mild has aged 2-3 months; mellow from 6-9 months; and sharp, from 12-15 months. Excellent for eating or cooking.
Cottage	The large or small drained curd of soured whole or skim milk. One of the few soft cheeses suitable for cooking.
Cream	An unripened American soft cheese that is popular for desserts. Like cottage cheese, cream cheese is a soft cheese suitable for cooking.
Edam	A mild, semihard cheese. It was originally Dutch cheese that now has several American versions. It has a bright red exterior rind and pale gold interior. Edam is primarily an eating cheese.
Feta	The most popular of Greek cheeses. White and crumbly, it has a unique flavor that is perfect for Hellenic cuisine.
Gorgonzola	A white and blue-veined Italian pressed cheese that may range from soft (very young) to semihard (aged). It is used in cooking, for desserts, or in sandwiches. An American gorgonzola is made in Wisconsin.
Gouda	Like gorgonzola, the mild-flavored gouda cheese becomes firmer with age. It was originally a Dutch cheese, that now has several American versions. Gouda is a popular dessert cheese.
Monterey	Also known as Monterey Jack, this California cheese is of two types: a semihard cheese and a hard cheese. Both are good cooking cheeses.
Mozzarella	A semisoft white cheese popular in Italian dishes. There are American versions but they lack the flavor of the Italian varieties.
Parmesan	A staple hard cheese of Italian cookery. American Parmesans, sold already grated, have only a fraction of the flavor of the original, ungrated cheese.
Provolone	An Italian hard cheese that has a smoky flavor and is used primarily for appetizers or sandwiches. The American version has little of the flavor of the Italian cheese.
Ricotta	An Italian cottage-type cheese. American cottage cheese can be substituted in almost every recipe calling for ricotta.
Romano	A very hard Italian cheese grated like Parmesan and used for cooking. There is also an American Romano.
Roquefort	A soft dessert cheese that is white with a characteristic blue veining. The veining comes from the penicillin mold that gives this cheese its sharp flavor.
Swiss	The common United States term for any of the Emmentaler or Gruyere cheeses. Used in cooking. (Not to be confused with the process cheese of the same name.)
Touloumisso	A spicy Greek cheese that is very good.

Quantities To Serve 50

FOOD	For 50 Servings	Size of Each Serving
BEVERAGES		
Carbonated beverages	25 16-ounce bottles	1 cup
Cocoa, for hot chocolate	3 cups	1 cup
Coffee, ground	1 1/2 pounds	1 cup
Coffee, instant	6 ounces	3/4 cup
Cream, for coffee	1 1/4 quarts	1 1/2 tablespoons
Fruit juice concentrates, frozen	54 ounces	1/2 cup
Fruit or tomato juice, canned	4 46-ounce cans	1/2 cup
Lemon, for tea	5 large	1 slice
Lemonade concentrate, frozen	78 ounces	1 cup
Punch	2 gallons	2/3 cup
Sugar, lump	1 1/8 pounds	2 lumps
Tea, bulk	4 ounces	3/4 cup
Tea, instant	1 1/4 ounces	1 cup
DAIRY		
Butter	1 3/4 pounds	1 tablespoon
Cheese, to shred	6 pounds	2 tablespoons
Cream, to whip	1 quart	1 tablespoon
Ice cream	2 gallons	1 large scoop
Milk	3 gallons	1 cup
MEAT, POULTRY, FISH		
Bacon	6 pounds	2 slices
Beef, boneless roast	25 pounds	8 ounces
Beef, rib roast	35 pounds	12 ounces
Chicken salad	6 1/4 quarts	1/2 cup
Chicken, to roast	35–40 pounds	6 ounces
Chicken, for dishes using chopped cooked chicken	20–25 pounds	
Fish fillets	13 pounds	4 ounces
Ground beef, for patties	12 1/2–15 pounds	4–5 ounces
Ground beef, for meat loaf	12 pounds	4 ounces
Ham, bone in, to bake	22–25 pounds	5–6 ounces
Ham, canned	14 pounds	4 ounces
Lamb, leg to roast	25 pounds	8 ounces

QUANTITIES TO SERVE 50 (continued)

FOOD	For 50 Servings	Size of Each Serving
MEAT, POULTRY, FISH		
Oysters, for stew	6 quarts	2 cups stew
Oysters, to scallop	6 quarts	1/2 cup
Pork chops	17 pounds (3/lb.)	5–6 ounces
Pork, loin to roast	25 pounds	8 ounces
Salmon, for salad	8 16-ounce cans	1/2 cup
Sausage	12 1/2 pounds	4 ounces
Shrimp, in shell	20 pounds	4 ounces
Shrimp, peeled	12 pounds	4 ounces
Tuna, for salad	16 cans	1/2 cup
Turkey, to roast	35–40 pounds	8 ounces
Turkey, for dishes using chopped cooked turkey	16 pounds	
Wieners	12 pounds	4 ounces
SALADS AND RELISHES		
Apples, for sauce	25 pounds	1/2 cup
Cabbage, for slaw	12–15 pounds	5–6 ounces
Carrots, strips	6 1/4 pounds	2 ounces
Celery, strips	6 1/4 pounds	2 ounces
Cranberry sauce	6 pounds	1/2-inch slice
Fruit cocktail	12 16-ounce cans	4 ounces
Fruit salad	9 quarts	3/4 cup
Fruits, canned	7 29-ounce cans	4 ounces
Lettuce	12 medium heads	1/4 head
Lettuce leaves	6 heads	2–3 leaves
Mayonnaise	1 quart	1 1/3 tablespoons
Nuts	3 1/4 pounds	1 ounce
Pickles	2 1/2 pounds	1 ounce
Potato salad	6 1/2 quarts	1/2 cup
Salad dressing	1–1 1/2 quarts	2 tablespoons
Tomatoes	30 medium	3 slices
Vegetable salad	10 quarts	3/4 cup

(continued)

QUANTITIES TO SERVE 50 (continued)

FOOD	For 50 Servings	Size of Each Serving
SANDWICHES		
Beef, roast, sliced	5 pounds	1 slice
Bread, sandwich	6 pounds	2 slices
Cheese, sliced	3 1/4 pounds	1 slice
Ham, baked, sliced	5 pounds	1 slice
Jam or preserves	1 1/2 quarts	1 sandwich
Peanut Butter	1 1/2 quarts	1 sandwich
VEGETABLES		
Asparagus, canned	14 pounds	4–6 spears
Asparagus, fresh	20 pounds	4–5 spears
Beans, dried	4 1/2 pounds	3 ounces
Cabbage	7 heads	1/8 head
Canned vegetables	14 pounds	1/2 cup
Carrots	13 pounds	4 ounces
Caulifloweretts	13 pounds	4 ounces
Corn on cob	50 ears	1 ear
Frozen vegetables	16 10-oz. packages	1/2 cup
Green beans, fresh	12 1/2 pounds	4 ounces
Onions, to cream	15 pounds	1/2 cup
Potatoes, to mash or scallop	15 pounds	1/2 cup
Potatoes, frozen French-fried	13 pounds	4 ounces
Sweet potatoes	25 pounds	8 ounces
MISCELLANEOUS		
Cake mix	3–4 packages	1 slice
Crackers	1 pound	2 crackers
Gelatin	13 3-oz. packages	1/2 cup
Ice, for tea	50 pounds	
Macaroni	4 1/2 pounds	3/4 cup
Minute rice	6 15-oz. packages	3/4 cup
Noodles	48 ounces	1/2 cup
Potato chips	3 pounds	1 ounce
Pudding	12 4-oz. packages	1/2 cup
Rolls	6 1/2 dozen	1 1/2 rolls
Soup, canned	20 cans	1 cup
Spaghetti	4 1/2 pounds	3/4 cup

Substitution Chart

	INSTEAD OF . . .	USE . . .
BAKING	1 tsp. baking powder	1/4 tsp. soda plus 1/2 tsp. cream of tartar
	1 tbsp. cornstarch (for thickening)	2 tbsp. flour or 1 tbsp. tapioca
	1 c. sifted all-purpose flour	1 c. plus 2 tbsp. sifted cake flour
	1 c. sifted cake flour	1 c. minus 2 tbsp. sifted all-purpose flour
	1 c. fine dry bread crumbs	3/4 c. fine cracker crumbs
DAIRY	1 c. buttermilk	1 c. sour milk or 1 c. yogurt
	1 c. heavy cream	3/4 c. skim milk plus 1/3 c. butter
	1 c. light cream	7/8 c. skim milk plus 3 tbsp. butter
	1 c. sour cream	7/8 c. sour milk plus 3 tbsp. butter
	1 c. sour milk	1 c. sweet milk plus 1 tbsp. vinegar or lemon juice or 1 c. buttermilk
SEASONINGS	1 tsp. allspice	1/2 tsp. cinnamon plus 1/8 tsp. cloves
	1 c. catsup	1 c. tomato sauce plus 1/2 c. sugar plus 2 tbsp. vinegar
	1 clove of garlic	1/8 tsp. garlic powder or 1/8 tsp. instant minced garlic or 3/4 tsp. garlic salt or 5 drops of liquid garlic
	1 tsp. Italian spice	1/4 tsp. each oregano, basil, thyme, rosemary plus dash of cayenne
	1 tsp. lemon juice	1/2 tsp. vinegar
	1 tbsp. prepared mustard	1 tsp. dry mustard
	1 medium onion	1 tbsp. dried minced onion or 1 tsp. onion powder
SWEET	1 1-oz. square chocolate	3 to 4 tbsp. cocoa plus 1 tsp. shortening
	1 2/3 oz. semisweet chocolate	1 oz. unsweetened chocolate plus 4 tsp. sugar
	1 c. honey	1 to 1 1/4 c. sugar plus 1/4 c. liquid or 1 c. molasses or corn syrup
	1 c. granulated sugar	1 c. packed brown sugar or 1 c. corn syrup, molasses or honey minus 1/4 c. liquid

Equivalent Chart

	WHEN RECIPE CALLS FOR . . .	YOU NEED . . .
BAKING ESSENTIALS	1/2 c. butter	1 stick
	2 c. butter	1 pound
	4 c. all-purpose flour	1 pound
	4 1/2 to 5 c. sifted cake flour	1 pound
	1 sq. chocolate	1 ounce
	1 c. semisweet chocolate pieces	1 6-ounce package
	4 c. marshmallows	1 pound
	2 1/4 c. packed brown sugar	1 pound
	4 c. confectioners' sugar	1 pound
	2 c. granulated sugar	1 pound
	3 c. tapioca	1 pound
BREADS & CEREAL	1 c. fine dry bread crumbs	4 to 5 slices
	1 c. soft bread crumbs	2 slices
	1 c. small bread cubes	2 slices
	1 c. fine cracker crumbs	28 saltines
	1 c. fine graham cracker crumbs	15 crackers
	1 c. vanilla wafer crumbs	22 wafers
	1 c. crushed cornflakes	3 c. uncrushed
	3 1/2 c. cooked rice	1 c. uncooked
DAIRY	1 c. freshly grated cheese	1/4 pound
	1 c. cottage cheese	1 8-ounce carton
	1 c. sour cream	1 8-ounce carton
	1 c. whipped cream	1/2 c. heavy cream
	2/3 c. evaporated milk	1 small can
	1 2/3 c. evaporated milk	1 13-ounce can
FRUIT	4 c. sliced or chopped apples	4 medium
	1 c. mashed banana	3 medium
	2 c. pitted cherries	4 c. unpitted
	3 c. shredded coconut	1/2 pound
	4 c. cranberries	1 pound
	1 c. pitted dates	1 8-ounce package
	1 c. candied fruit	1 8-ounce package
	3 to 4 tbsp. lemon juice plus 1 tsp. grated rind	1 lemon
	1/3 c. orange juice plus 2 tsp. grated rind	1 orange
	4 c. sliced peaches	8 medium
	2 c. pitted prunes	1 12-oz. package
	3 c. raisins	1 15-ounce package

	WHEN RECIPE CALLS FOR . . .	YOU NEED . . .
MEATS	4 c. diced cooked chicken	1 5-pound chicken
	3 c. diced cooked meat	1 pound, cooked
	2 c. ground cooked meat	1 pound, cooked
NUTS	1 c. chopped nuts	4 ounces, shelled 1 pound, unshelled
VEGETABLES	2 c. cooked green beans	1/2 pound fresh or 1 16-ounce can
	2 1/2 c. lima beans or red beans	1 c. dried, cooked
	4 c. shredded cabbage	1 pound
	1 c. grated carrot	1 large
	1 4-oz. can mushrooms	1/2 pound, fresh
	1 c. chopped onion	1 large
	4 c. sliced or diced raw potatoes	4 medium
	2 c. canned tomatoes	1 16-ounce can

COMMON EQUIVALENTS

1 tablespoon = 3 teaspoons
2 tablespoons = 1 ounce
4 tablespoons = 1/4 cup
5 tablespoons + 1 teaspoon = 1/3 cup
8 tablespoons = 1/2 cup
12 tablespoons = 3/4 cup
16 tablespoons = 1 cup
1 cup = 8 ounces or 1/2 pint
4 cups = 1 quart
4 quarts = 1 gallon
6 1/2 to 8-ounce can = 1 cup
10 1/2 to 12-ounce can = 1 1/4 cups
14 to 16-ounce can (No. 300) = 1 3/4 cups
16 to 17-ounce can (No. 303) = 2 cups
1-pound 4-ounce can or 1-pint 2-ounce can (No. 2) = 2 1/2 cups
1-pound 13-ounce can (No. 2 1/2) = 3 1/2 cups
3-pound 3-ounce can or 46-ounce can = 5 3/4 cups
6 1/2-pound or 7-pound 5-ounce can (No. 10) = 12 to 13 cups

Metric Conversion Chart

1 teaspoon = 5 milliliters
1 tablespoon = 15 milliliters
1 fluid ounce = 30 milliliters
1 cup = 250 milliliters
1 pint = 500 milliliters
1 quart = 1 liter
1 ounce = 30 grams
1 pound = 450 grams
2.2 pounds = 1 kilogram

The metric measures are approximate benchmarks for purposes of home food preparation.

Contributors' Index

Corine R. Allen
Virginia Alley
Lyn Allison
Barb Ames
Kitty Auker
Patti Bakke
Bonnie Bandemer
Peggy Bares
Cheryl Bargman
Ruth Barry
Bonnie Beard
Lisa Beebe
Becky Behmer
Gemma Benjamin
Dorothy Benning
Peggy Blair
Donna Brookbank
Lisa Broski
Betty Canfield
Linda Caruana
Kathy Cassioppi
Betty Chriswell
Judith Clark
Lynne Connelly
Bernice Corey
Margaret Brookes Crawford
Patrick Curran
Joan Davis
Sandy Davis
Sarah Davis
Peggy Dean
Henrietta Dotson-Williams
Sandy Dresser
Julie Maring Dreixler
Marilyn Duhigg
Dorothy Elson
Ann Ewing
Kappy Firch
Sarah Fletcher
Jeanne Floberg
Marianne Floberg
Debra K. Flynn
Stanley Folz
Peg Fourie
Dawn Franzen
Shelley Fridly
Beth Galbreath
Barbara Galloway
Marg Gang
Helen Gartner
Patricia Gibbs
Claire B. Ginsburgh
Pam Girardi
Mel D. Grell
Sue Grover
Evie Gruben
Erik and Anna Gulbrandsen
Karen Haas
Delores Hall
Mrs. Harley Hall
Portia Hanebuth
Colleen Hawkinson
Mary Healy
Terry Hodges
Judy Holder
Nancy Houk
Lauri Hovey
Anna Howard
Terry Ingrassia
Geneva Jacoby
Carol Johnson
JoAnn J. Johnson
Walita Johnson
Grace Kampmeier
Diana Keister
Dianna Kile
Jean Killingsworth
Sally Koepsell
Julie Koning
Bernice Kortendick
Sara Lane
Marilyn Lang
Diane Lewis
Elizanne Lewis

Jeanette Lindenmier
Anita Linder
Frances L. Liston
Ruth Little
Nancy Long
Johanna Lund
Ruth Lunde
Marjorie Lutz
Chris Magee
Colleen Magee
Jo Marshall
Cindy Mathison
Peggy McGaw
Joan Molenaar
Jane Naber
Dana Nailor
Kathleen M. Nebel
Shelley Nelson
Leanne Ness
Rita Ness
Brenda Nicholson
June M. Nilsen
Marilyn Olson
Debbie Oracki
Cynthia K. Patterson
Jo Pennock
Jenni, Jody and Jackie Peters
Barbara Peterson
Debbie Peterson
Betty Proctor
June Reents
Cinda Lee Rickey
Camille Rossi
Edward M. Rounds
Mary Anne Rounds
Martha Rowald
RRVCGS Outdoor Training
Mary Saxby
Andrea Schneider
Michele Schnorr
Talese Schnorr
Vicki Schramer
Barbara Schwengels
Adella Sefrhans
Barbara Shriner
Jane Skarka
Helen A. Smith
Kathy M. Smith
Nancy J. Smith
Barbara J. Snyder
Deborah K. Stienmetz
Krissy Swanson
John Terranova
Mary Tessman
Louise B. Trull
Shirley Tudor
Alyce Vincer
Michele Wallace
Jackie Waskiewicz
Diane Weber
Beth Whelpley
Nike Whitcomb
Betty Gail White
Alba Williams
Barb Willing
Cindy Willson
Fleur Wright
Kathie Ziegler

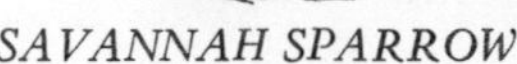

SAVANNAH SPARROW

Index

Microwave recipe page numbers are preceded by an m.

Aluminum Foil Cooking, see Outdoor Cooking
APPETIZERS
cheese
ball, 8
squares, Rita's, 19
cocktail sauce, classic, 14
cream puffs, miniature, 15
dips
apple, 11
broccoli, hot, m9
caramel, 12
chili salsa, m9
fruit dip, 12
green goddess dip, 8
liver dip, 10
orange-sour cream, 12
shrimp, 11
taco dip, Lynda's, 10
tomato, Terry Hodges', 10
finger Jell-O, 21
ground beef
meatballs, cocktail, cranberry, 15
nacho appetizer, 16
tostados, mini, 16
mushrooms, stuffed, 19
nacho
appetizers, 16
stuff, Stanley Folz's, 11
pate, braunschweiger, 8
pecans
cinnamon, 21
pizza
vegetable, cold, Colleen Hawkinson's, 20
vegetarian, 20
popcorn
balls, orange, Zillah's, 22
caramel corn, microwave, m22
sandwiches, vegetarian, 21
shellfish
clams casino, 13
crab
deluxe, 14
spread, hot, 13
shrimp
dip, 11
mousse, 14

BEEF
brisket, yummy, 48
chop suey, American, Peggy Dean's, 63
ground beef, see Ground Beef
pie, Italian, 50
roast
Italian, 48
steak
pepper steak, 49
Sunday dinner steak, 49
stew, see Stews

BEVERAGES
cocoa, terrific, 28
eggnog, cold, 24
orange Juliette, 24
punch
Champagne, 25
fruity, 25
islander punch, 25
real good, 26
recognition punch, 26
slush-slush, 27
tea punch, refreshing, 26
shakes, Johnny Appleseed, 24
slush
apricot, 27
summer slush, 28
Box Oven Cooking, see Outdoor Cooking

BREADS
- applesauce heirloom bread, 101
- banana
  - grandmother's, 101
  - strawberry, 102
- breakfast bread, 102
- coffee cakes
  - apple fritters, Patrick Curran's, 100
  - Mama Scheffler's, 100
- date-pecan, Aunt Marie's, 103
- elephant ears, 111
- English muffin bread, 110
- fritters, apple, Patrick Curran's, 100
- lefse recipe, 112
- monkey bread, 111
- muffins
  - apple-raisin, 104
  - Raisin Bran, 105
- pancakes, see Pancakes
- popovers
  - cold oven, Maggie's, 109
- poppy seed, 104
- pumpkin, 103
- rolls, pecan, miniature, 112
- white bread, Mary Lucas', 110

CAKES
- angel cake, strawberry, 132
- carrot-pineapple, 136
- cherry, Fanny Vogel's, 132
- chocolate
  - Creme de Menthe cake, 133
  - devil's food, one hundred dollar, 133
  - peppermint cake roll, 127
  - Texas sheet cake, Mrs. Curtis', 134
- Creme de Menthe cake, 133
- devil's food, one hundred dollar, 133
- family favorite cake, 134
- filling, see Fillings
- frosting, see Frostings
- oatmeal cake, Fran Artman's, 135
- peppermint-choco cake roll, 127
- pineapple-carrot, 136
- pound cake, cream cheese, 137
- rhubarb, Grace Kampmeier's, 135
- strawberry angel cake, 132
- Texas sheet cake, Mrs. Curtis', 134
- ugly duckling cake, 136
- war cakes, Mom Starke's, 137

CANDIES
- chocolate
  - fudge
    - cashew, 118
    - creamy, 118
- pralines, pecan, Mr. Peeples', 118
- see No-Cooking
- see Outdoor Favorites

CHEESE
- appetizers, see Appetizers
- souffle, 97
- soup, see Soups
- strata, ham, Helen's, 66
- three-cheese casserole, 96

CHEESECAKES
- Lafayette Parish cheesecake, 119
- no-bake, Barb's, 119

CHICKEN
- and dumplings, easy and inexpensive, Leisa's, 74
- biscuit casserole, 73
- breasts
  - in sour cream, 74
  - Parmesan, 76
  - party casserole, 70
  - rolls, tomato-stuffed, 77
  - sweet and sour, 78
- five-can casserole, 75
- Parmesan, easy, m76
- salad, hot, 78
- soup, see Soups
- supreme, 79
- with rice, casserole, 77

CHILI
- homecoming chili, 58
- pronto, m58

COFFEE CAKES
apple fritters, Patrick Curran's, 100
Mama Scheffler's, 100

COOKIES
biscotti, Italian, 150
brown-eyed Susans, 149
brownies, see chocolate cookies
cheesecake bars, 140
chocolate
biscotti, Italian, 150
brown-eyed Susans, 149
brownies, Girl Scout, 143
chocolate chip
easy, 147
monster cookies, mom's, 150
chocolate shot, 147
K-bars, 144
s'mores, m148
coffee bars, frosted, great-grandmother's, 144
date
pinwheel cookies, 148
sugared date-walnut squares, 145
gingersnaps, 146
holiday squares, 143
K-bars, 144
monster cookies, mom's, 150
oatmeal, Cape Cod cookies, 149
sugar cookies, Ramona Graupner's, 146
Waverly Wafer bars, 145
Croutons, 46

DESSERTS
banana split dessert, 114
cake, see Cakes
candy, see Candies
cheesecake, see Cheesecakes
chocolate
eclair dessert, 114
four-layer dessert, 115
Heath bar dessert, 115
moon cake, 120
mousse
au chocolat, 117
white chocolate, 116
tortes
bitter chocolate, 128
heavenly, 130
cookies, see Cookies
custard, coffee, 126
dirt cake, 116
fruit cobbler, quick, Ella Jo's, 121
Heath bar dessert, 115
lemon, love notes, 121
marshmallows, homemade, 117
moon cake, 120
mousse
au chocolat, 117
white chocolate, 116
Pavlova, Australian, 120
peek-a-boo cake, 123
pie, see Pies
pina colada wedges, 122
pineapple
Bennett's dessert, 122
popsicles, yogurt, 127
pudding, see Puddings
pumpkin torture, 125
strawberry, mille feuille, 126
tortes, see Tortes
Eggs
breakfast casserole, 67
breakfast pizza, 68

FILLINGS
almond butter cream, 138
Black Forest filling, 138
cream cheese, 139
see Frostings
Fire Starters, see Outdoor Cooking

FISH
bass, small-mouth amandine, baked, Betty Canfield's, 79
fillets
crispy, micromeals', m80
Parmesan, 80

orange roughy, 81
with tomato and basil, m81
salmon, supreme, baked, 81

FROSTINGS
chocolate sour cream, 138
coffee butter cream, 129
German chocolate cake topping, John Terranova's, 140
see Fillings
vanilla, 139

GROUND BEEF
appetizers, see Appetizers
chili
homecoming, 58
pronto, m58
egg rolls, 59
lasagna, easy, 60
meatballs
Swedish, 52
Cyndie's, 51
sweet-sour, Jo Marshall's, 52
meat loaves
Eva Swenson's, 56
microwave, m55
stuffed, ham and cheese, 55
mostaccioli, Velveeta, 57
olive Mexican fiesta, 57
pie, 60
pizza
fondue, birthday supper, 59
forgot-the-yeast pizza, Beth's, 61
potato casserole, 56

HAM
balls, 65
fettucini Alfredo, Kitty Auker's, 66
puffs, 67
strata, ham and cheese, Helen's, 66

Icing, see Frostings
Italian Sausage, beef pie, 50
Magic Kitchen System, see Outdoor Cooking

MICROWAVE
appetizers
caramel corn, m22
dips
broccoli, m9
chili salsa, m9
chicken Parmesan, easy, m76
chili, pronto, m58
fish
fillets, crispy, m80
orange roughy, m81
meat loaf, m55
s'mores, m148

MUFFINS
apple-raisin, 104
Raisin Bran, 105

No-Cooking, see Outdoor Cooking

OUTDOOR COOKING
aluminum foil cooking
chicken, in the garden, 163
desserts
apples
apple delight, 165
baked, 165
cake, in orange, 165
dinners, busy day, 162
ground beef, pizza loaves, picnic, 163
ham, heavenly, 163
muffins
corn, in orange shells, 164
popcorn, hobo, 162
vegetables
potatoes
scalloped, 164
supreme, 164
box oven cooking
ground beef
hamburger thrifty, 169
pizza, minute, 168
desserts
brownies, easy, 169
dump cake, Donna Jo Wait's, 169

fire starters
charcoal grill, 161
starter I, 160
starter II, 160
magic kitchen system, Beth Galbreath's, 178
how it works, 180
how to make it, 178
how to use it, 179
for frying or toasting, 180
materials needed, 178
tools needed, 178
no-cooking
beverage
peppermint-orange soda, 170
desserts
easy doozits, 171
gorp, 171
lunches, walking, 170
salad dressing, campers, 171
salad, walking, 170
outdoor favorites
bags of gold, 172
desserts
banana boats, 177
candy
doodlebugs, 174
eggs, baked, 172
ground beef
gooey gunk, 173
gumboburgers, Hazel Johannes', 173
in an orange, 172
shipwreck, 174
stew, campfire, 174
rice
chicken in the woods, 173
stick cooking
angels on horseback, 167
beef
shish kabobs, 166
dessert
s'mores, 167
frankfurters
mad dogs, 167
Outdoor Favorites, see Outdoor Cooking
PANCAKES
German, 105
with applesauce, 106
oven pancakes, polka-dot, 106
Swedish
thin, 109
Pastry, flaky, 154
PIES
apple, 151
bird's nest pie, 151
chocolate
fudge, fluffy, 152
lemon meringue, 153
mint tea pie, 152
strawberry, chilled, 153
tarts, Mrs. Lowry's, 154
PIZZAS
appetizers, see Appetizers
breakfast pizza, 68
fondue, birthday supper, 59
forgot-the-yeast, Beth's, 61
Polish Sausage, bake, 68
Popovers, cold oven, Maggie's, 109
PORK
bacon
fried, rice, 98
spinach quiche, 93
chops
baked, Gram's, 63
chop suey, American, Peggy Dean's, 63
ham, see Ham
kropp kakor, Krissy Swanson's, 64
sausage
breakfast casserole, 67
breakfast pizza, 68
POTLUCK
broccoli casserole, Colleen Hawkinson's, 158
dessert, fast, 158
drive-thru special, 157

no-pot answer, 156
salads
chicken, 158
cottage cheese, pronto, 157
potato, 157
survival traveling kit, 156

POTPOURRI
ant exterminator, nontoxic, 188
bath salts, effervescent, 187
blackboard cleaner, 186
canvas
fireproofing, 188
waterproofing, 188
coal flowers, 182
doggie biscuits, 188
egg dyes, natural, 185
furniture
lemon polish, 186
scratch remover, 186
humidity indicator, 185
ink
instant erase, 184
invisible, 184
modeling clay, 182
mosquito repellent powder, 187
newsprint transfer, 185
paint
finger paint, 183
poster paint, 183
plaster
modeling, crepe paper, 183
soap flakes plaster, 183
play dough, 182
poison ivy lotion, 187
vanilla, baker's, double-strength, 186
window cleaner, make your own, 186
writing surface, magic, 184

PUDDINGS
bread pudding
Aunt Lucille's, 124
Holland rusk, 123
persimmon, 124
raisin-rice, 125

Quiches
spinach, 94
bacon, 93
Rolls, pecan, miniature, 112
Salad Dressing, healthy, 46

SALADS
chicken, hot, 78
fruit
apple, taffy, 30
bubbling fruit, 31
Champagne salad, 31
cherry, 31
Marlow salad, 32
millionaire salad, 33
party salad, 30
pretzel salad, 33
strawberry pretzel delight, 34
seven-layer Jell-O, 37
Seven-Up salad, 38
sour cream Jell-O, 37
strawberry-rhubarb mold, 34
Waldorf salad, cranberry, 32
Manhattan deli salad, 38
seafood
easy, 39
tuna-cashew, 39
vegetable
Ameriental salad, 40
broccoli
and cauliflower, 41
crunchy, 41
Sarah's, 40
carrots, marinated, 41
coleslaw, 42
fiesta coleslaw, 43
frozen, 43
K. F. C. coleslaw, 42
rave coleslaw, 42
layered salad, 44
overnight salad, 43
pea, pantry shelf, Evie Gruben's, 45
Roman salad, 44
spring parfait salad, 45

Sandwiches
barbecues, perfect, 62
vegetarian sandwiches, 21
SAUCES
barbecue sauce
for pork, 64
Corine's, 65
cocktail sauce, classic, 14
corney dog sauce, 61
spaghetti sauce
Chuck's, 62
favorite, 69
quick, 69
SHELLFISH
crab bisque, 82
oyster stuffing, Louise Trull's, 97
see Appetizers
shrimp, stir-fried, 82
SOUPS
cauliflower, cheesy, Terry Ingrassia's, 86
cheese, 96
chicken-escarole, 75
chili, see Chili
crab bisque, 82
peanut, 94
pumpkin, 95
sausage, Sicilian, 68
spinach, cream of, my own, 95
STEWS
chili, see Chili
goulash, Hungarian, 51
six-hour stew, 50
venison, 70
Stick Cooking, see Outdoor Cooking
Stratas, see Ham
Stuffings, oyster, Louise Trull's, 97
Syrup, cinnamon, 109
Tarts, Mrs. Lowry's, 154
TORTES
chocolate
bitter chocolate, 128
heavenly torte, 130
coffee meringue, 129
hazel nut, 128
lemon ribbon torte, 131
mandarin torte, 130
rhubarb, meringue, 131
Turkey Sausage, 79
Veal
American chop suey, Peggy Dean's, 63
VEGETABLES
beans, western, 84
broccoli
casseroles
Colleen Hawkinson's, 85
favorite, 84
rice, 85
carrots
casserole, 85
orange, 86
corn, scalloped, different, 87
mixed vegetables
casserole, easy, 92
imperial, 92
medley, 93
potatoes
dilled, 88
hashed brown
au gratin, 87
deluxe, Marilyn's, 87
sour cream, 88
soup, see Soups
spinach quiche, 94
bacon, 93
sweet potato casserole, sweet and spicy, 91
zucchini casserole, 91
Venison Stew, 70

Order Form

RIVER VALLEY RECIPES

for those who cook...and for those who don't...

All proceeds and donations from **River Valley Recipes** benefit girls and young women in our communities. Through expanded outdoor programs and activities at Girl Scout Camp Medill McCormick, children build self-esteem, develop potential and learn to appreciate and respect nature.

CUSTOMER INFORMATION: (Person responsible for payment)

NAME ______________________________

ADDRESS ______________________________

CITY ______________ STATE ______________ ZIP ________

PHONE ______________________________

Please send ________ copies of RIVER VALLEY RECIPES @ $12.50 $________

plus $2.00 shipping and handling (per copy) $________

TOTAL AMOUNT $________

☐ Enclosed is my check for $____________

(Payable to Rock River Valley Council of Girl Scouts)

☐ Charge to my: ☐ VISA ☐ Mastercard

Account Number ______________

Expiration Date ______________

Signature ______________

☐ Additional donation of $________ is enclosed.

Mail Order Form to:
Rock River Valley Council
of Girl Scouts, Inc.
P. O. Box 1616
Rockford, Illinois 61110-0116

SHIP TO: (Person receiving shipment)

Name ______________	Name ______________
Address ______________	Address ______________
City ______________	City ______________
State __________ Zip ______	State __________ Zip ______
Phone (____) ______________	Phone (____) ______________

PLEASE ATTACH THE FOLLOWING GIFT STICKER. (Check one.)

☐ Merry Christmas ☐ Valentine's Day ☐ Get Well

☐ Thank You ☐ Happy Birthday ☐ Happy Holidays

☐ Happy Easter ☐ To Say Hello ☐ To and From

☐ Happy Thanksgiving ☐ Happy Hanukkah

☐ Other ______________________________

I would like the sticker signed TO: ______________________

FROM: ______________________

GIRL SCOUTS